THE FLAVOUR OF HOME
A SOUTHERN APPALACHIAN FAMILY REMEMBERS

The cover photo is an unidentified woman. The photo has been passed down through my mother's family for over one hundred years.

Earlene Rather O'Dell

The Overmountain Press
JOHNSON CITY, TENNESSEE

The author gratefully acknowledges the following for permissions to reprint previously copyrighted material.

Pickled Beets and Watermelon Rind Preserves from the 1936 Ball Blue Book® page 114, and Watermelon Rind Preserves from the 1969 Ball Blue Book® page 78. BALL and BALL BLUE BOOK® are registered trademarks of Ball Corporation and are used with its permission. All rights reserved. Readers should not attempt to use historical recipes, as given, but should consult the most current Ball Blue Book® for modern recipes and techniques.

Chinese Chews, Tawny Pumpkin Pie, and Southern Pecan Pie from FARM JOURNAL'S COUNTRY COOKBOOK, pages 139, 244, and 244, respectively. Copyright© 1959 by Farm Journal, Inc. Reprinted by permission of Farm Journal, Philadelphia, Pennsylvania.

Shrimp Salad and Mother Leone's Shrimp Sauce recipes from LEONE'S ITALIAN COOKBOOK by EUGENE LEONE, pages 242 and 242. Copyright © 1967 by Luisa Leone Mesereau. Reprinted by permission of HarperCollins Publishers, Inc.

Millie's Meat Loaf recipe from MY OWN COOKBOOK, page 92, by GLADYS TABER. Copyright © 1972 by Gladys Taber. Reprinted by permission of HarperCollins Publishers, Inc. For additional rights/territory contact Brandt & Brandt Literary Agents, Inc., 1501 Broadway, New York, NY 10036.

For my family and for the people
who shared Carolina Hill with me

To everything there is a season,
And a time to every purpose
Under the heaven . . .

Ecclesiastes 3:1

Contents

List of Photographs

Foreword

Pick the most colorful anecdotes from your family tree, discarding anything that is stiff or dry. Mix with vivid memories of your East Tennessee childhood, including detailed descriptions of folk games, old time country and gospel music, and throw in a few hair-raising true-life ghost stories for good measure. Add a treasure trove of prized recipes collected from family members, friends and neighbors. Leaven with wit and good humor, season with affection and pride. Blend ingredients carefully and thoroughly (for several years!), until you have produced a unique book which will appeal to the tastes and interests of a wide range of readers.

I am so glad that I encouraged Earlene Rather O'Dell to write the book you are about to read. When I first read the study of her family history and foodways project in cultural anthropology at East Tennessee State University several years ago, I enjoyed her lively down-to-earth writing style as well as her skillful combination of genealogy, folklore, and oral history along with carefully tested recipes. I felt that her work deserved a wider audience, and so I urged her to expand her manuscript and find a publisher for it.

Which she has done. It took a lot of time and effort, but Earlene, who has never been afraid of hard work, proceeded to gather more information, adding a fascinating chapter dealing with her family's "comfort foods" and an extensive collection of vintage photographs. I hope everyone who reads this banquet of delights Earlene Rather O'Dell has prepared with such loving care will enjoy it, learn from it, and share its bounty with their own families, friends and neighbors.

Richard Blaustein
Professor, Sociology and Anthropology
East Tennessee State University
September 5, 1999

Acknowledgments

The difficulty in writing my appreciation to the people who helped me in the writing of this book is that a multitude of people have had an influence. This book would not have been written if I had not been finalizing plans for a college course in Appalachian Culture. As I was reviewing the many stereotypes and theoretical interpretations of people and problems of Southern Appalachia, which are for the most part negative, I began thinking and writing about the differences in others' perceptions and my own more positive perceptions. As a result, I first have the writers of the more negative pieces to thank for getting me started.

Next, to two of my friends and former graduate professors at East Tennessee State University, Dr. Wendell Hester and, especially, Dr. Richard Blaustein, I appreciate your taking me under your wings again. I am especially grateful for Richard's insistence that I continue writing and expanding the short December 1995 epistle and for his helpful suggestions.

To my extended family (all my Greene, Vance, and Rather cousins—all forty-'leven of you—and especially to Aunt Beulah) thanks for loving and caring for me. Without you, your senses of humor, your influences on me when I was growing up, and your willingness to share your stories and memories, this book would not have happened.

To all the families and friends who lived on Carolina Hill and those who attended our church, I am grateful. Bert and Barbara Hartley Lerma, the kind of friends everybody should have growing up, have encouraged me all the way. Mrs. Young, thanks for treating me like a daughter. To Herbert Barker and Bernice Buckles, members of the Carolina Hill families, I appreciate your enthusiasm for this work and for your friendship all these years; I just wish I had not waited so long to write this. To Betty Honaker Gray, thanks for your sense of humor and encouragement. To Patsy and Larry, "Toodle" and Ray, Carol and all the others, thanks to you and your families for making those years special. And, to Lila McGinty, "my D.C. mom," thanks for looking out for me, caring for me, and continually encouraging me.

To my sisters, Reba, Marie, and Thelma, thanks for letting me invade your world and for all the things you did for me. To Tunis, Jim, and Henry, thanks for putting up with my sisters, too, and for treating me as you would your own little sister.

Lynette and Linda, thanks for being proud of your mom.

Many times during these last few years, I have heard a voice, referring to this book, saying, "Get to work!" That voice belongs to my husband, Ralph. He loves me and believes in me and that makes all the difference in the world.

Introduction

For years, Southern Appalachian people have been bombarded with the stereotypes attributed to all of the people living in the area and to their general lifestyle. I am a native of Southern Appalachia and have lived here most of my life. I know that many of the accepted stereotypes do not fit all of our people.

This is not an attempt to deny that some of the characteristics attributed to some of our people are correct. It is an attempt to show that even in the Southern Appalachians, there are *several* Appalachian lifestyles, not just the ones stereotyped—the ones which perhaps are exaggerated and often repeated.

This book centers on the extended Southern Appalachian family and the community into which I was born, grew up, thrived, laughed, cried, and survived to become whatever I am today. The community mentioned here particularly includes the church and the people who were our neighbors and friends on "Carolina Hill."

The one Appalachian value repeated throughout these chapters is "pride." As young people, we were taught to have pride in many things. Mainly this pride was interpreted as having self-respect. We were taught from an ancient admonition not to be boastful and not to think of ourselves more highly than we ought to think. Our family believed that religion, or having faith in something greater than ourselves, was very important. Even though we may not believe exactly as our ancestors believed, our faith is still important.

Our family also shared an appreciation of good food. Within our family we learned our traditional foodways—raising a garden, preparing, sharing, and finally, gleefully consuming the food. Family recipes, some of them passed down through several generations and still a cherished part of our Appalachian way of life—and some that are not quite as old but equally enjoyed, are included throughout the text with additional recipes found in the Appendix.

Chapter One begins with a discussion of the stereotypical views of Southern Appalachian people and their lifestyles. Some of the values important to our people are also included. Three chapters are devoted to the arrival in Southern Appalachia of the families which now make up my extended family, and include some of Mother's and Daddy's memories of growing up in Sullivan County, Tennessee, and Loudon County, Tennessee, respectively.

Chapter Five, "The Depression Years," reviews the memories of my brother and two sisters as they grew up during The Great Depression. The following chapter, "Going to Aunt Cindy's," describes several summer vacations when Mother took my sister Marie and me to visit Grandma's sister and family. Aunt Cindy was always a special person, and since we lived in town, the farming life she and Uncle Bob led was new and exciting to us.

Chapter Seven, "Seasons on the Hill," is focused especially on childhood and adolescent years spent in a caring, loving, and sharing neighborhood.

The final chapter includes the foods immediate and extended family members consider to be comfort foods—those foods we love to have (or would love to have) when we are down, homesick, or when the seasonal changes and sometimes dreary weather remind us of earlier days and the comforts of our homeplaces. Memories and stories from members of the family representing several generations are shared. Some of them were told to me years ago; others have been gathered since 1995.

The designation, "second cousin," as used here, is what some people refer to as "first cousin once removed." Since we had never heard this term used at home and were not accustomed to it, I refer to Mother's first cousins as my second cousins, as she always did.

Family members were asked an open-ended question: "What are your comfort foods?" As with many open-ended, unstructured questions (at least in this family) the answers were accompanied by many comments, jokes, laughter, and various food-associated memories. The conversations included the traditional foods served on special occasions, especially when company or the preachers came for meals.

Since most of the families represented here have been so interwoven for two centuries, I have not been able to determine the specific family or individual origin of some of the recipes. While the ancestry of these family members traces to France, England, Germany, Scotland, Ireland, Norway, and possibly Wales (the Rather family), with my husband also having Cherokee ancestry in his father's family, the food prepared and enjoyed by family members did not seem to have originated in any one particular country. And, as can be expected in a family as large as this, some commonalities in food preference and preparation exist.

Perhaps mention of the title should be noted. The British spelling of the word "flavor" has been used, not as an attempt to "get above my raisin'," but to indicate part of the family's heritage. The word "flavour" is used here to indicate not only the sights, tastes, and smells of the food served, but is expanded to the special qualities and characteristics of the places we call home and the home folks who gave us a feeling of belonging, of having a sense of place.

Chapter 1
Appalachian Values, Stereotypes, and Foodways

What is it like to be born and raised in Southern Appalachia? The answers are as many and as varied as the number of natives. To an extent, the answers may depend on whether a person has good or bad memories of growing up, the reaction to those experiences and memories, and the personal outlook formed throughout life. I believe that this is true, no matter where people are born and raised.

The people of the Southern Appalachian region, as a group, have been the subject of much stereotyping, laughter, debate, concern, and social programs (designed to alleviate the concern) since Albert Gallatin was Secretary of the Treasury during Thomas Jefferson's administration. A view that some outsiders have of the Appalachian people is one of a clannish lot of poor, downtrodden, ignorant, slovenly, strange creatures who need to be civilized according to some vaguely defined national standard.

While some may say that being called "a clannish lot" is a compliment because it refers to our ancestry, others know that this characterization conjures up images of famous family feuds, such as the Hatfields and the McCoys, which took place in other parts of Southern Appalachia. For the most part, neither these feuds nor the idea that all family members must always stick together, sometimes expressed as "blood is thicker than water," is realistic. While the ideal family *may* be one in which there are no disagreements, where everyone lives in peace and harmony, where no ill word is said to or about another family member, and where we "all live happily ever after," it is a rarity. In most families, including ours, there have been differences among some family members. Most of the time, we, like many other people, are very tolerant and very forgiving, and will take more or put up with more from individual family members than we would from acquaintances or strangers simply because "they are family." But, when the greatest degrees of tolerance and instances of forgiveness have exceeded that required of any human being, the line is then drawn.

Perhaps relatively few of us has had to draw that line; but, down through the generations, some of us have *had* to simply say, "No more."

Some immigrants to this area in the last twenty to thirty years, and some even more recently, believed that they were moving to an uncivilized land and actually expected to be abducted any time by people who came down out of the mountains. Expecting to find us always walking around without shoes, living in houses along dirt roads (with no inside plumbing and no television), making moonshine, wearing our clothes until they were stiff while the washing machines sat on the front porch where we "picked and grinned" every night, and wasting away because of a poor diet, these immigrants could not believe we had some semblance of civilization. Some of the newcomers probably were suffering from tunnelvision and were really shocked when they saw us as we are. They soon learned that these images and stereotypes did not always give a true picture of Southern Appalachian people.

The Southern Appalachian area was brought to national attention by popular television shows and the War on Poverty during the 1960s and 70s. The plight of our people brought outsiders rushing to give assistance. Many of the news reports and much of the assistance were centered in places which were unknown to large numbers of us. No one set of descriptions and no one set of stereotypes can describe or can be attributed to the entire region or its people

I visited a coal-mining area for the first time when I was in high school. The people in that community seemed no different from those at home. They had similar housing and transportation. The people my age were listening and dancing to rock and roll, using the same slang expressions, wearing the same styles of clothing, and eating the same food. They gulped junk food—hot dogs, hamburgers, french fries, chocolate nut sundaes, and *real* milkshakes—and consumed the same nutritious food—fresh or freshly canned fruits and vegetables from their families' gardens, homemade (and store-bought sandwich) breads, and the traditional meats of chicken, beef, and pork (including ham).

This reality was unlike the image portrayed on national television which many people believed was the reality for *all* people in Southern Appalachia. The one televised report which has remained indelible in my mind since the War on Poverty years was centered on a young mother who, with her several children, lived in a ramshackle, unpainted house. Her children (with dirty faces and dirty clothes, like most children playing outside in the summer) were romping and cavorting in a small yard of packed dirt surrounded by pasture and woodlands. The mother, expressionless, hair unkempt, her own clothes dirty and disheveled, was being interviewed by a reporter on national television. In response to a question about their diet, she stated that they had been eating only "water gravy" for their last two or three meals. She explained that the gravy was made from flour and water. Never had I ever heard of anything called "water gravy!"

Here I was, myself a young mother, not rich by material measures, who sometimes baked a tuna casserole (called "Surprise Casserole" because it surprised me when anybody would eat it) and stretched a little bit of chicken for a meal. But when I heard "water gravy," I sat there wondering, "What in the world?" I even asked Mother, who had lived in East Tennessee since her birth in 1902, about "water gravy." She had no idea what this was, either. I have since learned that "water gravy" is not the wallpaper paste-like mixture the young mother described; it is gravy made with the meat drippings, flour, and water (used instead of the milk to make cream gravy).

The young mother being interviewed seemed resigned to her lot, characteristic of fatalism, another stereotype attributed to Southern Appalachian people. She did not seem worried or upset that her children were not getting the nourishment they needed; although, their energy level did not seem to be lacking and none appeared to be ill. The grassy areas and woodlands surrounding the packed dirt yard may have provided wonderful, edible wild foods. Neither she nor the reporter mentioned this and dwelt only on "water gravy." In the same tone as she would say, "Bless her heart," Mother said, "She probably didn't know any better."

Since this report aired, I have questioned many times to myself, "Why didn't the young mother know better? Why didn't she seem to care? Why was she accepting of her lot?" Perhaps the answers lie in a combination of factors—peoples' internalization of certain values identified by Loyal Jones as "Appalachian values;" their monetary wealth or lack of it; their education (not necessarily formal, but practical); their determination; and their ability and willingness to take advantage of resources including the natural resources available to them. To me, the family's and the individual's outlook on life is the main factor. Though Jones wrote that, "The person who could not look after himself and his family was to be pitied," I tend not to pity, but to try to look beyond the condition to see why it has occurred and to look for solutions.

Such reports about people living in Southern Appalachia have resulted in programs which have benefitted some of the area's people and may have lessened their resistance to accepting outside aid which they previously saw as handouts —something to which independent-minded Appalachian people had an aversion.

As far as I know, our family never felt "exploited," as has been said about Appalachian people. The family worked hard at whatever they could do. Our extended family had varying degrees of wealth. In fact, some of us were downright poor, as were many other local families. However, I never heard the expression, "We're poor, but we're proud."

Some who use this expression may say it as a joke; others seem to use the expression as an actual expression of their "pride" in being poor; it is flaunted. In other words, being poor is a basis for bragging (which is in opposition to the supposed Appalachian value of modesty).

To me, this attitude is inconsistent with the sense of pride felt by many Southern Appalachian people. Pride is ingrained in some of the area's people and permeates many areas of their lives. It is the basis of their self-respect. They take pride in their work and in the fruits of their labor, in their talents and abilities, in the cleanliness and neatness of their homes—however tiny—and they take pride in their families. This sense of pride is connected with a sense of beauty found in simple, homemade things. The mother of one of my former students told me several years ago when we were discussing making sauerkraut, "I had the prettiest white kraut I ever had this year." I had never thought of kraut as being pretty, but this expresses the pride many Appalachian women feel and have felt for generations. This pride is a quiet, private, unassuming, internal attitude. If expressed verbally, this pride may be tempered as in the expression, "I'm kind of proud of my garden," which I used to hear Daddy say.

Traditionally, Appalachian women were extensively involved in planting, caring for, gathering, preserving, cooking and serving food for the many meals they would need to carry their families through the year. These activities are still practiced by many of our women—sometimes on a smaller scale and perhaps not for the original purpose, but done simply to keep in touch with the past. Some of us still can fresh vegetables in the summer because we still believe they taste so much better than commercially canned vegetables. And, there is that memory connection of seeing the rows and rows of canned vegetables sitting on the shelves in the old cellar just waiting for winter to come. Sometimes I don't know which is the more powerful—the taste of the food or the memories evoked.

Appalachian people, generally, have been a modest bunch. Some people have been known to invite others to have a meal with them by saying, "Come and go home with us for dinner if you don't mind poor folks victuals" (pronounced vittles). A variation might be, "You're welcome to eat if you don't care to take grub like pore folks."

After these invitations are issued, the guests, perhaps expecting the worst, may be dumb-founded when they see the table set before them loaded down with at least one meat (and plenty of it), several home-grown vegetables, homemade breads (biscuits or rolls and/or cornbread), cottage cheese, macaroni and cheese, salads, relishes (including homemade bread and butter pickles, sweet or fourteen-day pickles, and dill pickles—all homemade), jams/jellies (including homemade honey), and to top all that off—homemade shortcake made with wild strawberries slathered with fresh whipped cream, or perhaps lemon meringue pie, or apple pie, or rhubarb pie, peach or blackberry cobbler, or applesauce or spice cake, or perhaps, fresh coconut cake with boiled custard. . . And don't forget the coffee and the homemade fresh lemonade and the iced tea—and, in the old days, freshly made homemade butter brought from the spring house along with fresh milk. Yet, to the host/hostess, the meal may be just pore folks' grub—nothing special.

I never remember Daddy or Mother ever calling our food "grub" or "vittles" or their issuing such colorful invitations. The only thing I ever heard Mother say about the appropriateness or the quantity of dishes was when she was preparing a meal for company or after we had put the food on the table. Then, she sometimes said, "Well, it's not (or, "it doesn't seem like"] much, but I guess it'll do." This comment was said privately to the family, though, and nothing was mentioned when company arrived. Sometimes Mother would downplay compliments she received on the food, expressing that the bread or cake seemed a little bit "sad," meaning that it had not risen to her satisfaction.

Since the 1970s, folklorists and cultural anthropologists have studied foodways including the whole range of cookery, eating habits and nutrition. Some writers have expressed the belief that there is a paucity of research of food at the very personal level including the small-scale, community, church, or family-based events—events that create a sense of intimacy, belonging, and community. These feelings are sometimes rare commodities in modern American society.

Sometimes, even in Southern Appalachia, we tend to forget the importance of simple things. Just to remind all of us, the following pages are a small sample of my family's life in a little corner of the Southern Appalachians.

Chapter 2
The Family's Arrival in Southern Appalachia
OR
The Begats

Our family's maternal ancestral roots in Southern Appalachia trace to Watauga County, North Carolina, soon after the Revolutionary War, and back to 1765-66 when the first permanent settlers made their homes in Washington County, Virginia-Sullivan County, Tennessee. This area, which many of us still call home, was then known as the Holston Country. Thomas Sharp, his brother, John, and another unrelated person came here in 1765, cleared and worked some land during the summer, and returned to their families in Lancaster, Pennsylvania. The next year, they returned to settle. This time, they brought their families and other settlers with them. Thomas Sharp was my fifth great-grandfather. My paternal family came to Roane/Loudon County, Tennessee in the early 1800s from the Tidewater area of Virginia.

When these first families arrived, the area was known as the back country. It was still inhabited by the natives (usually referred to as the Cherokee), and in some cases the natives and the settlers were in conflict. As the story goes, two of Caleb O'Dell's sons were killed by some of the Cherokees.

One of Caleb's daughters, Catherine, married Jonathan Morrell. Catherine and Jonathan are my maternal ancestors. One of Caleb O'Dell's surviving sons, William, married Martha Morrell, a sister to Jonathan Morrell. William and Martha are my husband's paternal ancestors. This was the beginning of the O'Dell family in Sullivan County.

Samuel Vance was the first of my mother's paternal family to arrive in Abingdon, Virginia, in 1769. He was the son of Andrew Vance who had come to America in 1692 and died in Lancaster County, Pennsylvania, a few years prior to Samuel's migrating farther south. Andrew's sister, Elizabeth, married Joseph Jackson; they became the great-grandparents of Andrew Jackson.

Samuel Vance and his wife, Sarah (Coville), had nine children. One son, Samuel II, was my fourth great-grandfather. He and his wife, Margaret (Laughlin), had twelve children. One of their sons, John, married Mary (Polly) King. Mary's mother, Elizabeth, was the daughter of Thomas Sharp, referred to previously. Mary's father, William King, was the owner of the saltworks near Abingdon and established King's Boatyards in what is now Kingsport, Tennessee, to ship the salt down the Holston River which joins the Tennessee River farther downstream. It is said that the town of Kingsport is named for either William or his brother, James, who had the first iron works in Sullivan County, Tennessee. Both William and James later served in the Tennessee General Assembly, with William serving from 1815-17 as Sullivan County Representative. James's son James, Jr. was the founder of King College in Bristol.

David Vance, a brother to our fourth Great-grandfather Samuel Vance II, was the grandfather of Zebulon Baird Vance, former Governor of North Carolina. Long before I learned that "Zeb" was in our family, I read that he told someone, perhaps jokingly, perhaps not, that the Vances were run out of Scotland for stealing pigs. Evidently the family already had a liking for the taste of ham, particularly country ham—preferably home-cured—with "sop" (now called "red-eye" gravy). Here is a recipe for this long-time family favorite:

COUNTRY HAM WITH SOP (RED-EYE GRAVY)
This makes about 4 servings
1 pound thinly sliced country ham
Rinse the ham in cold water, but do not soak it. Pat dry.

Start pre-heating over medium heat, a well-seasoned cast iron skillet. Add the slices of ham. Cook the ham over medium heat until well-browned on both sides (about 3 or 4 minutes per side). Remove the ham from the skillet. Keep warm on a platter. Reduce the heat to low.

Into the ham drippings left in the skillet, stir in about 2 cups hot water*.

Stir the mixture well, scraping the bottom of the skillet to get all the browned particles included in the gravy. Let the mixture come to a boil. Reduce the heat and let simmer for a couple of minutes. If you like, you may strain the gravy through a sieve to remove the bits of ham. Or, serve as is, with the ham and hot homemade biscuits (recipe to follow). Many people add half water and half strong black coffee, but our Mother never added the coffee. She always left the ham in the skillet, added a little water, put a lid on the skillet, and steamed the meat until it was tender. Then she removed the ham; if needed, she added more water to the drippings and cooked it down to get it to the right strength.

If you are serving this for breakfast, it might be good to have a side dish of grits (although we never ate them at home), eggs, and plenty of fresh coffee to wash it all down . . . and lots of fresh fruit or fruit preserves or jam for any extra biscuits. And eat "lean" the rest of the day...because you probably will have already consumed more than a goodly amount of fat, cholesterol, and sodium.

While many things done and said by Cousin Zeb may not have been looked upon with approval, Clement Dowd, in his 1897 biography of Zebulon Vance, wrote that, "He (Vance) had plenty of self-esteem, but it was not that of one inflated by popular applause or indiscriminate praise, but only that of the man conscious of right motives and honest purposes.... He has been heard to say every man should have self-esteem and pride enough to keep out of bad company."

One of the speeches Zeb gave, a very profound address in my estimation—and back in those days he surely didn't have a speech writer— was given to the graduating class at Wake Forest College (now Wake Forest University) on June 26, 1872. The strength of his beliefs are evident in the words spoken. During the address, quoted in Dowd's biography, Zeb told the students, "Remember, too—and this above all—that there is no progress, no development, no increase, worthy of your efforts to attain, unless it be conceived in the fear (honor) of your Creator." He then tells the students that being exposed to new ideas in college may have caused some of them to doubt, to become skeptical, and to dismiss a simple faith and that he is aware that this happens. Then, he says, referring to students wanting to be different from others in their beliefs and believing themselves to be above others in their reasoning powers,

It sounds so large, too, to differ with everybody else. It smacks of genius...But be not deceived...The greatest intellects of the world have had all the doubts and suggestions you have thought new and peculiar to yourselves; they have sounded all the depths and shallows of human scepticism [sic], and have found it worse than folly. None can escape the conviction of the existence of a beneficent God—the grain of corn, the blade of grass, the flower and the forest, the seas and the heavens—all and everything, proclaim and prove that in spite of us....

In the closing of what probably was a very long graduation address, Zeb challenges the graduates to,

> Dismiss, my dear young friends, if you have them, all such ideas as those I have described, as skeptical and natural to you; and go forth to your positions in the world strong in the faith of that God from whom cometh every good thing; all true progress, all civilization, all genuine freedom, all desirable wisdom.
> ...Go forth, then and assume your duties in society, remembering what your liberties are worth, what they cost in their establishment. Remember the great and the good of every age have striven to perfect them, and that is your duty to seek diligently for the means and power to do likewise. Resolve, as you must become partisans—for governments are necessarily controlled by parties—that you will yet remain patriots. Labor incessantly to preserve bright and pure the sacred flame of liberty amid all the temptations and wayward tendencies of the age....

These words are unlike any I have heard spoken at any recent college graduation. In those days, speaking with political correctness evidently was not considered. People spoke from their own hearts and their own minds. Then, graduates were challenged to remember the past, to preserve the best, and to make the future brighter. Many times today, graduates and other people are challenged to succeed in their occupations or chosen professions, but unless spoken by a famous historic figure, the very basic underpinnings of success—self-respect, personal responsibility for individual actions, and a sense of duty—often are left out, as is any mention of a Higher Power.

The Vance family, generation after generation, has had a strong sense of personal responsibility and faith, a love of laughter, and, judging from the length of Zeb's speech, we also have shared another trait, as least among some of us—long windedness.

John and Mary King Vance, our third great-grandparents, had eleven children; the youngest was Leander, our great-great-grandfather. Leander married Sara Launa Crumley, the daughter of Jacob Crumley (son of George Crumley, Jr.). Jacob married a South Carolina native, Catherine Grier. Jacob was in the Battle of Horseshoe Bend during the War of 1812. He died in 1851. Jacob's grandfather, George Crumley, Sr., had come to an area of Sullivan County called "Chestnut Flats" sometime before 1769.

The Crumley house, adjacent to the Crumley Cemetery where many of our ancestors and extended family members are buried, is still occupied. Mother always called it the Jacob Crumley house.

Catherine's father, John Grier, was at one time a spy in the Revolutionary War. He served with John Sevier's North Carolina Regiment and was wounded in the right knee during the Battle of King's Mountain where he served along side some of our other ancestors. During the mid-1800s, John lived in Rush County, Indiana, near or with some of his children. The text of a letter John wrote to Catherine and Jacob, excepting one page which was lost before it was given to me, follows.

Dear Children,

I write to let you know that I am well at present thanks to the Lord for his mercies to me. Hoping these lines may find you all in health. I received your letter of July 30, 1837, which gave me great satisfaction to hear that you were all well. I returned from Richmond, Indiana, last Tuesday and I received my money and when I had paid what I owed I had not much money as would pay my expense to Tennessee and I tried to sell my next draw of money and could not get the value of it and I have to stay here till Spring then if the Lord spares me I will come as soon as the weather will permit me to travel. I have made about four hundred weight of tobacco of the best quality which I intend to make about fifty thousand cigars which sell one dollar and fifty cents a thousand and I will have more than one hundred bushels of turnips to my share. Another man and me gained and cleared the ground and go halfs. We are now offered twenty five cents perbushel and I think my tobacco and turnips will get me everything I want. I can dress myself in the best of broad cloth and camel and I will want for nothing only fresh venison and I do not expect any till I come home to Dry Creek and kill it. I have sold my gun. I have not heard from Ja... Grier since last Spring. William Grier was bound to be a tanner and he has quit the trade and gone to Boone County to James Grier and George was bound to a man and he has moved to the Blackhawk Purchase about 500 mi. Eli is not bound but will be in a few days. Subline lives with us. Robert made not crop but about two acres. He has hogs enough for his meat and thirteen for another year. Robert has been sick about two weeks. He caught cold ditching a road. He got fifty dollars for doing it—32-35 rod and he made $1.50 per day.

Give my best respect to Father Crumley and family, to Nathan Morrell and family, Isaac Morrell and his family, Samuel Jones and his family, and Squire Rockhold and his family, to Daniel Crumley and his family and John Crumley and family.

Sons, I want you not to neglect writing to me for I want to prove that I can lift a letter out of the office. I have got my mare and I intend to keep her. I have been offered sixty dollars for her but money cant buy her. I must conclude my letter.

You don't send us word how George is or where he lives.

October 22, 1837

John Grier
Robert Grier
Nancy Grier
Jacob C. Grier

Robert Grier was John's son. Nancy was Robert's wife and Jacob C. was their son. Nancy was the former Nancy Crumley, daughter of George Crumley, Jr. and sister to my Great-great-great-grandpa, Jacob Crumley. William Grier, mentioned in the letter, was also a son of John. William married Mary Crumley, a sister to Nancy and Great-great-great-grandpa Jacob. I suppose they decided to keep things in the family! Robert Grier, according to a newspaper clipping glued in a scrapbook made from *The Congressional Clube, 2nd Session, 40th Congress, 1868*, had skin cancer. The scrapbook, kept by Great-great-grandma Sara Launa Crumley Vance, also contained the following notices from unknown newspapers:

The subject of the following sketch, Robert Grier, was born in Carter County, September 5, 1808, and died in his home January 12, 1885, aged 76 years. He married Nancy Crumley in the year 1830 who still survives him. About the year 1834, they, in company with Mr. Haun and family, emigrated to the State of Indiana and remained there some five years. Not being satisifed owing to ill health, Mr. G. returned to Tennessee and settled in Sullivan County where he remained until he was called to that country from which none ever returns. Uncle Robin was a poor but honest man, generous and free hearted, and would divide his last crumb with the hungry. A better neighbor is seldom found ready at any time to accommodate even at the sacrifice of his own interest, the needy or afflicted. During the late war, aged as he was, he went to the front in search of a wounded relative and other friends and brought them home. He was a life long Democrat of the A. Jackson school and never feared to show his colors. For many years he was a member of the Lutheran Church and with Christian fortitude bore his last affliction without a murmur, said he was ready and awaiting his Master's call. 'Blessed are the dead that die in the Lord.' He has an aged wife and seven children to mourn his loss. But while they feel the sore bereavement they would not call him back to his sufferings. His end was peace and peace be to his ashes.

Ruthton. Feb. 17, 1885   A Friend

Ruthton was a community near the present-day South Holston Dam, near Bristol, Tennessee.

Island Mills, Tenn., Jan. 20.

Old Aunt Nancy Grier, wife of Robert Grier deceased, passed away last Thursday, and was interred on Friday in the Crumley graveyard. She was some 80 odd years old. One of her daughters, Caroline is lying at the point of death with no hopes of recovery.

Island Mills, Tennessee, was a community near the town of Bluff City. Today the area has lost its individual name and is part of Bluff City's rural surroundings. No year was given for Nancy's death. Family records indicate that Nancy died in 1890.

John must have loved to eat turnips, or perhaps they were a good crop to grow in that part of Indiana. Can you imagine having 100 bushels of turnips on hand? I can't, especially since I don't like cooked turnips! However, just before New Year's Day a few years ago, I decided that I would prepare a traditional New Year's meal for the family—my sisters who live in the area and their families included. While turnips are not one of the good luck, prosperity, or other virtuous foods eaten at New Year's, we happened to have some on hand. My husband had brought them home from a farm near where he plays golf. The farmer had told some of the golfers that they could come over and help themselves. So, they did. I remembered that some in the family did like that vegetable, and I made mashed turnips. Here is my recipe:

MASHED TURNIPS
2 to 3 pounds fresh turnips
1 tablespoon sugar
Butter
Salt to taste
Pepper to taste

Heavy cream or half and half
Parmesan cheese (optional)
Bread crumbs (optional)

Peel the turnips and slice into thick slices. Place in a medium saucepan. Pour in water just to barely cover the turnips. Add the sugar and a sprinkling of salt (more can be added later). Bring to a boil. Lower the heat and simmer until the turnips are just tender. Pour them into a colander to completely drain the water. Place the drained turnips back into the saucepan in which they were cooked. Place on low heat and add about 2 tablespoons of butter. Mash the turnips and butter together, adding salt and pepper as desired. Then, add heavy cream or half and half—a tablespoon at a time—just to make sure you don't add too much. (Since turnips are watery anyway, when cooked, they will not get as creamy as mashed potatoes). Keep blending the mixture together, adding more cream if you want; but you don't want to have a soup. Taste for seasoning again and correct, if needed. Place into a greased 1½-quart casserole dish. Sprinkle the top with grated Parmesan cheese and fine dry bread crumbs, if desired. Dot with butter. Bake 20-30 minutes in a 350 - 375 degree oven or until bubbly and golden brown. Or, just place the turnips into a serving dish and sprinkle the cheese over and serve without baking.

I doubt that Grandpa John Grier ever ate turnips fixed this way. My family never had, either. But I just could not fathom the thought of having plain old boiled turnips.

At some point in his life, John had owned a farm in Carter County, Tennessee, not far from North Carolina. It was to that area that he evidently had intended to return. However, at the time of his death in June 1844, he was living with Catherine and Jacob Crumley. John is buried in the Crumley Cemetery in Sullivan County, Tennessee.

Leander and Sara Launa Crumley Vance had one son, Jacob Leander, my great-grandfather, who was a baby when his father died. Sara took Jacob back to her parents' (Jacob and Catherine Crumley) home where they lived for awhile. She later married a man whose last name was Smith. Some of our relatives in the O'Dell/Vance/Crumley families referred to Sara as "Aunt Sairy Smith." She was their aunt, great-aunt or great-great-aunt, depending on the generation; but to some in the family, she was also a great-grandmother or great-great-grandmother.

Years passed, and Jacob Leander married Susan C. Morrell, the daughter of William and Susannah Vanderventer Morrell. William's father and mother were Jonathan and Catherine O'Dell Morrell, mentioned previously. Susannah's parents were Abraham and Mary Jones Vanderventer. Abraham was born in New Jersey in 1753 and died in Sullivan County, Tennessee in 1837.

Jacob and Susan had three children. A daughter, Sarah Launa, died when she was not quite twenty years old. Mother said that she got a rupture in her side from moving a chest of drawers. The other children were Cordelia Abbygate "Delia" who married Campbell Cole and William Leander Vance, our Grandpa. Grandpa was born in June 1877 and married Cornettie Elizabeth Green(e), born in July 1871 to John and Sarah Fidilla Trivett Green(e), of Watauga County, North Carolina.

This Greene family, headed by Jeremiah, came to North Carolina about 1750 with a group known as the Jersey settlers. They came from England to Massachusetts about 1635. One line of this family went to Rhode Island with Roger Williams. From Rhode Island, they went to New York and then to New Jersey before heading south to North Carolina. Jeremiah's son, also Jeremiah, was the father of Isaac, who lived to be 79 years old. Isaac was the father of 11 children, and reported had over 100 grandchildren and 100 great-grandchildren when he died.

Great-grandma Vance (Susan) with Grandpa and his two sisters—Sarah and Delia

Great-grandpa Vance (Jacob)
Mother Said That His Eyes Really Were Like They Are in This Photo

One of Isaac's sons, Solomon, had an inn, or more likely a stagecoach stop over, in Deep Gap (Watauga County), North Carolina, and was also a blacksmith. Sometimes I wonder whether any of the recipes served at his inn have been passed down through the family; if they have been, the recipes are no longer identified as "Grandpa Solomon's." According to one account, Solomon lived to be 85 years old and had 21 children, 160 grandchildren, 160 great-grandchildren, and several great-great-grandchildren. At least in this line of the family, our ancestors had exceptionally longer than average lives.

One of Solomon's sons was Larkin Greene. According to various years of the Census Reports of Watauga County, he was a blacksmith. Among Mother's old possessions was a strange-looking device made of hammered metal. Nobody knew what it was, but it was kept. After this device was passed down to me—I'm not one to throw anything away, either—I saw a reproduction of it in an Outer Banks, North Carolina, gift shop. It is a Patience Puzzle. Since it has been kept in the family, with no one in recent years knowing what it was, surely one of the relatives—more than likely Great-great-grandpa Larkin—made it. Sometimes when I look at that puzzle, I think that in today's society, the virtue of patience is almost as rare as that old toy.

Great-great-grandpa Larkin Greene married Lucinda Trivett, the daughter of Sallie Elrod and John Trivett, Jr. Among Sallie's and John's sons was Elijah. Larkin's and Lucinda's son, John Greene, married Sarah Fidilla Trivett. Sarah was the daughter of Elijah and Charity Irena Carlton Trivett. John and Sarah were first cousins. Despite the idea that all Appalachian people are a bunch of in-breeders, this is the only instance I found in our family of first cousins marrying. One of my cousins says that all this intermarrying is the reason that some of us have curved spines. Now, if I could just figure out where all my other weird characteristics originated....

Part of the Greene Family
Front Row: (Left to right): Uncle Clyde Greene (Grandma's Brother), Great-grandpa John Greene; Hobart Warren (a relative of Aunt Blanche), Great-grandma Sarah Fidilla Trivett Greene; Great-grandma Lucinda Trivett Greene; Grandpa Vance holding Uncle Cloyd [- - yes, little boys wore dresses then]; Grandma Cornettie Elizabeth Greene Vance holding Mother; and, standing at the right, Uncle Johnnie. Back Row: Grandma's Sisters and One of Her Brothers. (Left to right): Aunt Julia Greene Boyd (Lorena's and Lawrence's mother); Uncle Granville Greene; Aunt Brookie Greene Carrier; and Aunt Rosa ("Rosie) Greene Boyd (Conley's, Gene's, and J. Lee's mother)

In June of 1894, John and Sarah loaded up their belongings, including their children, into a wagon and left Watauga County, North Carolina, for a home over the mountains in Sullivan County, Tennessee. I have often wondered if they had an ordinary wagon or if they came over the mountain in what was known as a "North Carolina wagon." The backs of these wagons were supposedly higher than the sides to prevent possessions from falling out as they climbed those mountains. They brought a picnic lunch to eat along the way; but, none of their children or grandchildren ever thought to ask what they brought. Perhaps they brought fried chicken or cold roast beef, biscuits, potato salad or slaw made with vinegar, cake, cookies or fried apple pies, and perhaps fresh wild strawberries; and, to wash it all down, plenty of spring water or some herbal tea.

If Great-grandma Greene had made tea, perhaps she used mint. Mint tea on a hot summer day is so refreshing! This is the way I make it:

MINT TEA
2 cups of fresh spearmint
⅓ cup loose tea
1 quart of water to boil
6 or 7 cups of sugar
3½ quarts cold water

Place about 2 cups of fresh spearmint* into a heavy pitcher or heatproof bowl. Bruise the leaves with a wooden spoon to extract some of the flavor. To the mint, add ⅓ cup loose tea (or use 1 family-size tea bag). Bring 1 quart of water to boil. Pour over the mint and tea. Let this steep 4 or 5 minutes. Then strain the mixture. This will make about 1 gallon of tea.

To make the full amount, pour the spearmint-tea mixture into a gallon (or more) container. One of the crockery drink dispensers with a "faucet" near the base is ideal. Add 6 or 7 cups of sugar. Stir with a wooden spoon until the sugar dissolves. Add 3½ quarts cold water. Stir. Taste. Add more sugar if needed. To serve, place several ice cubes into a glass. Pour the tea over. Garnish with a lemon slice (or wedge) and a fresh sprig of mint.

If you do not want or need to make the full gallon at one time, cover the spearmint-tea mixture (without adding the sugar) and refrigerate.

For each quart of tea, into a 1½-to-2-quart pitcher, place 1 cup of the spearmint-tea mixture and 1½-to-2 cups sugar. Stir (with a wooden spoon) until the sugar dissolves. Then add water. Stir again. Serve as above. (If you sweeten the mixture after it cools, you may need to add more sugar, but some people do not like to sweeten tea and then refrig-

erate it because sometimes it becomes "cloudy").
You may use any kind of mint you like. Apple mint or peppermint is also good, but we prefer spearmint.

As the Greene family approached Bluff City, Great-grandpa John had stopped the wagon at the river to let the horses drink when a young man, William Leander Vance, saw one of John's daughters and said, "That one is mine!" "That one" was Cornettie ("Nettie") Elizabeth Greene. Evidently, Grandpa's grit, determination, and good eye were already very developed, because two years later, Grandma and Grandpa Vance were married.

Chapter 3
Mother's Memories and Stories

My mother, Susan Fidilla (Vance) Rather, better known as "Dilla," was born in a two-story log house in Cedar Grove (on Possum Creek), a section of Bluff City, Tennessee, in April 1902. When she was growing up, and even when we were growing up, she had no idea that she was related to famous, or infamous people. I remember that when we were studying about Andrew Jackson in elementary school, she said, "I never did think too much of him because of the way he 'carried on' with Rachel." Her saying that she didn't "think too much of him" was the same as saying that she didn't have too much respect for him. Of course, at that time, I had no idea what she meant by "carrying on," and I was too stupid or perhaps too smart to ask. When I found out that Jackson was a distant "Cousin Andy," Mother got a good laugh. We *all* did because of what Mother had said years earlier. She wasn't impressed merely with people's positions or how much money they had. She *was* impressed by what kind of human beings they were and how they treated other people. And did she ever try to teach us these same things!

When our daughters found out that they had some Cherokee ancestry from their dad's side of the family and that they were also related distantly to Jackson, they were mortified. The relation was not distant enough for them! One of our Cherokee-Appalachian friends once said, "Well, Jackson was a man of his time." Perhaps.

Two brothers, Johnnie and Cloyd (Claude), preceded Mother in birth. I have been told that Uncle Cloyd didn't like his name and changed it to Claude. But, Mother still called him Cloyd, as we did. He didn't seem to mind. The house in which the Vance children were born was on a corner diagonally across the road from where the old Mike Webb Store was built. Among Mother's possessions was a small, gold-edged light blue flowing into white semi-porcelain scalloped-edged plate in the center of which is written in gold: "M.E. Webb & Co. Cheapest Store on Earth Island Mills,

Tenn." (Since their beginnings, Bluff City and several of the outlying communities have had several name changes).

Several years ago, my husband and I went to the area to take additional photographs. Workers were busy tearing down the original Webb's Store, which had been closed and boarded up for years. We talked with the workers about the demolition and the history, and we talked about the old school which was torn down several years before this. Cedar Grove Freewill Baptist Church now owns this land.

While we were talking, I noticed a primitive farm table on the back of

The Old Mike Webb Store
In Process of Being Demolished

the workers' flatbed truck. The table had come from the store, and the foreman said I could have it for $10. The table, with its knife marks and wear
still quite evident, is now used again every day.

Grandpa Vance owned a large acreage going all the way back up Possum Creek and up what is now Hickory Tree Road. Mother loved living
in the log house. Her room was upstairs, and she had her own small crystal oil lamp that she took with her when she was ready to go to bed at night.
She said that the stairs went out of the front room. Out of the front room,
downstairs, you passed through another room, and then, into the kitchen.
At the side of the front room were two or three other bedrooms.

When she was about seven years old, Grandpa had a new house built up
the road. This house was not a log house, but was finished with wide clap-
board and had a blue tin roof. River rock columns supported the front
porch. Grandpa probably had picked up those rocks from his fields or had
taken the wagon the short way to the river to get them. I didn't think to
ask about this when I had a chance. Mother said that the new house had
four rooms downstairs and two rooms upstairs, but at that time, only one of
the upstairs rooms was finished.

Grandpa sold the older house and at least that part of the land to Mike
Webb. We believe that the log house burned some time after Mother and
her family moved. Mike built a two-story white house with a green roof
to replace the old log house. In recent years, the house has been remodeled and/or repainted. Today, within whispering—not shouting—distance

Mother's Second Home

Mother with Her Family
Mother, Uncle Cloyd, Uncle Johnnie, Grandma, and Grandpa

of Mother's second home, a new house has been built. Evidently, the owners plan to remove the older house.

Mother and her brothers went to Cedar Grove School which was to the side and back of Webb's store. A creek ran behind the school. Her best friend in these years and throughout her life was Zillah Webb who was later to marry one of their schoolmates, Karl Rhea. "She's the sister I never had," Mother said. Mother had always wanted a baby sister and she laughed and said, "I guess that's why I kept having babies!" And, have them she did—six of us. I asked Mother about her not having a baby sister or brother. She said that after Grandma had the first two children, the doctor told her that she should have no more children. But, Grandma still wanted a girl, so she defied the doctor's orders. I guess she was determined to try, no matter what!

Mother and Zillah used to go pick berries on the hills behind Mother's house. Zillah told me that she liked to pick blackberries. Mother said that she preferred to pick huckleberries rather than blackberries. There is a reason. Once, while she, Uncle Johnnie, and Uncle Cloyd were out picking blackberries, ". . . a black racer got after me," Mother said. "Johnnie and Cloyd told me to run and get on the fence, and I ran as fast as I could. I barely got up on the fence with that snake after me, and they came and killed it."

When we were children, we loved to visit with Zillah and Karl. She was a wonderful quiet-spoken lady whose bright and expressive eyes reflected her pleasure in the grown-ups' conversations. When someone made a statement or comment she agreed with, she would say, "Oh! Indeed!" I had never heard this and thought it was delightful. I still did when we took our children, along with Mother, to visit her. Karl had died years before, but I remember him as being such a happy, jolly person—as older people used to say—who was one of the favorite mailmen in Bristol. Zillah now lives in a retirement home. And, I think the expression, "Oh! Indeed!" is still delightful. I have never heard anyone else say it. It is unique to a very unique and special lady!

When I was twelve or thirteen, my sister Reba and her future husband Tunis took Mother, Mrs. Ragan (Tunis's mother), Marie—the sister just a few years older than I am, and me fishing at a cove on South Holston Lake. His ancestors had owned land there before TVA came in with the South Holston Dam. Since Tunis knew blackberries were growing there, Mrs. Ragan and Mother took buckets and went to pick them while we fished. This is the only time I know that Mother had ever gone on a real berrying since she and Zillah were young.

Cedar Grove School
(Used At the Time of This Photo As a Residence)

When Mother and Zillah were in school at Cedar Grove, where all ages were taught together, they had a teacher, a Miss Hicks, who was very hateful to them. They liked to giggle and have fun, especially during algebra, and Miss Hicks hated laughter. She was all business. Maybe this is one reason Mother hated algebra; she loved to laugh.

Mother did love English, though, especially poetry. I never knew this until one day in the 1970s when we were talking about school (this was when I had gone back to college to complete my degrees). For Mother's Day 1979, we gave her a copy of Robert Frost's poetry. The first poem she read from the book was "The Pasture." After she read it aloud, she said, "I love that poem," and her eyes just sparkled.

Perhaps it expressed her love of the land, the animals, and company— as in "you come, too." Perhaps it reminded her of a postcard she received from her Aunt Victoria (Uncle Granville Greene's wife) when she wrote,

> My dear little niece, I got your card a few dayes ago was glad to hear you had got well again I am about as usual rainy dayes not well & warm dayes better got a letter from your grand pa yes . . . [yesterday] was so glad to hear he was still better hope he will be well enough to come see me. you must come with him when he comes. Can't you come with your Uncle G . . .when he goes up there to see his pa you & your ma both come I'v got the pretiest little colt you ever saw one week old
> By by my little niece Your aunt, V.F.G.

The postcard is postmarked, "Jonesboro, Tenn. Mar 26 3 PM 1909." Jonesboro, now spelled Jonesborough, the oldest town in Tennessee, is located in Washington County, adjacent to Sullivan County. Aunt Victoria's maiden name was Farthing, also a Watauga County family.

She wrote to Uncle Johnnie on a penny postcard dated May 5, 1909, from Jonesboro,

> Dear Johnnie __ Oh! how I would of loved to of been there & went fishing with you all cach me a mess & come down & bring them to me & we will have a fine time I am so lonesome since Pa & Ma left I can't hardly stay at home so, you come & stay a few dayes with your Aunt Victoria

Another card that Aunt Victoria wrote from Jonesborough was to Uncle Johnnie and Uncle Cloyd. In it, she stated that Uncle Granville wanted them to come down and help him on the farm. Aunt Victoria must have

CEDAR GROVE SCHOOL STUDENTS PRE-1910. Bluff City, Tennessee. Female teacher shown very faintly on left, Virgie Crumley. Male teacher, far right, C.B. Jones. FRONT ROW (LEFT TO RIGHT): Guy Cox, Robert Bowery, Unknown, Clarence Simerly, Unknown, Claude Vance, Cecil Simerly, Unknown, Dorius Keaton. SECOND ROW: left to right): Grace Simerly, Leon Simerly, Unknown, Unknown, Dilla Vance, Edith O'Dell, Eva O'Dell, Zillah Webb, Bessie Riley, Lorena Rhea, Willie Crumley. THIRD ROW (left to right): _____ Morrell, Burley or Bill Morrell, Bryan Webb, Lilly Simerly, Juda Simerly, Texie Cox, Mae Crumley, Bertha Rhea, Mertie Crumley, Virgie Buchanan, Mae Moss, Lena Greene. FOURTH ROW (left to right): _____ Cox, Unknown, Stella Keaton, Maude Jenkins, Minnie Morrell, Clara Rhea, Cordie Morrell, Ira Crumley, Mary Anne Riley, Ann Reece, _____ Lackie, Belvon Jenkins, Sudie Harmon, Clayton Cox. FIFTH ROW (left to right): Unknown, Belmont Rhea, Frank Riley, Johnnie Vance, Ernest Simerly, Karl Rhea Alfred Boyd, Joe Crumley, Bob (?) Morrell, Jim (?) Morrell, Ed Cox, Unknown, Sampson Cox. The two Morrell children beginning the third row and Minnie, Cordie, Bob, and Jim Morrell were children of John Morrell. (Ann Reece, in this picture, and the other Reece children in the following pictures, were sisters and brothers to B. Carroll Reece, former U.S. Congressman from Tennessee).

(Photograph Courtesy of Mary Boyd Jones, daughter of Lee and Grace Simerly Boyd)

CEDAR GROVE SCHOOL STUDENTS. December 21, 1910. FRONT ROW (left to right): Jim Simerly, Andy Riley, Dona Simerly, Truman Crumley, Eva O'Dell, Lorena Rhea, Willie Crumley, Ardith Coffey, Dilla Vance, Leon Simerly, Sudie Harmon, Belvon Jenkins, Edity Riley (?), Teacher Ida Fine. SECOND ROW (left to right): Bessie Riley, Laura Reece, Belmont Rhea, Zora Coffey, Collis Coffey, Claude Vance, Johnny Bowery, Mertie Crumley. BACK ROW (left to right): Raleigh Reece, Cecil Simerly, Maude Jenkins, Mary Anne Riley, Clara Rhea, Millard Reece, Robert Cox, Mandy Ann Reece, Frank Riley, Clarence Simerly. (Note: Ardith, Zora, and Collis Coffey were the children of Grandma Vance's sister, Ermine, who married Elbert Coffey. Zora became a nurse and worked for many years in the nursery at Bristol Memorial Hosptial where she took good care of our children when they were born).

Figure 11. CEDAR GROVE SCHOOL STUDENTS. Post-1910. FRONT ROW (left to right): Worley Webb, Lawrence Simerly, Reford Cawood, _____ Hardin, Billy Glover, Howard Jenkins, Ronald Harmon, Edrie Cawood, Anna Boyd, Lennie Glover, Bertha Hardin. SECOND ROW (left to right): Eva O'Dell, Lennis Harmon, Nellie Mae Woodring, Hazel Jenkins, Grace Simerly, Leon Crumley, Maggie Jenkins, Daisy Webb, Nena Simerly, Victoria Boyd, Ival Woodring, Ida Hardin, Nannie Kate Ealey, Ethel Riley. THIRD ROW (left to right): Mertie Crumley, Clementine O'Dell, Zillah Webb, Bessie Riley, Teacher Alice Hicks, Dilla Vance, Edelle Boy, Sudie Harmon, Teacher Kate Hicks, Anna Mae Glover, Leon Simerly, Marie Harmon, Beulah Harmon. FOURTH ROW (left to right): Ronald Simerly, Truman Crumley, Caleb Glover, Clarence Simerly, Frank Riley, Claude Vance, Belmont Rhea, Cecil Simerly, Paul Boy, Andy Riley, Belvon Jenkins, Willie Crumley, Edith O'Dell, Lorena Rhea. (Note: Mother is standing next to Miss Hicks; I'll bet Mother was really happy. Was Miss Hicks still trying to keep Mother in line?) (Photograph courtesy of Mary Boyd Jones, daughter of Lee and Grace Simerly Boyd).

been very lonely. Some of her immediate family still lived in North Carolina, I believe, and the rest of the family was in East Tennessee. She and Uncle Granville had no children.

Even at country schools in the early 1900s, school pictures were being made. Sometimes the pictures were made of the whole student body with teachers. When the school children at Cedar Grove had special performances for the community and during Commencement Exercises, sometimes an admission fee of 15 cents was charged, and refreshments were served. Uncle Cloyd and Aunt Blanche kept some of the programs, which weren't really noticed until after their deaths.

Closing Excercises

Cedar Grove

Tuesday, February 8, 1916

———

Closing exercises Cedar Grove School 1918

Program 1:30 p. m.

Chours ... .Welcome to All

Invocation........ ....Rev. E. A. Gentry

Prize Contest

A Brave Little Boy ....Theo. Crumley

Small Dress Making............ ....Rubby Webb

Johnny Sleepy Head..................... ....Parks O'Dell

Willies Tea Party...................... ....Hazel Jenkins

The Drummer Boy.............................Haskell Mottern

Home Measurments.... ....Edrie Cawood

A Bothered Boy ....Howard Jenkins

Don't Bury Me Deep.............. ... .Nannie Ealey

Bound to Do It...................................... Reford Cawood

A Little Girl's 'plaint ....Daisy Webb

A Grevious Complaint...............................James O'Dell

Her Papa...... ....Nena Simerly

Promoted.. Lawrence Simerly

The Little Grave ....Leon Harmon

....Leon Crumley

Little Orphans ....Grace Simerly

Willie Wanted to Die.............................. Worley Weeb

Washington and His Hatchet...................Ronal Simerly

....Truman Crumley

Metal Contest

....Victoria Boyd
Little Jim......... ....Ethel Riley
Columbus..James Simerly
Papa Begins to Shave.............................Victor Broyles
.... Marie Harmon
Little Willie and the Apple.......................Andrew Riley
The Dying Soldier.................................Verlin Mottern
Nobody's Child.... .... Ardltlr Coffey
The Irish Maid.....................................Lorena Rhea
A Scene In a Tenent House....................... Edith O'Dell
Your Mission..James Broyles
Ride of Jennie McNeal.........................Eva O'Dell
The Rum Maniac.................................Below Jenkins
Mona's Waters.............................. ....Willie Crumley
The Last Hymn..... ....Lena O'Dell
.... Myrtle Crumley
A Tribute to Grant............................ .... Zella Broyles
Night After Shiloh................................Dilla Vance
Alameda...Zillah Webb
The Fountain of Youth.......................... Lee Broyles
Two Brothers................................... Belmont Rhea
Curfeu Must Not Ring To-night...................Edelle Boy
As The Moon Rose..................... ....Clemma O'Dell
Tommy's Prayer...................................Bessie Riley
Dialogue............................... .... To Aunt Emily's
Quartet...Little Builders

USHERS
Johnnie Vance, Cecil Simerly, Paul Boy, Frank Riley

Program 6:30 p. m.

Quartet......................... Massa in De cold, cold Ground

Monologue......................................The Water Melon

Backtown Spirits

Drama—I Act...................................Time—One Hour

Dialogue

Getting the Bag to Hold

Hazel Adams III Acts.....................Time One Hour and

Forty-Five Minutes

Awarding of Prizes, Medals and Certificates of Promotion

USHERS

Belmont Rhea   Claude Vance

1916 Program of Closing Exercises
Cedar Grove School

Closing Exercises
Cedar Grove
Wednesday, March 13, 1918
1 O'Clock, P. M.

Program

Song	...Welcome Year
Invocation	Rev. H. D. Chapman

RECITATIONS

I Love My Papa	Ruby Simerly
A Happy Accident	Thelma Jenkins
A Piece	Glenna Rhea
Take-It-Back-Day	Nannie Bess Broyles
A Little Speech	Murrel Cawood
A Little Girl's Soliloquy	Sallie Kate Broyles
Drill	Upside Down

RECITATIONS

Mathematics	Viola Broyles
The Birthday	Edrie Cawood
Ordering A Brother	Hazel Jenkins
	Maggie Jenkins
	Ella Fae Woodring
Dialogue	The Spelling Match
Class Exercise	The Days of The Week

RECITATIONS

The Difference	Theo Crumley
Johnny Sleepy-head	Howard Jenkins
Willie's Exercise	Arvile Harmon
The Mother of A Soldier	Reford O Cox
Drill	Come Play With Me
Dialogue	Keeping Store

RECITATIONS

Little Blossom	Daisy Webb
My Ideal	Leon Crumley
Grandma's Mistake	Nena Simerly
If We Only Understood	Nellie Woodring
Catch The Sunshine	Lenos Harmon
The Master Is Coming	Gladys Broyles
Papa's Letter	Nannie Ealey
Comedy	A Meeting of The Young Ladies' Club
A Comedy	A Crumpled Rose Leaf
Dialogue	Waiting For The 2:40 Train
Dialogue	From Punkin Ridge

REFRESHMENTS

Concert
6:30 P. M.

Drill	Red, White and Blue
A Drama in Two Acts	The Last Loaf
A Comedy in Two Acts	Timothy Delano's Courtship
Pantomine	My Old Kentucky Home

AWARDING OF PRIZES   DISMISSION

USHERS

Cecil Simerly	Lester Sharp
Frank Riley	Belmont Rhea

ADMISSION 15 CENTS
REFRESHMENTS

The McGill Printing Co., Bristol, Tenn

Closing Exercises Cedar Grove School 1918
Note that many of the students from 1916 are no longer listed on this program.
They had completed their years here and had moved on to other things.

Grandpa started teaching Mother to cook when she was about eight years old. Grandma was ill much of the time, and Mother had to help with the work. She was too little to reach the table to do the mixing, so she stood on a little stool to make the biscuits, cornbread, and other foods. She made biscuits every day for ever so many years after that!

This is one of the recipes for Buttermilk Biscuits that Mother had kept over the years. I really doubt that this is the recipe she first learned because most people in the early 1900s probably were still using lard instead of what we call "shortening." These are still good biscuits:

BUTTERMILK BISCUITS
2 cups sifted flour
2 teaspoons baking powder
1 teaspoon salt
¼ teaspoon soda (baking soda)
2 to 3 tablespoons shortening
⅔ cup buttermilk

Combine together the flour, baking powder, salt and soda. Cut or rub in shortening. Add buttermilk to make a soft dough, stirring just enough to make ingredients hold together. Turn out on lightly floured board and knead gently for half a minute. Roll out and cut. Bake on an ungreased pan. Bake at 425 degrees for about 10 minutes.

Mother learned to steam meat to make it very tender. The technical term for the steaming method she used is *braising*. She learned to coat meat with flour and seasoning and then brown it in shortening. When all pieces were browned, water was poured over the meat; the skillet was covered, and the meat simmered for an hour or so, until it was fork-tender. She did this with fried chicken, cubed steak, and pork chops, and much later, with pot roast. Beef and pork roasts were boiled or simmered until they were so tender no knife was needed to cut the meat. (That's the way we had these cuts of beef and pork at home). Here is the method Mother used:

BOILED BEEF (OR PORK)
Choose about a 3-pound blade or chuck roast. If using pork, use a shoulder roast or pork loin. You can also use this method for back-bone and ribs, if you are lucky enough to know someone who still raises and butchers their own hogs, or if by chance, you can find the backbone and ribs in the grocery stores or perhaps in a butcher shop. Many times ribs are available, but not the backbone. I don't really know what difference, if any, in taste there is, but "backbone

AND ribs" were the tradition.

Wash the meat. Place in a deep pot. Cover with water. Over medium heat, bring the water to a boil. As the water begins to simmer and foam begins to form on the top of the water, begin skimming the foam off with a large spoon. (Try not to pick up the water as you are doing this). When the foam stops forming on the top, add salt—close to a tablespoon. Cover the pot and let the meat simmer for 2 to 3 hours or until it is very tender. Check the broth and taste the meat to see if you want to add more salt; if so, add the salt and simmer about 15 more minutes. This can be refrigerated in the broth and served, after heating, the next day.

It was the tradition in our family for the meat (beef and pork) to be served with boiled potatoes. In addition, when pork was boiled, sauerkraut was cooked in a saucepan to go along with the meat, potatoes, and broth.

To serve with boiled potatoes: About 30 to 45 minutes before you are ready to serve the meal, and before the meat is really done, peel and cut potatoes into halves or quarters. Add them to the boiling meat and broth. (This will help take care of the saltiness if you happen to add too much salt.)

To serve: Remove the meat to a large platter. Place the boiled potatoes either around the meat or in a separate bowl. Strain the broth through a sieve and serve in another bowl or in a gravy boat. Be sure to have plenty of hot biscuits for soaking up that wonderful broth!

Evidently, Grandpa Vance was a stickler for the quality of the food and how it was prepared and served. Perhaps this was why Mother would preface some meals with, "I guess it'll do."

After the food was put by for the winter, the women started their needlework. Grandma made much of the family's clothing. She also made embroidered and candlewick bedspreads and crocheted items used as dresser, table, or overstuffed furniture protection as well as decoration. Some of our relatives wove coverlets, but we are not sure that Grandma did this. Some members of the family also did tatting.

Recently, Raymond, Uncle Johnnie's second son, gave me a piece of fabric which was woven by Grandma. The note, written by Raymond's mother (Aunt Ida) and attached to the fabric, said that this was part of a straw tick covering made by Grandma before they came here from North Carolina. Ticks were used then as we use mattresses now; but, this was the first I had heard of anybody in the family using straw ticks. I was familiar with the feather ticks, though—I slept on one when I was very young and still have it. The fabric Grandma wove is from yarn so soft it feels like silk. I can just see Grandma as a young girl sitting at the great wheel spinning the yarn and then sitting at the big loom weaving it into this wonderful fabric.

Grandma also made quilts. At one point in their lives, Grandpa sold men's clothing. Grandma used some of the small sample material swatches to piece a quilt almost like today's comforters. The different-sized swatches were sewn together to make a full-sized top. Then, Grandma used the turkey-track embroidery stitch to form a border around each swatch. This top was then put together with cotton batting and a grey flannel-like backing. All layers were then tacked together with a heavy pink embroidery thread. This is still used sometimes on our bed during the winter.

The traditions of sewing our own and/or our children's clothing and quilting has remained with some of the family to the current days. Some of us still embroider, crochet, and knit. Much of the needlework is still done only in the fall and winter months, as was the tradition.

Grandma (or one of the great-grandmas) also did "turkey work"—fine-lined red embroidery (the outline stitch) on white backgrounds. This type of work seemed to have been common among people of German ancestry. Two of the turkey work pillow shams in our family which were never finished off for use as pillow covers are now framed. The quotations embroidered on the two pieces say much, I believe, about the overall philosophy of this extended family.

The first piece, depicting a lady lying in a bed of flowers while an angel with its wings shaped like those of a butterfly looks over, states, "I slept and dreamed that life was beauty." On the companion piece is embroidered a lady with her hair up in a bun. She is wearing an apron over her dress and has a broom in her hand. The embroidered quotation on this piece, "I woke and found that life was duty," is perhaps an embodiment of the Protestant Ethic by which this family lived.

Much of their lives was centered on their families, their religion and the church. It was in their churches that some of them learned to read music, to sing, and to play musical instruments. Yes, some still "pick (or play) and grin," as the common saying goes. But, to Mother's frustration, I never learned to read shaped notes. About the time she was trying to teach me this, Reba (with some help from Marie at times) was trying to teach me to play the piano by reading the regular-shaped notes. To me this was much easier even when singing than remembering which shapes "do," "re," "me," etc. were. When I finally learned to play the piano, at first and perhaps later, the family sometimes grimaced instead of grinning—especially after I learned to play "Beautiful Dreamer" with both hands. I used to play it over and over and over until somebody would yell, "Quit that!"

The churches held singings often, as well has having camp meetings in the summer. One of the old postcards Mother kept was from one of her cousins or a friend, who asked if she had been attending the singing and said, "I would like to attend, but it's been too cold." The card, signed "C.B.," was postmarked at Emmett, Tenn. Dec 28 1918." Emmett is a community near South Holston Dam/Lake.

Many of the singings and all of the camp meetings involved the consumption of food. Sometimes they had dinner on the ground after the first two-to-three-hour-long morning services and before the night services. They probably needed much fortification for the fire and brimstone preaching common in those days.

Another special event that Mother loved attending was a singing school. A visitor would come to the church and teach the people how to sing (using the shaped notes, of course) and they would learn new songs. During the late 1970s or early1980s, we had planned to take Mother to Watauga County on Good Friday since we had a day off from work and school. Mother had said that she always wanted to see the place where the family lived before moving to Tennessee. Prior to our trip, I had written to some of the officials in Boone who very kindly looked up some of the land records for me; so, we had at least some starting point.

The day we were to go, Mother was not well enough to make the trip, but we went on so we could at least take pictures for her. In the process of finding the homeplace, our daughter spotted a small cemetery on top of a hill. We took the gravel road up to the cemetery and found the graves of Elijah (who lived to be 81) and Charity Trivett and some of the other relatives. At Trivett's store, across the highway from the cemetery, we were told that this was the Adams Cemetery and that a man, Clyde Greene, who lived just off the highway, a relatively short distance down the road, took care of the cemetery. The people at the store said that he might be able to help us. When I called Clyde, I told him what we were looking for, and asked if we might visit with him. He said, "Why, yeah! Come on!"

As we started up the walkway toward the house where he was waiting in a crisp white shirt and pressed, faded, bib overalls, I told my husband, "He's a cousin, alright!" Some of the Greenes have carried with them some common mannerisms and facial and structural characteristics. Sure enough, he was a distant cousin on both the Greene and Trivett sides of the family. Clyde said that until recently, when he found out he had some heart trouble, he had always walked to the cemetery to cut the grass and weeds, and make sure everything was in order. He said that sometimes he still walked there, but not always. As we sat and talked about the family, past and present, it was as if we were in the home of one of the closer relatives.

When we began to leave, Clyde, in his 80s, said, "I wish you would stay and eat supper with me and then go to the singing school," which was being held at the little church down the road from his house. That would have been nice, but we still wanted to find where Grandma had lived, which we did. Sometimes since, I have wished that we had stayed and spent more time with Clyde and had gone to the singing school with him. We heard the next year that he had died. Singing and other forms of music have been a strong influence on this family for a very long time.

Another family tradition was to have the preachers come for meals. Mother remembered that a Preacher George Barker used to come to their house fairly often. Later, I learned that although George Barker was married to a daughter of Mother's great-uncle Solomon Greene, he was still called "Preacher George Barker." The blessing was always asked by the preacher. Mother said, "I never could figure out why he always said the same thing, especially since he was a preacher."

Of all the farming seasons, Mother's favorite time was threshing. She loved the colors, the smells, the rhythm of the work in the fields, and all the company this time brought. At various times in the year, they would have other special food-related occasions. These included corn shuckins', bean-hullins,' apple butter making, and molasses stir-offs.

Every year, the entire family would gather in a hollow near Crumley Cemetery and near Great-grandpa John Greene's house to make molasses. The mule or oxen, attached to the press, walked around in circles while men fed the sorghum cane stalks into the press. The juice from the cane was collected in a large vat placed at the base of the press. This was then boiled over an open fire until it was just right. One year, Mother got too close to one of the boiling pots; her foot slipped, and one of her arms went into the scalding, sweet, sticky mass. Grandpa grabbed her and stuck her arm into a bucket of cold water, but she still had severe burns. This would have turned some people against ever eating molasses again, but Mother always liked good molasses meaning that it was of the right consistency, flavor, and color. I have seen some homemade molasses that has a greenish tint and some that turned to sugar almost as soon as it was put into the jars; sometimes, people also "cut" the molasses with Karo or other corn syrup which dilutes the stronger flavor. Mother would have said that these molasses were "not fit to eat." These days, I use molasses mainly to add to gingerbread and other dishes, but Mother and Daddy liked molasses with butter and biscuits as a part of their winter breakfasts. Sometimes the butter would be blended into the molasses and the biscuit dipped into this mixture. That tasted pretty good to me sometimes, but I never made it a habit.

Mother had marked this recipe in a booklet of recipes using Snow King Baking Powder. The booklet had Mick and Mack No. 2 (one of the markets that used to be located on Moore Street on the Virginia side of Bristol) stamped on the front. The recipe had been a county fair winner in Wilson County, Tennessee from 1923-27. The recipe was by Miss Louise Granstaff, Lebanon, Tennessee. The booklet stated that the recipe was being used by the County Demonstrating Agent. Of course, this was before my time, but I remember Mother's gingerbread!

GINGERBREAD

¼ **cup sugar**
¼ **cup molasses**
¼ **cup shortening**
Few grains of nutmeg
⅓ **cup milk**
1 egg
1 cup flour
1 teaspoon Snow King Baking Powder (I think you'll have to use a substitute brand these days. I know that I've never seen this brand).
¼ **teaspoon salt**
¼ **teaspoon (baking) soda**
½ **teaspoon each ginger, cloves, allspice**

Mix together egg, butter, sugar and molasses. Sift dry ingredients together and add milk to first mixture and next (add) dry ingredients. place in greased and waxed paper-lines pan. Bake in quick oven 375 degrees, approximately, until the bread starts to pull away from the sides of the pan.

When I make Gingerbread, I like to serve it with Lemon Sauce. This was one of the very few things I liked about school cafeteria food when I was growing up—they always put Lemon Sauce over the Gingerbread. I have had this recipe for years, but as far as I know, this is not the recipe used by the cafeterias when I was in school.

LEMON SAUCE

½ **cup sugar**
⅛ **teaspoon salt**
2 tablespoons cornstarch
1 cup boiling water
2 tablespoons butter
Juice of 1 lemon
1 teaspoon grated lemon rind

In saucepan, mix first 3 ingredients. Stir in water and cook, stirring until thickened. Remove from heat and add remaining ingredients. Serve on hot gingerbread, bread pudding, apple desserts, cottage pudding, or steamed pudding. Makes about 1¾ cups (about 6 servings).

Talking about molasses reminds me of something that happened in one of my classes several years ago. We started a chapter in sociology dealing with culture and I asked the class what a "cultured person" was. I started getting the generally accepted characteristics of a cultured person as one who is well-read, one who is educated, one who appreciates fine art, the ballet, opera and other classical music, one who is rich, one who has traveled a lot, etc. Finally, after about five minutes of this, one of the older students sitting toward the back of the lecture hall, rared back in his seat and in his long, drawn-out, exaggerated Southern accent said, "Wael (well)..., I've always heard that a cultured person uz (was) one who could drag a hog-lard biscuit through molasses without breaking it!"

The class broke into fits of laughter and then came the puzzled expressions....What in the world was he talking about? So, after we settled down somewhat, I asked what molasses are and what hog-lard biscuits were. Some of the students thought molasses came from bees or from a tree and they had no idea what hog-lard was. Somebody finally said that the lard was the fat from a hog. I asked if they just chopped up the fat and put that into the biscuits; they had no idea. When I explained the rendering process, they thought that was a revolting idea. This discussion led some of the classes later to request that we make molasses on campus. I thought that this would be too difficult for them to handle, but we did make apple butter in the huge pots over open flames...or at least some resemblance of apple butter. They had to peel the apples and carry through the whole process to putting it into jars. Some of these students had never even peeled an apple, so this was an experience!

In addition to the ordinary crops the family raised, Grandma raised hops and made her own wine—for medicinal purposes, of course. When I first learned that hops were used in beer making, and not knowing then of the medicinal value of hops or that they were used in baking yeast breads, I wondered why Grandma, of all people, would have raised them because my Grandpa and Grandma were teetotalling Baptists—Grandpa having gone the route from being baptized in the Lutheran Church, and then belonging to the Methodist-Episcopal Church, and finally becoming a hard-core ("hard-shell") Baptist. Grandma also raised flax (to be used in weaving and also for medicinal value) and ordered other herbs from the Indiana Botanical Gardens; her catalog remains in our possession. (Incidentally, Indiana Botanical Gardens is still in operation).

When Mother was very young, she "took" spinal meningitis, as she said. Grandma, trying to give Mother some relief from this infection, went to the cabinet where she kept the medicine, herbs, etc. She meant to get the calomel which was used, essentially, to clean out the system. Instead, she gave Mother strychnine. I have forgotten what Mother said Grandma did, but I would have panicked! Strychnine has been used in small doses to stimulate the nervous system…but…My dear! Perhaps the dose Mother was given was just enough to allow her to get better and survive. She was one of the relatively few to beat this disease during that time.

Mother remembered her Grandma Vance (Susan C. Morrell Vance) as being "such a sweet woman" who made good cookies. Mother always loved to go visit her and to have her visit them. Among the recipes Mother kept was one written on very old paper and labeled "Grandma's Cookies." I don't whether this was the recipe that Great-grandma Vance used to make the cookies Mother liked, nor not. Perhaps it is. Here is the recipe:

GRANDMA'S COOKIES

1 cup of sugar
½ cup of lard
½ cup of buttermilk
1 teaspoon soda (baking soda)
1 teaspoon baking powder
1 egg
2 cups or as much as needed of flour
Vanilla (I suggest ½ to 1 teaspoon)

Put sugar in pan. Sift flour soda, baking powder and salt together. Put in on top of sugar. Add egg, then lard and pour in milk and flavoring. Stir; make a real soft dough. Roll thick (½ to ¾ inches). Leave 1½ inches in between cookies. There were no baking directions. Everybody back then just knew how hot those wood-burning stoves needed to be. I suggest that you set the oven somewhere between 350 to 400 degrees, depending on your oven, and bake from 10 to 15 minutes or until golden brown.

Thelma remembers that Mother said that one of her grandmothers once had skin cancer on her nose. She had come to stay with Grandpa and Grandma Vance and the family. Grandpa and Grandma Greene lived just up the road and often, other family members lived with them. While Great-grandma Vance was living with them, Grandma and Grandpa asked an Indian doctor to come to treat the cancer. Mother said that he stayed with them for a few days and treated her grandma. Before the doctor left, the cancer on her nose just peeled right off, and as far as is known, she never had cancer again.

Great-grandma Vance had lived with Mother's Aunt Delia, a sister to Grandpa, who married Campbell Cole. They lived in or near Damascus, Virginia, at that time. Some of the postcards Great-grandma wrote to Grandpa and Grandma Vance between 1910 and 1913 state that she cannot come down to see them because she has a "paine" in her side; sometimes her back hurts, too. Another card written in 1913 by Clyde Cole, Aunt Delia's son, tells Grandpa Vance that, "Ma is a little better, I think, she said she would look for you up in a few days and she said she may be able to go back with you and she may not."

By March 3, 1914, Great-grandma Vance was living with Grandpa and Grandma. She received a postcard from her granddaughter, Thelma Cole, addressed to "Mrs. Susan Vance…c/o W.L. Vance." Also, in April of 1914, she received an Easter postcard, postmarked April 10 Bluff City, Tenn., from her brother, Joe Morrell. Great-grandma Vance died May 15, 1914.

Since Mother's family lived nearer the Greene relatives, she saw them and visited with them more. She used to walk through the woods to go to her Grandma and Grandpa Greene's and to her Great-uncle Solomon Greene's, Uncle Solly, as he was called. Mother did not like to walk though those woods alone, however. She said, "I was afraid."

Mother's Great-grandma Greene, Lucinda, lived with Uncle Solly and his family. Mother remembered her vaguely as being "a little fleshy woman who always wore a scarf or bandanna tied like a turban around her head and she was hard of hearing." Mother said that Uncle Solly's children had it hard—they not only had their grandma living with them, but the schoolteacher lived with them as well.

Several years ago, on a Saturday morning, my husband and I started to a country auction of personal property. I had read the directions to the auction in the newspaper, but it was not until we were on our way up the road past Mother's home place that I realized the auction must be at "Uncle Solly's place." One of the first people I saw was Lorena, the daughter of Grandma's sister, Julia. She said that, "Yes, this was Uncle Solly's." The house remained in the family. She showed me around the house some and told me that when they were young, Uncle Solly's sons slept upstairs.

Among the personal effects being auctioned were fancy frosted, scalloped-edged dishes, identical to the ones passed down through Mother's line, and out of which company had been served many times at our house. Additionally, in the upstairs were old cobbler and wood-working tools, primitive twig tables and plant stands. Among other things downstairs, was a companion to what I call a spinning chair, still with original dark green paint, which has been passed to us. The chairs, lower than dining chairs, were homemade; the seats have wide pieces of oak, I suppose, woven in a primitive manner. In our family the chair has been used ever since I can remember for seating when company came to eat meals at our house. Sometimes, the seat would be piled high with cushions so one of the children too large to sit in the high chair could be boosted high enough to be able to eat at the table.

Boxes of books were also sold during the auction at Uncle Solly's. For some reason, at auctions, my husband and I are attracted to books although at other times, he tries to steer me clear of bookstores. We happened to get two or three boxes of books. Several Bibles were included as was Baptist literature including the Minutes—programs and proceedings—of the forty-second and forty-third sessions of the Three Forks Baptist Association of North Carolina. These sessions were held at the church at Flat Top in 1882 and at Mulberry in 1883. The proceedings of the Holston Association of Baptists (Tennessee) from 1938 and 1944 were also included in those boxes. The Holston Association meetings were held at Chinquapin Grove Baptist Church (outside of Bluff City) and the First Baptist Church, Bluff City, respectively.

The Three Forks Association minutes are especially interesting. The back cover of the 1882 minutes included notice of Wake Forest College at Wake Forest, North Carolina. Six faculty members were listed as well as an unnamed tutor. These faculty taught Greek, Modern Languages, Moral Philosophy, Natural Sciences, Mathematics, and Latin—one for each discipline, perhaps. Expenses per term of five weeks were as follows: "Tuition $30.00; Incidental Fee 3.00; Contingent Deposit 2.00; Library Fee 2.00; Room (furnished) for each occupant 6.00; Room (unfurnished) for each occupant 3.00; Board, per month $9.00 to 10.00." Can you imagine!? The Fall Term began September 1 and the Spring Term began January 15. Fees for 1883 did not change. Would that some things didn't change!

The 1882 Report on Education to the Three Forks Association given by Elder E. F. Jones, states in part,

Education in the sense of mental and moral training is a necessity. If our minds and morals were developed as our bodies are, we would be a race of mental giants. In order that the minds and morals of the young people of our country be developed we must take fast hold of institutions of learning and support and patronize them.

We are glad that the people of our hill country are interested in general education, but we need academies for the better training of our children. Our high school at Boone is not in such a condition as we would have it, therefore we recommend that the Association take hold of that property and finish the house; place a good teacher there and use efforts to build a good school, or sell the property and locate a school in a place more suitable to build a high school.

The people back then were concerned, as in today's time, with having good teachers. And, they were concerned about the mental and moral development of their children. When some people talk these days, it seems that they tend to believe that theirs are original concerns which other generations have not had.

The surnames of Green and Trivett appear often in the minutes. David Green was a "Licentiate," a licensed minister. M.S. Trivett, possibly Mastin S., one of Great-grandma Greene's brothers, was Chairman of the Temperance Committee in 1883. His report to the association began, "Your committee (we) are happy to report that there are no members of this association engaged in making or selling ardent spirits." "Ardent spirits" here means strong alcoholic beverages or the "hard stuff," which would include moonshine. Their homemade wines probably were not included in the "ardent" category since these wines were used, "for medicinal purposes, only." The surname of Farthing in the Minutes is plenteous. Since Uncle Solly's Wife's (Bette's) maiden name was Farthing, these documents were probably handed down through her family.

Aunt Bette, or someone in that family, had cut quilt patterns from pages of an old botany textbook which had her name written inside. These patterns were then placed back in the book from which they were cut. Some of the patterns have been tacked together with thread, while others are pinned together with a straight pin. When I found the patterns, I wondered how often she and other family members used them to make the colorful and warm quilts so needed during the long winter months at their little house in the hollow.

One of our second cousins, Hazel, daughter of Grandma's brother, Clyde, told me that Aunt Bette wore bonnets with big wide brims at the front and a ruffle or something at the back which always matched her aprons.

When Mother and her family lived at Cedar Grove, during the growing season, especially, Grandpa took some of his vegetables, fruit, etc., into Bristol to sell. He would load up the wagon with produce and eggs, leave early in the morning, and be gone most of the day. For church and other occasions, they had a buggy or a surrey. And, when the occasion was very informal, or for pleasure, they rode horseback. Grandma rode side saddle, like a lady. Sometimes they rode bareback with just a cloth thrown over the horse. One of the horses they had was a Roan. Another was a Chestnut named Charlie who once bit Mother on the shoulder.

Grandma churned and made butter for Grandpa to deliver to her regular customers in town. One of these customers was a Jewish lady who always had to have unsalted butter and Grandma made this especially for her. She wrapped the butter in a special paper that Mother knew only as butter paper. Mother said that when they lived in the log house, they had a wooden churn, but when they moved to the blue-roofed house, they got a new churn. She didn't say, but the new churn probably was crockery.

On at least one of the trips into town, Uncle Cloyd went along with Grandpa. He asked a little girl if she wanted to buy some "pie plant." The girl turned to her mother and asked, "Mother, do you want to buy some rhubarb?" Uncle Cloyd became very embarrassed because this was the first time he had heard "pie plant" called rhubarb. I heard just the other day that some people in New England still call rhubarb "pie plant," as some people here probably do.

One year near Thanksgiving, Mother and I were discussing what we would have for dinner that year. Turkey, of course, was mentioned and she said she would rather have chicken and dumplings. On their farm, Grandma raised turkeys but they never had turkey for a meal. Mother said, "Papa said they were too expensive." Evidently, those turkeys got a special diet which the chickens didn't get. When Mother finally did eat turkey, she decided that she didn't like it as well as she did chicken.

Lemons were also expensive. "Papa would buy lemons for the Fourth of July because they were too expensive to buy all the time and Mama would make lemonade." Mother always looked forward to that special treat. Mother taught me pretty early to make Lemonade. Here's how:

LEMONADE

3 lemons, washed and cut in half, horizontally
1 cup sugar (or more to your taste)
Approximately 1½ quarts cold water
    Squeeze the lemon juice. Use one of the "old-fashioned" lemon

juicers with strainer attached to it, if you have one; if you don't, roll the lemons on your work surface to soften them before cutting them in half. With a small spoon, remove any seeds that may have slipped into the juice. Pour the juice into a 2-quart pitcher. Add the sugar. Then, add the water. Slice one of the squeezed-out lemons and put the rinds into the mixture. Stir with a wooden spoon (I always used Mother's old wooden spoon that had been in the family a long time) to make sure the sugar dissolves. Let set for about 5 minutes, if you can, to let some of the flavor from the lemon rind seep into the lemonade. Place ice cubes into glasses and pour the lemonade over. This amount may serve about six people, depending on their thirst.

In the spring, one of Mother's favorite dishes was Grandma's fried peas. In fact, even though she would eat them other ways, Mother said that "fried" was the only she ever really liked them.

In addition to all the edibles which were raised or which were available for the picking on their farm, Grandma raised pea fowls, or peacocks. The peacocks were supposedly good "watch dogs" and were also valuable for their brilliant feathers which some of the women wanted for decorations on their hats.

After graduation from Cedar Grove School, some of Mother's friends went on to school at the Normal School in Johnson City, which is now East Tennessee State University. She received a postcard dated Apr 20, 1914, from a friend, Mary Anne Riley, who was attending the school. Mary Anne wrote, "Hello Dilla, How are you enjoying these cold spring days? I like here very much. We have a good school. There are over five hundred in school. Ans. soon and tell all the news."

We never knew why Mother never went on to the Normal School or to another college. Perhaps Grandpa thought girls didn't need to further their education; or, maybe he thought it was waste of money; or, perhaps Grandma and/or Grandpa wanted to keep Mother home to help them. Uncle Johnnie did go on to some school which was in or near Morristown, Tennessee. Mother received a postcard from him dated January 5, 1917 in which he wrote, "I am getting a long fine. I like my boarding place fine to. Went to school last night and did not get in until late..."

Some time after Mother finished school at Cedar Grove, Grandpa decided to sell the farm and move to Athens, Tennessee to help one of Grandma's brothers on his farm. Mother's Uncle Granville and Aunt Victoria had moved to Athens from Jonesborough. Mother said that Grandma was against the idea and told Grandpa that it would never work, that they would never get along; but Grandpa was determined to go help because Uncle Granville kept after him to come.

Mother had a pet dog, a toy poodle named Trixie, that she left with her first cousin, Dilla Sharp. While they lived in Athens, the dog died; Mother said it died of black tongue it got from eating raw potatoes. After her dog died, Mother never did want to get attached to another dog. But, she almost did in her later years when a young mixed German Shepard set up camp at her house. She began calling the dog Trixie and started feeding it. I told Mother one day that if she wanted to keep the dog, we would take it to the vet for all the things that were needed and she agreed. So, one day, we went down to Mother's and took the dog to get it examined, to get the shots, and to get her spayed. When we retrieved Trixie from the vet's, I called Mother and said, "We're bringing Trixie home." Mother said, "Oh, no, I don't want to get attached to another dog. That's not my dog. You all keep her." And, we did. . . for as long as Trixie lived. She was an awfully good dog.

The family had lived in Athens for awhile, but things just did not work out. Grandma had proved to be right. Grandpa made at least one trip back up here in 1919. Raymond, Uncle Johnnie's son, gave me a postcard that Grandpa wrote to Grandma, addressed to "Mrs. W.L. Vance Box 69 Athens, Tenn." which was written on a Friday and postmarked at Bristol, Tenn. on July 11. He wrote,

> Dear Nettie I don't expect I will get home before Sunday if I do then. I am just run to death nearly. I am at Bristol [and] am going out on the river start[ing] now. Will have to come back here tomorrow if everything works all rite. Will be home Sunday unless I get through in time to hit the train Sat. but I wont. That's all. W.L. Vance

In looking at these old cards, I started seeing some commonalities in the way people wrote. They did not write their feelings down on these cards except to express their physical "paines" as Great-grandma Vance wrote about, or to express their loneliness as Aunt Victoria did. Great-grandma always signed her cards with either, "Your mother, S.C.V.," or just "S.C.V." In the card Uncle Johnnie wrote to Mother, he signed it, "Your brother, J.V." And, then, here is Grandpa writing a card to Grandma addressed to Mrs. W.L. Vance and then signing it W.L. Vance instead of signing it "Will," as he was known to most people. Instead of signing off with "Love," as we tend to do, he just wrote, "That's all." I guess that they just didn't want the people at the post office reading anything that would cause gossip. And, perhaps Grandpa wanted to make sure that they knew Grandma was not getting mail from a strange man. At least Grandma got a "Dear Nettie," and she was probably lucky to get that!

I wonder if Grandpa came back up here to try to buy back their farm or to buy another farm. Nobody ever mentioned it. Some time after this, Grandpa moved the family to just outside of Lenoir City, where they lived just down the road and around the corner from a good-looking guy who started asking Mother for dates. They dated for about a year and then, he popped the question.

Grandma made Mother's wedding dress. I remember few of the details Mother described except that the dress was navy blue crepe with a lace collar. I believe Mother said that the dress had long sleeves with lace cuffs, as well. Mother was so proud of that dress and she was so happy. Mother and Daddy never made it to the church to get married, however. No... nothing like that...

When Daddy had a stroke in 1962, Hobart, our brother, came in from Denver and went to Lenoir City to get some of the records and to be sure that all of the papers were in order if and when they were needed. One of the things he was looking for was where Mother and Daddy were married. Then he found out.

I asked Mother about it and she told me that the preacher came along as they were driving to the church and suggested that instead of driving all the way in to the church, he marry them there. So, he proceeded to perform the wedding ceremony at the side of a country road with Mother and Daddy still sitting in the buggy. It didn't seem to bother Mother a bit. And, when you think about it, it is kind of romantic—being married out in the middle of the country with wildflowers blooming all around. Besides, not all people need to have a huge, or modest, church, and a fancy wedding to feel that they are properly married. The things that matter most are the feelings and beliefs people have and the commitments they make to each other and to someone beyond themselves.

Lorena said that she guesses she was about 10 years old when her mother, Great-aunt Julia, took her and her brother Lawrence to Lenoir City when Mother and Daddy started housekeeping. She said, "Zillah (Webb) and Claude (Uncle Cloyd) went, too; but, they only stayed for the weekend. But, we got to stay for a whole week and I had a birthday while we were there." Lorena said that they went on the train. I asked her if she remembered what she wore. She said that she wore patent leather shoes and we talked about her probably wearing some kind of a hat because all ladies wore hats for such occasions then—no matter what their age. Lorena said, "Uncle Will and Aunt Nettie had a big house. Your mother and daddy had rented a small house in town." She continued, "I remember Uncle Will taking us to the train station in the wagon." This trip to Lenoir City and

Mother and Daddy About the Time of Their Marriage

back to Bristol is the only train trip Lorena ever took.

The family stayed in Lenoir City where my brother, Hobart, was born. Grandpa and Grandma decided to move back to Sullivan County—this time to Bristol. Mother and Daddy either moved with them or came up here to live soon after.

When our daughters were growing up, Mother told them that after she met Daddy, "THAT was IT!" I think Daddy was the only person she ever dated that she loved. And, when he went away from us for awhile, the way I like to look at death, in 1976, she missed him sorely. Sometimes this feeling came out at seemingly odd times—like while watching the nightly television news. While watching an anchor we refer to as "Cousin," Mother would say once in awhile, "Oh, he reminds me so much of Oscar when he was younger."

Mother and Daddy Still in Lenoir City

Chapter 4
The Rather Family

Daddy As a Young Man

The Rather family originally settled in the Tidewater area of Eastern Virginia. The first in the family to come to America from Wales or England were Samuel and Anne who lived in Prince George County in the mid-1700s. Their son, William, was a teamster during the Revolutionary War and lived in Dinwiddie County, Virginia during the 1780s. William and his wife, Sarah Williamson, had ten children. The oldest was Jessee.

Jessee was our Great-great-great-grandfather. He married Frances Dillon in 1788 in Prince Edward County, Virginia. Both Jessee and Frances were born in Virginia and died in Roane County, Tennessee. Jessee's house burned in February 1854; he died in the fire. Frances had died about ten years before.

The oldest son of Jessee and Frances was John, our great-great-grandfather. Their other children were Stephen, William, Devereaux, James, Daniel, who was a doctor during the Civil War, Betsey, Patsey, and Sally. All of these children were born in Virginia but are found in Census Reports of Roane County, Tennessee taken during the 1800s.

Great-great-grandpa John Rather was born about 1790 in Virginia and served in the War of 1812. He married Margaret ("Peggy") Reyburn daughter of Thomas Reyburn, who lived in the same area of Tennessee as the Rather family. In his will, Thomas left some money to John for his wife, Peggy. He gave money to his other sons-in-law for their wives, also. If this happened today, some women would revolt!

A Loudon County, Tennessee historian told me several years ago that her family used to live next to the Rather family and that the land was taken by eminent domain by the government. This land is included in the restricted area of Oak Ridge next to the K-25 plant which was involved in the Manhattan Project. John and Margaret are buried at the New Bethel Baptist Church Cemetery (AEC#16 - Atomic Energy Commission), within the area taken by eminent domain.

John and Margaret had several children including Jessee James, known as James, who was our Great-grandfather. Daddy told me, when I was little, that James had been a scout during the Civil War. I thought that was important, thinking that he was a lookout or a spy. Daddy tried to explain to me that he hid out and wouldn't fight for either side. But, in my little mind, I just knew that he was a spy. I guess thinking that was more exciting.

Aunt Beulah, the wife of Daddy's brother, Jessee, "Jack," told me there were stories about Great-grandpa James killing two Yankees and burying them under his smokehouse. She said, "Well, they did find some bones under there, but they could have been any kind of bones!" She also said that during the Civil War, a bunch of men were after him and he put the horses' shoes on backward to confuse the men who were chasing him. I have heard other people say that their relatives did this, too. They must have thought that the enemy was really dense.

Daddy told me that one day, Great-grandpa James was at home and some of the Confederates came after him. Great-grandma went to the front door while Great-grandpa ran out the back, got a horse from the barn, and rode away. Daddy said that the men came back another day while nobody was home and took all the livestock and horses and burned the house and all the buildings down.

After the war, James' brother, William, left Tennessee and moved to the Oklahoma Territory. Daddy said that when he was young, some of the relatives who had moved west came to visit, but he didn't remember too much about them. One of William's (Uncle Billy, as some called him) descendants gave me most of the information on the family before their moving to Tennessee from the Tidewater Area.

Grandma Rather's father (Elbert "Eb" Shaw) served in the Civil War. Later on, he came up to Washington County, Tennessee, adjacent to Sullivan County. I believe, but am not sure, that he had relatives living in Washington County at that time. He had to travel a distance of more than one hundred miles to join the Union Army. Later, he was wounded in a battle at Etowah Creek and spent several months in the hospital in Chattanooga, near the battle site. Then, he was furloughed home and was listed on the Muster Out Roll. Yet, when he applied for a pension, the pension was denied; the reason given: desertion.

His pay sheets indicate that he was either present, in the hospital, or furloughed home; and then, the name Elbert appears no more. However, "Elsworth" and sometimes "Ellsworth" do appear. Even then there were mistakes being made? When he joined the Union Army, "Eb" was described as being twenty-one years old, five feet eleven inches in height, with blue eyes and light hair; he was born in Monroe County, Tennessee, and was a farmer.

In the application for pension papers, Great-grandpa Shaw's statements were witnessed by Grandpa Rather. It was eery to see Grandpa's signature because it was almost identical to Daddy's. I learned from Census Reports that Great-grandpa Shaw could not read or write.

In responding to a request from the people in Washington to send a statement from some member of his unit, he stated that he did not know where anybody from his unit now lived. He said that he had known about one who had lived in Blount County but that this person had died. Evidently, after so much paper work and additional requests for statements which were impossible to find, he gave up on trying to get his pension. I wonder if anybody in Washington ever checked the pay sheets. He had a severe eye injury and a debilitating injury to his hand which prevented him from doing the farm work he had always done.

Daddy, Oscar Oliver Rather, Jr., was born in Loudon County in November 1897. His parents, Oscar Oliver Rather, Sr., and Mary Etis Shaw Rather, had a farm just outside Lenoir City. He had two sisters, Virgie and Katie, and three brothers, Jessee, Herman, and Raymond. Grandma Rather died February 9, 1923, of cardiovascular disease and tuberculosis. I also learned from a copy of her death certificate that her mother was Sallie Tommason (in other places, this name is spelled Thomason or Thommason, depending on which person is doing the writing, I suppose). Grandma had several brothers—Joe, Charlie, and Henry—and Mother and Daddy kept remembering the name Philip; but Aunt Beulah said that she didn't know of any Philip. Aunt Beulah told me that Grandma and Joe were twins. Mother always like Grandma Rather; and, her other daughters-in-law did, too.

I have been told that I (and Hobart) got our red hair from Grandma Rather. If Grandma's daddy, Eb, had light hair, as the records indicated, perhaps his hair was red, too. Hobart's hair was always darker red than mine—almost brown. When I was little, I didn't think I really belonged in this family because none of the rest of the family had hair the color of mine. And I didn't think that I looked anything like anybody in my family. I was just sure I had been adopted!

Grandma Rather *Grandpa Rather*

Daddy talked some about growing up but I do not remember his talking about any particular foods except popcorn and watermelon. He raised some popcorn one year when he was young, sold it, and bought a small camelback trunk to store his clothes.

He talked about going fishing and spoke about "trot" lines which were placed across the river. When I was little, I thought he was saying, or meant, "trout" lines. He also talked about seining, not for minnows as some people do today, but using the large nets with bottom weights and floats on top. I believe that he must have really liked to fish, because when he talked about it, he would get a sparkle in his eyes. However, I never remember him ever going fishing after I was born. And, I'll bet he missed it!

Some of the Shaw relatives lived in Sweetwater and Daddy used to talk about walking down there and of walking to Norris, where the TVA dam and lake are now located. But, I never recall that he ever mentioned going hunting on any of these trips.

The family lived in a two-story log house where Daddy was born. By the time I remember seeing it, when I was about eleven, it had been covered with siding. Daddy said that he slept upstairs. Sometimes during the winter, snow would drift through some of the cracks in the chinking between the logs and he would wake up with snow on his bed. During this time, he had a pet "flying squirrel." The squirrel would come into Daddy's room through an open window and if the door going out of Daddy's room was closed, the squirrel would start gnawing at the bottom of the door to get into another room. Visible marks of its efforts remained, I guess until the house was torn down.

Since Hobart was about 19 years older than I, he remembered some things about Grandpa, and the farm. Hobart said that for some reason, Grandpa used to keep an old pistol hanging over his bed. He said that Grandpa promised he wouldn't marry again, after Grandma died, until his youngest left home. He kept that promise. In addition to raising tobacco and an abundance of watermelons, Grandpa also had bee hives and took the honey from them.

Among Mother's recipes was one labeled "How to Make Honey." This doesn't sound like a recipe Grandma Rather would have had since Grandpa kept bees. These directions appear to be for someone who had little access to the real thing. It is interesting, to say the least!

HOW TO MAKE HONEY
7 pounds white sugar
7 tablespoons bee honey

1 level teaspoon alum
1 quart boiling water
Boil 5 minutes.
No other directions were given. I suppose that after boiling, it is just put into clean sterilized jars and sealed.

Hobart said, "Grandpa used to take me out very early in the morning while it was still dark to show me how to catch birds. And, do you know what he did?" Expecting a joke or smart-aleck reply because we never knew what Hobart would come up with, I answered, "No. . . put salt on their tails?" Hobart said, "No, he moved up to the nest very quietly and carefully and shined a flashlight in their eyes. He said that the light would stun them so they wouldn't move."

Mother told me that Grandpa Rather was close with his money but she didn't say anything beyond that statement. Hobart said that one day, Grandpa went to town to withdraw his money from a bank to deposit it in a different bank. Hobart didn't know why he was doing this. "When Grandpa got to the second bank, he had lost the money, he thought, but found it in his pant cuffs."

Hobart continued with another story:

In the old days, when Grandpa still had about 1600 acres, he took a load of wood to Lenoir City. Grandpa said that he had never had such a response on the road or on the street when he got into town. Everybody was speaking and waving, 'Hello,' 'Hello,' 'Hello,' Grandpa said over and over, tipping his cap, as gentlemen did then. And, all this time he still couldn't figure out why everybody was being so friendly. When he got to the place he was taking the wood, he found out—there was a lizard sitting on his cap!

Everybody said that Grandpa always wore some kind of hat. Some people can never remember him being without one. In all the pictures we have of him, he had on a hat with a brim.

I hope I never forget two stories Hobart told me about Grandpa and Daddy. The stories, as told by Hobart, follow:

During the harvest one year, Grandpa had some people helping him. At dinnertime, everybody went to the house to eat. When people sat down at the table, Grandpa looked around and said, 'Somebody's missing,' and he got up to go looking for the missing person. On the steps of the back porch, Grandpa found him—a little black

boy about 13 years old.
Grandpa said, 'What are
you doing out here?' The little boy said, 'I'm eating my
dinner.' Grandpa said,
'Anybody who can work
with me can eat with me!'
And, after that, the little boy
was always at the table.

The Rather family was also
Baptist—at least by the time
Daddy came along. This story
places Daddy at church instead of
in church.

When Daddy was twelve
or thirteen, a revival was
being held at the church—
out in the country—no
street lights or anything.
Daddy and some of his friends

Children at Grandpa Rather's Farm

had sat in those services most of the week listening to people praying for 'the Lord to come.' Daddy and the boys got tired of it and
decided to 'lay out' of church one night. This was on one of the last
nights of the revival and there was no moon, no stars, no light, what-
soever. One of the boys had a 'pet crow.' They took the crow outside
the church where the people still were praying for 'the Lord to
come.' The boys rigged up a string of rags or something and tied
the string to one of the crow's feet; then, they set the rigged-up contraption on fire. They let the crow go and it started flying around
the outside of the church. When the people in the church saw that
fire flying around the church, it scared them to death! Daddy said
that they were falling all over each other trying to climb out the windows and run out the door! They thought that the Lord really HAD
come, and they were terrified!

My brother asked me, "What happened to their faith *then*?"
Daddy did grow up and get over playing pranks at the church. Years
later, he and Mother were charter members of our "home church" where he
was Treasurer for several years and a Deacon. But, he still liked to play

practical jokes other places.

Another story that was told in the family has more than one variation. Hobart said that Daddy told him the following:

> One night at church in 'Bat Hollow,' someone was praying for the Lord to send them some sign. About that time, an owl, outside the church sang, 'Whoo–Whoo?" The man praying answered, 'Just anybody, Lord!'

I think that the funniest variation was told by Mother. In this version, an older woman was praying for the Lord to send her a man. An owl outside the window sang, "Who? Who?" The woman answered, "Just anybody, Lord!"

Thelma can remember the watermelon and strawberries they had to eat when they went to Grandpa Rather's, but, she says, "I know we ate meals there because we spent the night; but, I don't remember them."

In our family, many times, fresh strawberries from the garden were eaten with cream. Just in case you've never tasted strawberries this simple way, you're in for a wonderful treat:

STRAWBERRIES WITH CREAM
Gather fresh ripe strawberries early in the morning. Gently wash the berries to get any sand, dirt, or straw off. Pinch the green tops off the berries. These days, you can purchase a gadget made just for this purpose, but the old thumb and forefinger still do the job just as well, if not better. Cut the very large berries in half, vertically. Leave the smaller berries whole, or cut them, as well. Place into a bowl large enough to hold the berries you are fixing. When the berries have been prepared, sprinkle with granulated sugar. Shake gently to make sure the berries have had some contact with the sugar. Cover the bowl and refrigerate until you are ready to serve. When you are ready to serve the berries, place an individual serving of berries with some of the syrup that has been formed into a dessert dish. Mother used her footed green-swirl Depression Glass dishes many times. Pass heavy cream—use the cream as it is—don't whip it—for each individual to pour over the berries, as desired. We always used the top cream from the milk — before the days of homogenization. Beware: Some people may ask for a soup bowl!

In more recent years, I have found another delicious way to use the fresh strawberries. And, I really like this better than the sugared strawberries with cream. It is reminiscent of having fresh strawberries with Clotted Cream in Covent Gardens. Here's the recipe:

FRESH STRAWBERRIES WITH CREAM CHEESE AND SOUR CREAM SAUCE

1 (8 oz.) package cream cheese, softened
7 to 8 tablespoons sour cream
2 cups sugar
Fresh strawberries

Wash and cap the strawberries. Let dry on paper towels. Leave berries whole if possible. Whip together the cream cheese, sour cream, and sugar. Cover and refrigerate until serving time. The sauce can be made a day ahead of serving, but if possible, do not wash and cap the strawberries until almost serving time.

To serve: In a dessert bowl, put an individual serving of berries. Spoon on some of the sauce. For "fancy," garnish with a fresh mint leaf and a very small strawberry—or a larger one cut in half, placed cut-side down on the cream.

Reba remembers that Grandpa had a big watermelon patch across the road from the house and that there was a big old persimmon tree in the pasture at the back of the house. I don't know whether anybody in the family ever really did anything with those persimmons except to eat them after the first hard frost, but I make a pretty good Persimmon Pudding from the persimmons my husband and I go out looking for in the fall. Here is the recipe:

PERSIMMON PUDDING

A note of caution: Be careful about the area where you "forage" for wild persimmons. You really don't want to use any that have fallen on chemically-treated grass or other contaminated areas. Wash the persimmons well (use the "wild" or "native" kind—not the supermarket variety—unless you must). Put the persimmons through a food mill, or canning colander, to remove the seeds and the skins.

2 cups persimmon pulp
1¼ cups all-purpose flour
1 teaspoon baking soda
½ teaspoon baking powder
½ teaspoon salt

1 cup sugar
2 eggs, beaten slightly
2 tablespoons butter, melted
1 cup milk
½ teaspoon grated lemon rind
1 teaspoon vanilla extract

Mix the dry ingredients together. In another bowl, place the slightly beaten eggs and the melted butter which has been allowed to cool slightly. Add the milk and the dry ingredients alternately, blending well. Fold in the persimmon pulp and the lemon rind. Then, add the vanilla. Blend in well. Pour into a greased 9 x 12-inch baking pan or Pyrex baking dish. Bake in a preheated 350 degree oven for 40 to 50 minutes. If you are using a glass baking dish, the pudding may take less time to bake. You may want to set your oven at 325 for the glass dish. You can serve this with vanilla ice cream, whipped cream, or hard sauce. But, it is good served plain.

Reba said that once, the night before they were going to Grandpa's,

I literally couldn't sleep all night. I remember looking out the side window—this was before the house next door was built; in fact, there were few houses beyond our house. I could look out and see the distant street lights and the stars. When we got to Grandpa's,

Having Watermelon at Grandpa Rather's in the Earlier Years

Mother and Daddy told him that I had not slept I was so excited. Grandpa said, 'I know why you were excited—to get down here where the piano was!'

Pearle, Grandpa's second wife who he married several years after Grandma's death, had a piano. Reba said, "I didn't try to play the piano. I just looked at it and touched it." Everybody in the family really seemed to like Pearle. I believe that they really missed her when she died. Pearle must have been like a grandmother to some of the children.

I never to got to know Daddy's brothers and sisters too well. His older sister, Virgie, died long before I was born. The youngest sister in the family was Katie; I knew her better than any of the brothers and sisters because she came to visit us once or twice when I was in junior high school or high school.

Aunt Katie's older son used to come to our house when I was tiny; I was still sleeping in Mother's and Daddy's room. The only thing I remember from his visits then was that he liked to laugh. When I saw him later, he told me that one of the times he came to visit was near Christmas. I believe that this may have been when he was in service. He said that we had a lot of oranges and tangerines and that he and Hobart and some of my sisters and their friends started playing ball with those oranges and that Daddy got up when he heard all the racket and told them to stop it. He thought they were going to tear the house down. One of the girls who was at our house that night stayed so long that when they took her home, her parents had locked the front door and she had to climb in a window.

I never remember talking to Uncle Jessee, but I remember being at their house when we made that trip when I was about eleven. When he died, some of us went to the funeral. It was then that I first really talked with Uncle Herman and Aunt Ella, I believe, and got to meet Uncle Raymond Rather.

Uncle Raymond and one of his sons who then lived in the Midwest, made a surprise visit one Saturday after that, visiting with us and going to see Daddy for awhile. Uncle Raymond went to have supper at Thelma's, and when he got back, we played Rook, his and Daddy's favorite card game. We thought they would spend the night, but Uncle Raymond wanted to go on to Lenoir City. I learned later that this was the way he always was: when he took a notion to go, he went.

Uncle Herman, Aunt Ella, and one of their sons came to visit Daddy and Mother once, before Daddy went away for awhile, and I found out that Aunt Ella was really funny. Uncle Herman was a dear; of all the ones in the family that I did get to know a little, somehow, he reminded me more of

Daddy. Maybe it was because he always seemed to have a twinkle in his eye.

In the mid-1980s, on the first Sunday in May, part of the Rather family met at Melton Hill Dam/Lake for a reunion where I met more of my cousins. By this time, most of Daddy's generation was no longer living, but, Aunt Beulah was there. When they were planning the reunion, somebody was wondering whether any of us would come. Mena, Aunt Beulah's daughter-in-law, said, "I told them Earlene would if nobody else did!"

I got to know part of Uncle Jesse's family more than others. Maybe it was because Mother and Aunt Beulah wrote to each other more than the others, and Gib, their older son, was the one who called us when anything happened down there. He and I got to be the bearer of bad news for awhile. When they came for Daddy's and Mother's funerals or the visitation before, they stayed longer than others and we talked much more. I used to write to Aunt Beulah and ask questions about the family's birth dates, etc. In one of the letters, she wrote to me, "I see that you're still shaking the family tree; you'd better be careful, some nuts might fall out and hit you!" She is so funny!

After we practically stuffed ourselves at that reunion dinner, we sat and talked and the stories just kept coming. At one point, Marie said, "Earlene, are you writing all this down?" But, I couldn't write fast enough! I wish I had taken a tape recorder! When our conversation turned to talking about Grandpa, Anna Mae said, "He was one of the quietest people I ever knew." Aunt Beulah, in her own special way, said, "Well...he fell in love awfully fast!"

Some time after Pearle died, Grandpa married his third wife, a woman whose first name was Elizabeth. She used to make green grape pies; and, she was a fortune-teller of sorts who read tea leaves. Aunt Beulah said, "Every time it rained, she said that a girl who was killed at the crossroads came and out danced on her grave." She continued, "Pap was afraid of her; he was afraid she was going to poison him and he divorced her after fourteen months!" Uncle Jessee and Aunt Beulah always called Grandpa "Pap."

Aunt Beulah said that Grandpa's left index finger was crooked and nobody knew why. This was not attributed to his third wife's talents, however. She also said that Grandpa used to play tricks on Lena (Helena), his sister. So, I guess that Daddy, and later, Hobart, learned to play practical jokes by having a good example!

Grandpa had one half-sister named Nan. The half-sister was born to Great-grandpa James and his first wife whom he divorced. Aunt Beulah told me one time that Grandpa never remembered his mother and never knew what happened to her. He was told when he got older that she died when he was twelve. Some believe that she might have gotten sick and had to be hospitalized.

Late one night, when I was in the second grade, the telephone rang. Daddy got a call from Lenoir City saying that Grandpa was ill. He had been working out in the garden when he became ill from a blood clot. I remember seeing Mother trying to get Daddy some clothes packed so he could leave.

This was really hard for him to do emotionally and particularly physically this night because that day, he had been hammering a nail at work and had his thumb on the nail so that when he hit it, the nail went through his left thumb. His thumbnail and the bones in the first joint of his thumb were crushed. This was one of the oddest things, I think, to ever happen. Daddy was always a perfectionist about working with tools, or anything for that matter, and ordinarily never would have done anything like this.

Daddy needed to get to Lenoir City in a hurry. He called his office because he remembered that a truck loaded with lumber was due to go out soon; so, he got a ride down on that truck. It was quicker than waiting to get a bus or the train; and, we had no car. But, Grandpa died before he got there.

Hobart, who was still living here then, and some of my sisters went to Grandpa's funeral. I cried to go, but Marie and I had to stay home with Mother. Even though Grandpa died in 1947 and we visited there some when I was a baby, I don't remember him. I wish I did.

When Uncle Jessee and Aunt Beulah got married, or soon after that time, they lived in a little log house that was across the field from Grandpa's house. I can still "see" that little house from my first remembered trip to Daddy's home place.

When we were talking on the phone once, Gib told me that Grandpa gave Uncle Jessee thirteen acres of land. Then, Uncle Jessee and Aunt Beulah moved into the house with Grandpa; and, after he died, they lived in the house and worked the farm. Gib said, "Every two weeks, Grandpa went to town to have wheat and corn ground. If he didn't have any wheat, he would take extra corn to trade for wheat. On the way home, he would stop once in awhile and buy a pound of coffee, but that's all."

Gib said, "One time Uncle Oscar (Daddy) went to the dentist with me because that's the only way I would go. And, he laughed at me because I was scared." Maybe Daddy thought that if he made light of the situation, Gib wouldn't be so scared. Some of us were and are not quite as tough as Daddy when it comes to enduring pain. I don't know whether he ever laughed at me when I had to go the dentist or not, but I know that he got

Aunt Beulah and Uncle Jessee's children — Gilbert (Gib), Susie, and Ken Rather

pretty disgusted with me when I was scared about going.

Now, years later, the old Rather house has been torn down; but, Gib and Mena have built a new house on the same site. Gib likes to cook so Mena said that's why he had two sinks put in the kitchen.

Many houses now dot the land my family used to own. Daddy said that the land used to go all the way to the river. Relatively few acres of the original farm remain in the family, with Gib. But, he and Mena are carrying on the traditions of raising watermelons and having a large garden. One recent summer, they canned almost 200 quarts of green beans, not to mention the corn, tomatoes, and other food they canned or put in the freezer.

Aunt Beulah now lives downstate near her daughter. Up until just a few years ago, she was going to the Senior Citizens Center several times a week sometimes to quilt and always "to aggravate the 'old men'," she said. I am so glad that I am part of this family!

Chapter 5
The Depression Years

My sisters, being older than I, which to some like Thelma who helped wash my diapers was more of a curse than a blessing, have memories I sometimes wish I could have shared. Of course, sometimes I furnished a good excuse for Thelma to get out of helping with the supper dishes. "I had you trained to ask for me to rock you to sleep," she said. Perhaps this was

Thelma just prior to their move to the Virginia farm.

little compensation. Later, Reba, "had to practice the piano for church," and she got out of doing the dishes. When Marie and I came along, after the Depression, we had few excuses to get out of doing the dishes.

When I asked Thelma and Reba about living during the leaner years, Thelma said that Daddy moved them to the country in Virginia because he thought he could make a better living for them there.

Reba said, "I *caused* the Depression! I was born in 1929!" She also said that Mother and Daddy had told her that during the Depression, Daddy was having a hard time paying the house payments and he decided to sell the house and move to the country. Grandpa Vance offered to help him make the house payments because he just owed about $500 on the house, but Daddy wouldn't let Grandpa help. I guess that Daddy, being the independent-minded soul that he was, thought that taking care of his family was his responsibility.

Thelma said, "We had about 13 acres. We had chickens, cows, and hogs, and always had milk and butter. And, we had our own hams." When I asked about being poor, she said that everybody was, but that they still had plenty to eat. She said that sometimes people would come by begging for food in exchange for helping with some of the farm work.

Reba said that one day, all the other children had gone to school where they were going on a picnic. "I wanted to go on a picnic, too," she said. "So, Mother put some leftover beans from the night before and some other things into a little tin cup and took me on a 'picnic,' up beyond the pond, behind the cow pasture, on the hill." In the wintertime, sometimes during the day, Mother would cook beans on a little stove they had in a bedroom instead of heating up the big kitchen stove. "She would fry potatoes, open home canned tomatoes, and fry cornbread for lunch. Just she and I would be there and I remember that so well," Reba said.

Thelma said that since they lived just over the hill from the school, she and the older children went home for lunch when they lived in the country—unless they had a picnic or something—and she, too, remembers those home-cooked meals. "That was good eating!" she said.

Fried cornbread is still a family favorite. Despite the idea that southern people put sugar in their cornbread, we never did. In fact, most of us do not like sweetened cornbread at all; the sweetness seems to hide the good flavor. To make the fried cornbread, you may use the recipe for Hobart's Cornbread (see Index) or you may use one of the following variations.

FRIED CORNBREAD
1½ cup white corn meal
¼ cup flour (optional)

½ rounded teaspoon salt
¾ teaspoon baking soda
1 egg, slightly beaten
1 cup, or more, buttermilk
Shortening for frying

Mix dry ingredients together. Add egg. Stir. Then, add the buttermilk. Blend well. The mixture should pour from a large spoon easily—a little thinner than the consistency of pancake batter.

If needed, add more milk.

To fry: Heat a cast iron or other heavy skillet over medium heat. In the skillet, place about 2 tablespoons solid shortening (in earlier years, some people used lard or reserved bacon grease). When the shortening has melted and the skillet is sufficiently hot for frying, for each piece of bread, pour in about ¼ cup of the cornbread batter. If you use a large skillet, you can fry about three at a time. When the batter begins to puff up and looks a bit dry around the edges, flip the bread over and brown the other side. Keep adding enough shortening to the skillet so that the bread will "fry" and be crispy. Keep the bread warm while you are frying the remaining batter.

Serve hot with plenty of butter. . . and if you're like us, we like cooked dried beans, and at least some freshly sliced tomatoes and onions, or Chow-Chow, if not the added greens and fried potatoes. Now that's an old-fashioned meal!

Do not use oil; it doesn't have the same effect. And, butter or margarine does not make for crispy bread. An even easier way to make Fried Cornbread is to buy cornmeal mix, add an egg, and sufficient "sweet" (homogenized) milk to make the batter. This is NOT the traditional way to make it, though.

Since Daddy and Mother had a garden, some of their summer suppers probably included the Fried Cornbread with freshly cooked green beans cooked with new potatoes. This is the way Mother used to cook this dish when I was little, and I'm sure she cooked them like this during the Depression, also:

GREEN BEANS WITH NEW POTATOES
2-to-3 pounds fresh green beans
Water
Salt to taste
Salt pork (streaked meat/streak o' fat-streak o' lean)

8-to-10 small new potatoes

Wash, break off the tips, and remove any strings from the beans. Break into 1-inch pieces. Put into a large pot. Cover with water. Add a bit of salt. When the water comes to a boil, add about a 2-inch-wide slab of salt pork which has been rinsed in water.

Cover the pot and reduce the heat. Let the beans cook slowly for about 2 hours. Check every so often to see if you need to add more water. Don't let these cook down completely dry.

When the beans have become VERY tender, but not mushy, and have changed color, and a taste-test tells you they are going to be good, it's time to add the potatoes.

Mother always used the tiny white potatoes; I like to use the red ones. Either can be used, but choose a "waxy" variety. Wash and scrape the potatoes with a paring knife. You don't really peel them—just scrape off that very thin skin. These days, I just peel a thin strip off the skin around the middle of the potato and leave the rest of the skin. Remove any deep "eyes" or blemishes. Add to the beans.

You may need to add a bit more water and some more salt, but don't overdo the salt. Let the potatoes cook in the beans for about half an hour, depending on their size.

If too much water remains, remove the pot cover and keep on low heat for a few minutes.

You may substitute margarine or some other seasoning instead of the salt pork. The dish will not taste the same, but your arteries may thank you for not overtaxing them, and the beans and potatoes will still have good flavor.

This may serve 4-to-6 people.

Serve with Fried Cornbread and, if you have them, fresh tomatoes and onions—or make some Cole Slaw—or try Cucumbers and Onions in Vinegar. The recipe follows.

CUCUMBERS AND ONIONS IN VINEGAR

**Wash, peel, and thinly slice cucumbers—enough to serve for
  one meal—3 or 4, depending on the size, usually**
**4 to 6 green onions, or Spring onions, cleaned and sliced into
  rounds (or about ½ cup onion, chopped)**
Salt to taste
½ cup apple cider vinegar
½ cup water

Combine cucumbers and onions. Sprinkle with salt. Mix together the

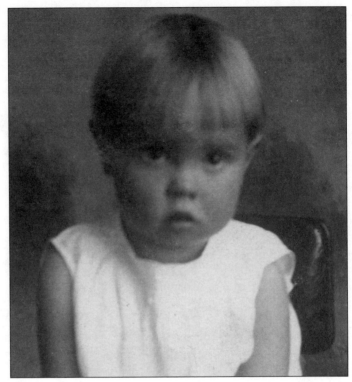

Reba a couple of years before her singing debut.

vinegar and water. Taste a tad and if this is not sour enough, add a bit more vinegar. It should be sour, but not overpowering. Pour over the cucumbers and onions. Refrigerate until ready to serve. This may serve 4-to-6 people.

Mother sometimes cooked fresh green beans and she added some fresh corn to it. She also mixed the two together if she had some leftover green beans and some leftover whole kernel corn. Somebody in the family called it Succotash. When I finally saw what some other people called Succotash—green lima beans mixed with corn—I thought, "That's not Succotash!" But…what did I know?

Reba remembers that in addition to all the other animals they had on their farm, they were at least exposed to horses. One of the families from town used to keep their horses in a field next to our family's house and Reba met the daughter of that family. Later, when the family moved back to town, they went to school together.

Being the baby of the family then, Reba wanted to do everything the other children did, including going to school where all grades were taught in one room. Sometimes, she got to go. She said, "Oh, the teacher didn't try to teach me; I just sat there and absorbed what the other children were learning." When she was about five, she was included in the school's Christmas Program. This was to be Reba's singing debut. She said, "I remember I got my doll from Santa Claus early that year because I was going to use it in my song"—a song that she remembers to this day:

Santa Claus brought me a dolly
And her eyes are oh so blue
And she goes to sleep so jolly
Don't you wish you had one, too
Here she is now I brought her
Along for you to see
I think she's very pretty
I think she looks just like me

When they were living in the country, Daddy always walked to work and back home at night unless somebody gave him a ride. Sometimes, it would be dark at night before he got home from work. They had a dog named Shorty. One night when Daddy came home after dark, Shorty wouldn't let him into the front yard; he thought Daddy was a stranger. Mother had to call the dog to the back of the house so Daddy could get into the front door.

Daddy moved the family back to town after a few years because he thought the children were not receiving the best education they could have. Wherever they were in school, he made sure to buy their books rather than their just paying a fee to use the books during the school year so they could study during the summer.

Thelma said that even when they moved back to town, "People still came by the house begging for food or saying they would work for food, and they would. Of course on the farm, there was always work they could do. But, we always had something for them to eat. They never left without something."

One weekend when Thelma was about nine years old, Grandma and Grandpa took her to visit with Aunt Julia, Grandma's sister, and her husband, Uncle Robert Boyd. Thelma said, "Lorena was dating Parks O'Dell at the time and Aunt Julia tried her best to get me to go into the living room where Lorena and Parks were sitting and say, 'Uncle Parks, I want a stick of gum.' I wouldn't do it," Thelma continued, "but Aunt Julia kept trying."

Mother and Daddy With Their First Four Children

Parks did become a cousin when he married Lorena, but he wasn't an uncle. In fact, Parks was a long-distance cousin on the Vance-Morrell side of the family even before he married Lorena—going all the way back to when the O'Dells and Morrells married—but we didn't know that until a relatively few years ago.

Reba said that Grandma Vance used to make dresses for them. "I don't remember how old I was; I was probably in the second or third grade by this time. When we wanted or needed a new dress, we had a Sears catalog; and, with Mother and Grandma, we would look through it and pick out what we wanted. They would buy the material and Grandma would make the pattern from brown paper and then sew the dresses."

Some time after the family moved back to town, Daddy and Hobart got pneumonia. I remember hearing them talk about Hobart having double pneumonia. He also got pleurisy and had to go to the hospital to have the fluid drained. Mother said that it was so hard on her to have both of them sick. And, remember, she had the other children to take of, too. From listening to Mother talk about it, I believe that she thought sometimes that she might lose both of them.

After this, Daddy got Bright's Disease which was an almost fatal disease at that time. Hobart quit school and went to work to help support the family. He said that he remembered sitting at the kitchen table with Mother planning what to do with the money he had earned. Daddy finally did recover; he credited Dr. Rock for curing that Bright's Disease and saving his life. Dr. Rock remained our family's doctor—still making house calls—until he retired.

Even after the family moved back to town, they kept a cow. Reba said that the cow's name was Pet. Sometimes Pet was kept in the pasture which was probably about a mile and a half from the house. The pasture was called Blackley's Field. At other times, she was kept in the barn at the back of the house. "Hobart helped Daddy take care of the cow, and, after awhile, Daddy gave her to Hobart," Thelma said. "Hobart sold her; and, with the money he got, he bought the radio." This radio, a large floor model with all kinds of knobs for changing stations, tones, and different bands on the radio, was in our dining room when I was little. This is the radio that the older children and Mother and Daddy listened to for all the news, comedy programs, and music. One special feature of this radio, and maybe one of the reasons Hobart bought it, was it had short-wave. He used to sit and listen to that radio for hours, evidently, and could pick up some things on it that other people could not get on their radios. When you think that this was probably during the build-up for World War II, he probably heard some pretty interesting and perhaps some pretty scary things.

That radio lasted for years. After the Depression, Marie came along; and, then, here I came. And, that radio was still blasting as it did for many years after! We wish it still did.

Chapter 6
Going To Aunt Cindy's

Aunt Cindy As A Young Lady

Marie and I share some of the same childhood memories. Some of the best of these memories are of going to Aunt Cindy's and Uncle Bob's for a week during several summers. Aunt Cindy was Irena Lucinda Greene Sharp, a sister to Grandma Vance.

Mother would get the old brown-speckled and striped, paper-covered suitcase from a closet next to our fireplace in the dining room, where old treasures were stored, and start packing our clothes. We were going to Aunt Cindy's! Knowing how I packed for our two children, my husband, and me for a week's trip, I cannot imagine that this suitcase is all she used, but I can recall nothing else and neither can Marie.

How we got to the bus downtown that would take us to the country, we do not remember, but after what seemed to me to be an endless trip, we arrived at Lorena's house to have lunch, spend the afternoon, have supper, and then go to Aunt Cindy's.

Lorena and her family—two daughters about our ages and her husband— also lived on a farm. They had a hammock hanging between some trees which I thought was wonderful until I sat in it the wrong way and was flipped out backwards. At this age I was already "Miss Coordination?"

Neither Marie nor I could remember what we had to eat at Lorena's— probably because we were so excited. As far as we know all of our relatives are good cooks. Not long ago when I talked with Lorena, I asked if she remembered. She said, "You know, I was just thinking about that the other day and I couldn't remember everything, but one of the things I probably had was lemon pie." I asked if she would give me her recipe, and here it is:

LORENA'S LEMON PIE
1 cup water
1-to-1½ cups sugar
3 tablespoons corn starch or 5 tablespoons flour
2 or 3 eggs, separated. Reserve whites at room temperature
for making the Meringue
Juice of one lemon or 1½ tablespoons lemon juice
Pinch of salt

Boil sugar and water. Mix flour (or cornstarch) with water to make a paste. To the egg yolks, add lemon juice and salt. Pour into the boiling mixture and stir well. Remove from fire. Let cool.

PIE CRUST
Lorena said that she got this recipe from Frances O'Dell, a lady who goes to her church. She said that this crust freezes well. This recipe

makes enough crust for two double-crust pies OR four single-crust pies.
4 cups all-purpose flour
1 teaspoon salt
1 teaspoon baking powder OR 1 teaspoon cream of tartar
1 tablespoon sugar
Sift the above ingredients together.
Work in 1½ cups or a little more shortening
Beat 1 egg, ½ cup cold water, and 1 tablespoon vinegar together.
Add to the other mixture.
Mix well (but do not knead). Divide into four equal portions.
Use very little flour when you roll this out. Roll the dough out a lit-
tle larger than the pie plate. Place the rolled out crust in a pie plate.
Dock (prick) the bottom of the crust and around the sides with tines of
a fork a few times so it won't blister while baking. Flute the edge of
the crust. Bake at 425 to 450 degrees, depending on your oven, 12 to 15
minutes or until the crust is just very lightly browned. Remove from
the oven. Let cool while you make the meringue.

MERINGUE
3 egg whites which should be room temperature—not chilled
A pinch of salt (about ⅛ teaspoon)
A pinch of cream of tartar (about ⅛ teaspoon)
3 to 6 tablespoons sugar
In a large mixing bowl, add the salt and cream of tartar to the egg
whites. Beat until soft peaks begin to form; gradually add the sugar and
continue to beat until stiff peaks form.

To finish the pie:
Fill the cooled crust with the lemon filling. Top with the meringue
making sure that the meringue touches all edges of the crust. Bake at
350 degrees until the meringue is golden brown.

I remember one afternoon after Lorena's husband, Parks, got home, it
stormed. When we left to go on to Aunt Cindy's, it was dark and the car
had to go through water and mud to get there. I cannot remember exactly
what happened when we first got to Aunt Cindy's. But, knowing the way
she always was, she probably came running out the door of their screened-
in back porch, and down the back walk to the back gate to give us hugs.

Then, we would bed down for the night. Poor Mother. Even though
there were beautifully furnished rooms upstairs where Marie and I used
to play sometimes, until Mother caught us, during the day. When it got to

be nighttime, we became scaredy cats. Mother put up with two squirming brats in bed with her the whole week in a downstairs bedroom.

We were fascinated by the pretty dressers with white scarves on them, the pretty crystal and frosted glass powder dishes, and silver dresser sets. We loved to pretend primp. Mother didn't want us messing with those nice things because she was afraid we would break something.

In addition to all these fancy things, I was in more awe of the great wheel which was in one of the upstairs rooms, hoisted up close to the rafters so that it would be out of the way. I didn't know it then, but one of our Greene ancestors made that wheel and it stayed in the family until Aunt Cindy's daughter, Dilla's, estate was settled probably. I had wanted to buy it from her years ago. But, she said then that she would like to keep it for as long as she could, that someone in the Greene family had made it, but that after her, she wanted someone in the family to have it. We don't know where that wheel is today but we have the memories.

I believe that Marie especially remembers trying to play the old pump organ Aunt Cindy had. It took both of us to get any sound out of that organ! I remember that sometimes, I would sit on the floor and put all the strength I could muster into pushing those peddles so Marie could play some "music."

One year a panther, it was called, had been up in Uncle Bob's woods beyond the high meadows and the barn or at least it was somewhere close enough to cause some alarm. Late one night, I woke up to an awful noise and was scared. Mother said, "Oh, it's just a dog barking out in the road!" But, the only dog I had ever heard barking at night was Pepper, the red cocker spaniel who belonged to my friend, Barbara, who lived next door to us. All Pepper did was to stand and howl at the train whistle blowing blocks away from our house!

In the mornings, we went for breakfast into the bright, airy dining room. We always had lots to eat, but the things I remember most during these weeks are the biscuits, homemade butter, and honey I ate for breakfast. Marie remembers some of the other food we had there—tenderloin, gravy, and apple float or apple snow. Recipes for apple float and apple snow follow:

APPLE FLOAT
To one quart of cooked and sieved apples, add six tablespoons of sugar. Flavor to taste with freshly grated nutmeg. Beat four egg whites until they form stiff peaks. Fold the apples into the egg whites a spoonful at a time. In another medium serving bowl, place two cups of heavy

*cream to which has been added sugar and nutmeg to taste. Spoon the
apple mixture onto the cream.*

APPLE SNOW

*Peel, core, slice, and cook 12 large cooking apples, Winesap,
Granny Smith, or your favorite, in enough water to keep the apples
from sticking to the pan. Place the cooked apples in a colander or food
mill and process. Add sugar to taste while the apples are hot . Beat 12
egg whites until stiff peaks form. Fold the beaten egg whites into the
apples. Eat with cream.*

At Aunt Cindy's, we got to feed the chickens. I also saw a hen lay an
egg for the first time in my life and I was totally shocked! Uncle Bob tried
to teach us how to milk the cows. He took us up the hill to the barn where
the cows had gathered at milking time. He showed us how the cows had
to be cleaned before milking and the technique of milking, positioning
the milk buckets just right and showing us the proper grip. The only problem was when we tried it, we only got a squirt or two, and then, the cow
kicked over the bucket. Uncle Bob got very frustrated and sent us back to
the house.

Sometimes in the early mornings, the truck from the milk plant in Bristol would come pick up the milk which had been put in large metal cans.
Then, Aunt Cindy cleaned and scalded the cans for the next milkings. All
the clattering woke me up. I remember that one year, she made cottage
cheese and I watched how she made it. Mother proclaimed the cheese, "the
best I've had in years!" Marie said that Aunt Cindy would read the calen-
dar and could tell which days the cows would be fresh. By the time we
were spending the weeks with Aunt Cindy, since we lived in town and
did not have a cow, Mother had started buying cottage cheese and other
dairy products from Piedmont Dairy in Bristol which delivered all these
things to our house in a truck.

I remember one day when we were at their house; it was raining outside
and Uncle Bob was sitting in his chair on the screened-in back porch. Their
dog was curled up sleeping at his feet. I was sitting beside the dog and
began to pet it. I was so content because we didn't have a dog at home,
only a cat once in awhile. I kept petting the dog, and evidently he got
enough of it because he woke up and snapped at me. It scared me and I
began to whimper. What made it worse was Uncle Bob saying, gruffly,
"That will teach you to let sleeping dogs lie!" Uncle Bob probably was
glad when our week-long visits ended.

On their farm and in their garden, Aunt Cindy and Uncle Bob raised
just about everything they needed to eat including having honey there. She

canned sausage and other meat; this, along with the canned vegetables and fruits were stored in the cellar which was entered through a huge door with heavy metal ring for lifting it in the floor of their back porch.

At the side of the yard, beyond the cut grass, were the vegetable and flower gardens. Aunt Cindy planted a large flower garden, both annuals and perennials, so they could be seen from the road. One of the annual flowers she grew was touch-me-nots; her's were the first I remember seeing. She also had flowers that were called "Pretty Me Nights;" these are now usually known by the less descriptive name of "Four O'Clocks." The vegetable garden was planted behind the flower garden.

During the week we would walk up the road to visit some of the neighbors, all relatives of Uncle Bob— "Aunt Hattie" and "Aunt Jennie" Sharp. What we didn't know then was that we, also, were distantly related to the Sharp family. Sometimes we walked down the road to visit with Dilla, her husband, and stepchildren. Sometimes we got to play in the creek in front of their house.

Sometimes, Dilla's younger stepson would come up to Aunt Cindy's. He would get out in the front yard and Marie and I would peek out the windows upstairs. He would pick berries off the big holly trees in the front yard and throw them up at the windows and we would pretend to get out of sight. He got caught and was told to quit doing that. We also got caught and were told to get away from the windows, but that didn't keep it from happening again. I don't believe that we ever got a spanking for it, though.

One afternoon during the week, we went down to the old log spring house, back of the garden, where the black walnuts were stored. We learned, but not very well, to crack black walnuts on an old flat iron by holding the walnut between the left fore-

A Young Dilla Sharp with Her Dolls and A Young Friend

finger and thumb and striking it with a hammer. We struck more fingers and thumbs than walnuts. Mother took some of the black walnuts home to make our Thanksgiving and Christmas black walnut cakes.

MOTHER'S FAMOUS BLACK WALNUT CAKE

2 cups sugar
1 cup shortening
3 cups applesauce
2 small cups seeded raisins or any kind of preserves (Sometimes, Mother used 1 cup of the raisins and 1 cup of watermelon rind preserves, but no other kind) A small cup is a little less than a full measuring cup
2 cups black walnuts
2 teaspoons baking soda dissolved in 2 tablespoons hot water
2 teaspoons vanilla extract
4 cups all-purpose flour
½ teaspoon salt

Cream sugar and shortening. Add applesauce, walnuts, and raisins or preserves. Add soda which has been dissolved in hot water. Mix flour and salt together. Add to the applesauce mixture. Add vanilla. Bake at 350 degrees in loaf pan (1 hour) Or layer pans (less than 1 hour).

NOTE: I never remember Mother baking this in a loaf pan, tube pan, or in layer pans. She used a baking pan, about 9 x 15-inch size. In the later years, she never made watermelon preserves during the summer and used only raisins in the cake. These preserves were more trouble to make than other kinds; but Daddy loved them.

The recipe for Mother's Watermelon Rind Preserves which came from the 1936 edition of the *Ball Blue Book*® follows:

WATERMELON RIND PRESERVES (1936)

4 pounds watermelon rind, white part only
4 oz. slaked lime (calicum hydroxide)
2 oz. ground ginger
8 cups sugar
Spices, if desired

Dissolve the lime in 2 gallons cold water. Cut rind into small pieces of uniform shape and size. Soak overnight in lime water. Drain and rinse through two changes of cold water and soak in clear water for 3 hours. Take the rind from the water after 3 hours and drain. Add the *ginger to 1 gallon water then add rind and boil 20 minutes. Add sugar and sliced lemon to 3 quarts fresh water. Bring to boiling, add rind, and if desired, add cinnamon, allspice and cloves to taste. Cook until it is clear and tender. Pack in clean, hot sterilized jars and seal immediately.*

By 1969 when I had begun to can for my own family, this recipe in the Ball Blue Book® had changed a bit. But, I never attempted it. This is the 1960s version:

WATERMELON RIND PRESERVES (1960s)
1½ quarts prepared watermelon rind
2 tablespoons slaked lime OR 4 tablespoons salt
2 quarts cold water
1 tablespoon ground ginger
4 cups sugar
¼ cup lemon juice
7 cups water
1 lemon, thinly sliced

To prepare watermelon rind...trim green skin and pink flesh from the thick watermelon rind; cut into 1-inch pieces. Dissolve lime or salt in 2 quarts water and pour over rind. Let stand 2 to 3 hours if lime is used, or 5 to 6 hours if salt is used. Drain; rinse and drain again. Cover with cold water and let stand 30 minutes. Drain. Sprinkle ginger over rind; cover with water and cook until fork-tender. Drain. Combine sugar, lemon juice and 7 cups water. Boil 5 minutes; add rind and boil gently for 30 minutes. Add sliced lemon and cook until the melon rind is clear. Pack, boiling hot, into hot Ball jars, leaving ¼-inch head space. Adjust caps. Process half-pints and pints 20 minutes at 180 - 185 degrees in hot-water bath. Yield: about 6 half-pints.

NOTE: If lime is used, the preserves will be crisper. Slaked lime (calcium-hydroxide) should be available at drugstores or farm seed stores. If a spicy preserve is preferred, tie 1 stick cinnamon and 1 table-spoon whole cloves in a cheesecloth bag and add to sugar mixture.

During the year, Aunt Cindy saved up pretty flour sacks. At that time, the larger quantities of flour and animal feed were packaged in cloth rather than paper. This cloth usually had flowered designs. Aunt Cindy gave Mother the clean, pressed cloth which Mother made into school dresses for us. I remember one year I wore the new dress with tiny blue-flowered print to school which everybody loved until I said, "It's made out of a flour sack." Then, everybody laughed. But, I thought it was special! Still, I really did not like to wear that dress to school anymore.

Also during the week, Aunt Cindy made Marie and me necklaces and bracelets of pretty old beads. Marie's were made of larger beads, mine of smaller, and they were varying shades of blue. Marie's beads sometimes were yellow. At least once, Aunt Cindy placed tiny crystal beads between the colored ones. Some of these beads still exist and are treasured.

On our last night at Aunt Cindy's, Dilla would arrive carrying her ice cream freezer and all the fixins' in her arms. We were going to have home-made ice cream! The old hand-crank ice cream freezer took a seemingly endless time, but the wait was worth it! What a treat!

The next day, we went home…until possibly another summer. Neither Marie nor I can remember how we got home from Aunt Cindy's. Perhaps that's because our minds were still on the good times we had at that special place. We never knew why we were taken to spend the weeks at Aunt Cindy's. I don't think we ever asked. It was enough for us to know that we were going. Maybe we just thought that Mother wanted to spend some time with Aunt Cindy and she took us along because Daddy and the older sisters were working. And, I never thought of it any other way until I was just writing this.

One summer, we took our children to a working farm in the Shenan-doah Valley that had what were called "farm vacations." We had a cabin with two bedrooms, a living-dining-kitchen combination, and a bath. The cabin we had and the other cabins were converted sheds and other farm buildings. The owners had found a box turtle and had anchored it outside our cabin, because coming from the "city," they didn't know whether the girls had ever seen a turtle or not. They had. I believe that this was the year that a turtle with one leg missing and another injured one had appeared almost on our doorstep. We "doctored" it, somebody named it "George," and he stayed around awhile; then he was gone. But, he came back at least two more years after that. Then, we saw him no more.

During the time we were at the farm, the girls got to gather eggs from the hen house and put them into oak splint egg baskets. They got to hike in private woods and at the end of the day, they played with the owners' Airedale dogs. Not long ago, one of our daughters asked, "Mom, why did you all take us to the farm that summer?"

I told her that by the time they were that age, none of the family I knew had a working farm I could take them to and that I wanted them to know what it was like to be on a farm for a little while. And, it still didn't "hit" me until now…

Maybe that's why Mother took Marie and me to Aunt Cindy's! We were the only two of her children who had never spent any time on the farm. She loved the farm and maybe she wanted us to know what it was like—just a little bit.... But, still, the reason matters little, especially now. We went to Aunt Cindy's and we never will forget it!

Chapter 7
Seasons on the Hill

Marie and I were born in a big house on Carolina Avenue in Bristol. The house was on the top of a hill and could be seen for blocks, partly because of the high-pitched tin roof. When Marie was born, Reba cried because she said that she wanted to be the baby.

When I was born, I guess everybody just threw up their hands! The night I was born, Hobart went to visit with the neighbors, the Buckles family, across the street. According to Hobart, Mr. Gray Buckles said,"'Well, it looks like the stork is visiting Oscar's house again.' Joe Bush, one of the Buckles' relatives who was also visiting, responded: 'Hell, that ain't no stork! That's a duck! The stork's done worn its legs off!'" So, I came into the world with laughter echoing on Carolina Hill.

One year when we returned home from Aunt Cindy's, Daddy had built a big swing for Marie and me. The posts were four-by-four wooden posts embedded in deep holes filled with concrete. The posts had been treated to resist termites and a large metal pole, embedded inside each of the posts connected them at the top. The actual swings were attached to that pole. Instead of rope or other material to hold the swing seats, Daddy had used heavy-duty

My Favorite Picture of Marie, About Age Six

chain. He had bored the right-size hole in boards at least three-quarters of an inch thick for the seats and had threaded the seats onto the chains, with the chains underneath reinforcing the seats. Not many daddies would have gone to all this trouble, but he wanted to make sure that this swing set was safe and that we couldn't tip it over. That swing lasted for years, outlasting several times over the purchased metal swing sets.

Daddy also made us jump ropes out of heavy cotton roping that he had knotted on the ends to make handles. Marie and I had our own individual ropes; mine was a wee bit shorter. We were the only neighborhood kids to have a long rope which required two people to turn, one on either end while we kids jumped in the middle. Daddy made the long jump rope the same way as he had made the shorter ones.

During some summer evenings after the supper dishes were done, some of the neighborhood kids would gather at our house and the mothers would turn the rope for us out in the street while we jumped and chanted such things as:

> Cinderella dressed in yellow
> Went upstairs to see her fellow.
> How many kisses did he give her?
> One... two... three... four...
> (While we jumped, we counted,
> until we missed a jump. Then,
> it was somebody else's turn).

Another of the chants was:

> Teddy Bear, Teddy Bear,
> Turn around.
> Teddy Bear, Teddy Bear,
> Touch the ground.
> Teddy Bear, Teddy Bear,
> Tie your shoes
> Teddy Bear, Teddy Bear,
> What's (or "Tell") the news.
> One... two... three...
> (Here we counted, again,
> until we missed, and another
> kid took a turn).

In the Teddy Bear chant, we had to act the words out by turning around, touching the ground, and pretending to tie shoes. Anytime we goofed up, our turn was over. Marie remembers that Mrs. Barker, Betty Jean's and Herbert's mother especially liked to turn the rope. Since there was little traffic on our street, we rarely had to move.

We played Rock School on the first set of concrete steps leading up to our yard from the parkway, the grass which separated our property from the street. Our steps were higher, so we always played there. On the short walk from the street to the beginning of the steps, we drew the grid and played Hop-Scotch. We played Hide and Go Seek, Tag, Freeze Tag, and Kick the Can. And, we played Mother, May I? Already in our play we were supposed to be learning proper grammar? If so, it didn't "take" because when we wanted permission to do something, we still asked, "Can I?" We also played Jacks and Marbles. My favorite marbles were my steelies and my best maroon and white shooter.

Mother didn't like for us to play Red Rover or Crack the Whip because she thought they were too rough. I played these games at school, though; and, I usually fell down or got a bruised arm from some bigger and stronger kid trying to come through the line while we were playing Red Rover. I may have been chubby around the middle, but my wrists were tiny. When we played team sports in school, unless it was volleyball or badminton, I usually was the last kid to be chosen for a team and I knew the reason. I couldn't hit the broadside of a barn when we played softball and I rarely could hit the basket when we played basketball. I learned about 15 years later that my depth perception was a bit off; perhaps this had some effect on my playing some of those sports, but I accepted the fact that I was not very good at most sports and it didn't bother me. It did bother some of my physical education teachers, though.

One day when Mother was in her later years, we went to visit and found her sitting in the den watching a baseball game on TV. I asked why she had the game on and she said that she loved baseball. All these years I had never known! She said that they used to play baseball at Cedar Grove and other places and that she could hit the ball really well and that she could run fast. She loved it!

A game we played in large groups when we were probably too young for the other games was Drop the Handkerchief. We made a large circle with all the kids facing inward. Someone was given a real hankie and that person was "It." "It" walked, sauntered, or ran around the large outer circle behind the other kids' backs. Then, ever so sneakily, "It" would casually drop the hankie behind someone. The person who had the hankie dropped behind his/her back, had to pick it up, and chase "It" around the circle, trying to tag him/her before arriving at the empty space in the circle.

If the old "It" got back to the empty space without being tagged, the person carrying the hankie was the new "It." Some days, I was "It" a lot because I couldn't run as fast as some of the kids.

When I was in the middle grades of elementary school, one of the favorite things we did during the summer was to trade comic books, or funny books, as we called them. I had a stack of those things, which I wish I had saved, at least a foot high. Sometimes we took trading so seriously that we set a specific time to meet and trade books. At times, we traded two-for-one, depending on how much we valued a particular book.

After a storm or big rain in the summer, some of us floated homemade boats in the limestone-lined gutters or ditches at the edge of the street. When our children were little, I remembered this and we made little sail boats out of plastic banana split dishes. When they went out in their little slickers to sail their boats, one of the neighborhood women told them not to do that because they would get sick. One of them said, "Mother said we could!" They didn't get sick; and, they had fun.

I remember one summer when we were little, some of the girls in the neighborhood came to ask Mother if we could come to a play at their house on a certain day. Their parents had quit raising chickens and had converted the chicken house to a playhouse for the children—complete with curtains and all. On the day of the play, Mother made me clean up and put on a clean pinafore and I had to have my hair freshly plaited into pig tails. The meaning: "If it was a play, you dressed nicely to go." I believe that the "admission" was one penny. After the "play," which was to me no different from when we played house, we had Kool-Aid and cookies or some kind of refreshments. The kids who played at my house sometimes got all of the above and they weren't charged an admission fee. I just couldn't understand that!

Some summer evenings after the sun went down and darkness came, several of the neighborhood women would come over and sit on our steps and talk with Mother. None of the mothers had jobs other than being homemakers then, and this was their time to relax after putting up with us all day, canning, or whatever their daily schedules were. Sometimes, Mrs. Buckles ,"Haggi," would tell us ghost stories. She was a wonderful storyteller who seemed to make the stories come to life. The street light across the street shone through the forsythia bush on one side of our yard and the mock orange tree on the other side cast strange shadows. Sometimes after her stories, I was almost afraid to make the short walk to our second set of steps to the front porch.

Mary was Mrs. Buckles' given name. But, years before I was around, some of the neighborhood kids at that time started calling her "Haggi" after some cartoon character. The nickname stuck and sometimes she even referred to herself as "Haggi." In Daddy's memorial book, she signed her name Mary Buckles and then after that, she wrote "Haggi."

I think everybody on the hill loved Haggi. And, she loved everybody, not just the people who lived on the hill. Any time a family had some illness or sadness, Haggi was there to offer her help. I could always tell the urgency of her mission by how fast she walked. If she had her arms bent at the elbows with her hands out front of her almost in fists, walking as fast as her skinny little legs could carry her, a straight-ahead gaze in her eyes with a set expression on her face almost like she was gritting her teeth, it meant that there was business of some kind that needed her attention. Other times, she would just walk slowly with her hands to her side, looking around at the sky or birds flying over, or look at something on the ground. This meant she was probably just going someplace for a friendly visit.

After we moved away from the hill, I still went back to visit her. She was always the same. Luckily, our children got to know Mrs. Buckles. They just called her, 'Buckles.' She treated them the same as she had treated me when I was little and even when I was grown up—with kindness and love.

Thelma remembers that when she was little, Daddy used to play Hide and Go Seek with her and the other children, including the Buckles' children—Jim, Charlie, and Dot. I suppose that by the time I came along, he was too tired. I never remember his playing this game with us.

I never knew Grandpa Vance—he died a few months before I was born—and I remember only a few things about Grandma Vance. She died when I was about three. Once she came to visit and brought Marie and me each a little pottery dog. These were little containers for plants. Marie's was brown with some orange-tone highlights; mine was white, shaped like a Scottie dog, with light brown pointed ears, and some brown on the tail and feet. I still have mine and I guess Marie still has hers.

The next time Grandma came, I asked her what she had brought me and kept waiting for her to pull something out of her big carpet-like bag. She said that she had not brought me anything. I couldn't believe that! Grandma didn't bring me anything and I started to cry. She became perturbed and yelled for Mother to come and "do something with her."

My first food-associated memory was when Grandma Vance was sitting beside me at our dining room table. The table which sat at least ten people was surrounded. Among other things on the table were biscuits and gravy. As the food was being passed, I told Grandma that I didn't want any gravy, and I put my hands over the biscuit, kind of crossed, so she wouldn't give me any. She was busy, talking to somebody across the table, and had forgotten, or had not heard, what I said. So, while she was talking, she continued to spoon out gravy; then, she spooned some on my biscuit—only my hands got the gravy.

When she was staying with us, not long before her death, a lady stayed with us to help Mother with all she had to do. I disliked that lady because she tried to make me eat peaches at lunch one day when I did not want peaches, probably the first time anyone ever had to try to get me to eat.

Although I remember little of my eating habits when I was very young, I have been told that when we went to Grandpa Rather's when I was a baby, they gave me watermelon and I ate so much Mother said she was afraid I would be sick.

Sometimes, we had so much company that Mother had to have two sittings at that big table in the dining room. When I began eating with the grown-ups, they let me start eating with the "first table" and I still would be eating with the "second table." I really did eat slowly; and I surely never went hungry!

The family who lived next door to us when I was tiny, well, the tiniest I've ever been, always raised pigs. When the weather became cold enough, word went around that they were going to kill a hog. I heard a loud pop and Mother said that's how the hogs were killed. She let me look out one of the bedroom windows. I saw a man carrying a long narrow brown object. I

Old Photos Don't Lie. But, is this the first table or the second table?
Me at about age 3

guess that is the first time I ever saw a rifle. Later, I saw the hog hanging up in the doorway of their barn/garage. Mother explained, when I asked, what the people were doing, but I do not remember all the details she told me then.

I barely remember parts of World War II, but I remember that we had those dark, dark-green window shades. Sometimes at night during an air raid, we had to keep them pulled all the way down. Somebody told me that airplanes that flew in the sky dropped bombs that killed people. They had probably told me when I asked what bombs were. Anyway, I became the laughing stock of the kids in the neighborhood because when I was outside playing, if a plane came over, I ran into the house screaming.

One day on the back of the newspaper, I saw a big scary drawing of a man with stringy wild hair and bulging funny-looking eyes. His mouth was wide open and his teeth looked like fangs. He was reaching forward with fingers that looked like they had claws for fingernails. I asked Thelma who that was. She told me that those were the people we were fighting in the war. I asked why he had those long fingernails. She said they were long so he could come open people's doors. She knew how to shut me up, didn't she? It scared me, but I don't know whether it bothered my sleeping at that time or not. But, later, I remember some nights I was afraid to go to sleep until I heard Reba and Marie sleeping. Thelma had a bedroom by herself, the front bedroom, but I didn't get up to go see if she was asleep yet. When I heard the other two sleeping, I figured that if they thought it was safe to go on to sleep, I guess I could, too.

I remember the afternoon all the sirens in Bristol went off, the church bells were ringing, and everybody was crying. I asked Mother what was going on and she told me that the war was over. For once, I don't think I cried about anything. I couldn't quite figure all this stuff out. And, I just stood and watched and listened. The people who had originally lived next door had moved, and the mother of that family came driving over to the Buckles' house, jumped out of the car, and ran in with arms outstretched to hug everybody. Mother said that she was happy.

I had seen the Red Cross decals on most people's front door windows and once in awhile, I had seen a gold star, too. The older houses had a large window—either a square or oval shape—in the front door during those days. Mother had told me that the red crosses meant that people had given money to the Red Cross, but that didn't mean much to me, then. It meant much more later when I got my Red Cross First Aid certification, which I used many times in my first job in college and it meant even more later when I lived in Clara Barton's house. Mother told me that the gold star meant that the people's son had been killed in the war.

The first memorial service I was ever taken to in the church was for William P. "Billy" Mitchell on September 3, 1944. Billy was one of Thelma's and maybe Reba's friends. Billy, Sonny to his family, had been a Technical Sergeant in the Army. Billy's mother was one of my first Sunday School teachers. Catherine, "Toodle," his younger sister, was one of my friends. She says that she remembers the crossed sword formation and the twenty-one-gun salute given to Billy in front of the church. I just remember the big flag and seeing everybody cry.

When I was little, and even not so little, my favorite place to be was outside in the yard. I loved playing under the cherry tree in the backyard and beside the smokehouse under a sweet shrub bush. One of the "picnics" Mother fixed for some of my little friends and me were toasted cheese sandwiches which we ate under the sweet shrub. Later that year, one of these little friends, Mikey, had a really bad cold and fever. His mother had given him an aspirin to try to break his fever and had turned around to the bedside table to pour his water. When she turned back around, he was choking on the aspirin that he had already put in his mouth. She tried to get it dislodged, but he died minutes later.

My best friend who had moved next door when I was three, was Barbara. Besides arguing over the property line between our houses, we had food-eating contests. One of the contests was to see which one could make the worst faces while eating a stalk of raw rhubarb. But, oh, the rhubarb pie tasted so good! Here's the recipe for my family's favorite pie:

STRAWBERRY-RHUBARB PIE

This can be made into a plain Rhubarb Pie by increasing the amount of rhubarb called for here to 4 or 5 cups and increasing the sugar to 1¾ to 2 cups. The Rhubarb Pie is the favorite of one of our Cherokee-Appalachian friends.

**3 cups rhubarb, washed, lightly peeled of strings and cut into
1-inch pieces
2 cups fresh strawberries, washed, capped, larger one cut in half
or quarters
1½ cups sugar
3 tablespoons cornstarch
¼ teaspoon salt
1 tablespoon butter
1 recipe plain pastry (Basic Pastry for Pies, see Index)
9-inch pie plate preferably a fairly deep glass one**

Prepare pastry and while it is chilling, prepare the fruit, putting it into a large bowl. Combine sugar, cornstarch, and salt. Sprinkle over

*the fruit. Toss, gently, to distribute the dry ingredients. Let this rest
while you roll out the crust. Divide the pastry in half and roll one half
out to ⅛-inch thickness. Place in pie plate, allowing the pastry to extend
an inch beyond the edge. Then, roll out the other half of crust. Spoon
the strawberry-rhubarb mixture into the shell, dot with butter, and
cover with the top crust. Press together the edges of the bottom and
top crusts and fold slightly upward, making sure that the edges are
well sealed. Flute or crimp the edges. Cut several vents in the top crust.
Bake for 40 to 45 minutes at 400 degrees. Serve with vanilla ice cream
or whipped cream. But, I like it best just plain.*

Once when Barbara and I talking long-distance, she recalled another
story involving that small bank we argued over years ago and the property line. As Barbara tells it,

> One day, your mother wouldn't let you come out and play. I
> stood with my toes exactly on that line on the bank and yelled, 'Mrs.
> Rather, please let Earlene come out to play.' Your mother would
> not answer, so I yelled louder, 'Mrs. Rather, PLEASE let Earlene
> come out to play.' She still wouldn't answer. Now, I have never been
> a 'Miss Goodie-Two-Shoes' whatever other people perceived, and
> I thought, 'Well, humph!' And, I marched right across your yard—
> remember the walk that divided your yard and went through the gar-
> den? I was really encroaching on the boundaries! So, I went over to
> that gooseberry bush—remember your mother made those goose-
> berry pies—and I stood at that gooseberry bush and ate gooseber-
> ries, and ate, and ate, and ate some more! I went home then, and
> got so-o-o sick, and Mother couldn't figure out what had made me
> sick. To this day, I cannot stand to even look at a gooseberry—not
> even in the grocery store in Topeka!

Barbara's family moved when we were in early elementary school. I
was a grade ahead of her only because I was a few months older. Barbara's new house was in the first subdivision built near King College,
called King College Park.

During the summer, we would visit each other and I spent nights at their
house several times a year. About halfway between our houses was Hylton's Store. When we visited each other, our mothers would give us a
nickel each to buy candy. The store was our meeting place, she walking
from her house, I from mine. With that nickel, we could buy a whole bag
of candy from the large display case in the store. We bought Mary Janes,

Dum-Dums, chocolate-covered raisins, Jaw Breakers, Malt Balls, Tootsie Rolls, Double Bubble Bubble Gum, Tootsie Pops, and licorice sticks. The licorice made our mouths and tongues a disgusting black color, but we loved them.

Barbara and her younger sister went through a childhood trauma because of knowing Mrs. Hylton. She told them that there was no Santa Claus! If she had known the word blasphemy then, I'm sure Barbara would have used it! Instead, they told Mrs. Hylton that she was lying. She laughed at them which made the experience even more traumatic!

In comparison, the Santa Claus revelation came to me during one summer when I was playing with Betty Jean, across the street. Somehow Santa Claus was mentioned during our playing. Betty Jean, a year or so older than I was, told me that there was no Santa Claus. I began arguing with her. Her brother, Herbert, who was a few years older, told her to shut up. She didn't, and I went home very angry with her.

After supper, as we were preparing to do the dishes (I helped even then), I told Mother and my sisters how Betty Jean had lied! They started laughing and told me that Betty Jean was right, that there was no Santa Claus. Mixed emotions came flooding in. I was still angry with Betty Jean, and here my family was saying the same thing she had said, so I accused them of lying to me. I felt just awful. I said, trying to strike back, "Just for that, I am not helping with the dishes!" I got spanked! And, I helped with the dishes after all this had happened to me, snubbing from crying the whole time.

Not long ago, I talked with Herbert. We talked about the fun we had growing up on Carolina Hill, the good neighbors we had, and especially how lucky we were. All of those neighbors looked out for us and cared about us. Herbert said, "You know, the kids today, most of them, don't have that." I agreed. We doubt that this can be attributed to the supposed fact that today's people are too busy to care about other people.

When I spent the night with Barbara, her mother made meatloaf, mashed potatoes, and peas for supper. Barbara and her sister always made a hollow in their mashed potatoes to contain the peas—a sort of "bird's nest." When we went upstairs for the night, we took sandwiches made from the leftover meatloaf and dill pickles to eat for a snack. The next morning, we woke to the smell of onions in the room, but we didn't mind.

One of the first meat loaves I learned to make is very simple and I don't remember now who told me how to make it, but here is the recipe:

SIMPLE MEAT LOAF
This will serve 4 to 6 people

1 pound ground beef (preferably ground round)
1 cup fresh bread crumbs OR 1 cup quick oats
1 egg
1 medium-large onion, chopped
1 teaspoon salt
1 can condensed tomato soup, undiluted

Set the oven to preheat at 350 degrees. Lightly grease a heavy skillet or baking pan with shortening and set aside. In a mixing bowl, combine the beef, the bread crumbs, the egg, onion, and salt. Mix together a little bit. Add one-half of the can of undiluted soup. Combine thoroughly. Form into an oval-shaped loaf and place in the prepared pan. Bake for 30 minutes. Remove from the oven and spread the remaining half can of soup over the meat loaf. Return to the oven and bake for an additional 30 minutes.

Serve with mashed potatoes and peas. Children may like to make a "bird nest," like my friends did. Or, you may make a nest for them, sometimes just to get them to eat their vegetables.

The recipe I use for meat loaf now is different from most recipes I've seen. I started making it when our older daughter, Lynette, was in college. It is the family's favorite and both of our daughters now make it.

MILLIE'S MEAT LOAF
This recipe comes from Gladys Taber's My own cook book: From Stillmeadow and Cape Cod. I first started reading articles that Mrs. Taber wrote for a popular magazine—when the price of the magazine was about a quarter. Those were the days when I was "dying" to move to Maine, but Ralph wouldn't budge. The recipe is said to serve 4 or 5 people but unless people eat two or three slices at a sitting, it will serve 4 or 5 people with enough leftover for the next day's sandwiches. The recipe is one made by Mrs. Taber's friend, Millie.

1 pound ground chuck
1 egg, well beaten
½ cup dried bread crumbs
1 ½ cups milk
¾ cup diced sharp cheese
1 teaspoon salt
½ teaspoon pepper
½ teaspoon celery salt

¼ teaspoon paprika
1 medium-sized onion, chopped
1 medium-sized green pepper, chopped

Mix all ingredients well and turn into a greased loaf pan. Bake about 1 hour at 350 degrees.

Our favorite pastime at Barbara's house was playing in Cedar Creek which ran behind her house. There we would pretend to swim in the shallow water, watch the snakefeeders, or dragonflies, catch crawdads (crawfish/crayfish) and were sure we saw snake holes in the creek bank. We also went exploring in the King College Woods long before roads went beyond or behind King College. We sat on the moss-covered ground under the trees and watched the birds, found "treasures" in the creek, and gathered what we thought were beautiful flowers; "old wild apricots" was Mother's name for them. They were passion flowers.

When my brother and I were older, we talked often on the telephone. By this time, he was living in Colorado. We talked much about growing up. Most memories were quite different, but one special memory we shared was of the King College Woods. He said that he used to sneak off from church and go there sometimes even though he knew he would be punished for sneaking off and laying out of church.

During the colder seasons when we had to stay inside at Barbara's house, one of our favorite things to do was to get old blankets and pillows and put them down the stairs—our makeshift version of an outdoor slide. Barbara's mom did not mind our doing this, but, her dad did. I don't know the reason. One day as we were happily sliding down the steps, the car came into the driveway. Barbara's dad had arrived home from work earlier than expected. We were a tangled mess, falling all over ourselves, trying to get all those blankets and pillows back up the stairs before he came in the door!

My Favorite Picture of Hobart

Barbara and I looked forward to a spring event at King College and in Bristol which took place when the dogwoods were in bloom. Much like a May Day celebration, the Dogwood Festival was held near the Chapel in a tree-shaded cove. A king and queen were crowned. Girls in long pastel-colored dresses wearing matching picture hats and escorted by finely dressed young men composed the court. A play or musical was presented for entertainment. Our mothers dressed us in our finest clothes and black patent leather shoes, and again we met at the store. This time, we bought no candy.

After a few years, a reception was held following the program. The tables were set with crystal and silver. Punch was served by dignified elderly women. Fancy sandwiches, cookies, nuts, and mints filled the table. This was my first fancy party.

When I went home and related this story, I was told by one of my sisters that the reception was for the students at the college and their parents and that I should not go again. The next year, the weather was rainy and the festival activities, including the reception, were held in the gym. The party did not seem as special—perhaps because the canopy of leaves in the cove was missing. And, yes, I did stay for the reception. When I saw that some of my other friends and their mothers who had no connection with the college were staying, I reasoned that if they could, I could, too. But, I never told my family.

I loved for spring and summer to come. This meant I could be outside more. I climbed our cherry tree where I sat and "surveyed my kingdom," but my "kingdom" was not "still" and I did not sit and ponder too long; there were too many insects to study, including measuring worms of various sizes! Other people called these tiny creatures inch worms. One cool day, when I was about eight years old, while looking out a kitchen window, I saw a luna moth on our big lilac bush near the sweet shrub. The moth sat there for a long time; finally, Mother gave me a Range-tec glass pan for collecting the moth. No, I didn't remember the brand of the pan; I have it now and I looked on the bottom of it to see what it was. I never remember Mother cooking anything, ever, in this pan. But, after finding this moth, it was always a special pan to me. After I brought the moth in, it began to warm up, its wings became dry, and Mother saw that it could fly. She told me that it was time to take it back outside. I took it back to the lilac bush, this was perhaps my first lesson in ecology.

When the ground in the garden was dry and warm enough to allow plowing, Daddy asked the Hagaman family on the next street to come plow for him. They came with their work horses and we could hear the men yelling, "Gee," "Haw," and "Whoa," much of the morning. Later, they would come back to harrow the ground. The sounds of the men giving commands to the horses and the click-clack of the simple machinery was much more pleasant than the varoom-varoom sounds of today's modern tractors!

Daddy explained that the ground could not be worked if it was wet because this would make clods rather than fine soil good enough for planting. After the Hagamans sold their horses and quit plowing our garden, Daddy never did find anyone who could do the work as well as that family.

Mother and Daddy saved seeds from one year to another, especially tomato seeds. Mother would clean the seeds off in water and place them on small pieces of white fabric. After they dried, the cloths were rolled up and stored in brown paper bags for the next year. Daddy made seed flats from lumber he got where he worked. Seeds were started in these flats early in the spring and placed at the kitchen windows.

The first fresh spring vegetables we had included mustard which came up every year. Sometimes when we ate the greens cooked fresh from the garden, Mother would add a few very young dandelion leaves, but we never ate dandelions by themselves. These days, dandelion greens are considered to be really special. This past spring, one market in Atlanta had fresh dandelion greens for $1.69 a bunch. All we have to do is go out and pick them before they bloom, but most of the time, we're too lazy.

Before the mustard became too old and strong and went to seed, Mother canned enough for the winter. We usually ate these greens simmered in salted water until tender and then seasoned with some grease which was fried out of salt pork just before the greens were done. The greens were served with vinegar to pour on as desired, soup beans, cornbread, and fried potatoes. Sometimes, we had Oven-Browned Potatoes, instead of fried ones. Here is the recipe:

OVEN-BROWNED POTATOES

If made just right, these potatoes are nice and crusty on the outside and moist but almost "mealy," one of Mother's expressions, on the inside.

Wash, peel and cut potatoes into halves or quarters. (Prepare at least one potato for each person you are serving and you may want to use some extras; these are habit-forming for some of us). Boil in slightly salted water for about 10 minutes. Drain the potatoes in a colander and let "dry" while you melt ½ to 1 stick of butter or margarine. (This depends on the number of potatoes you are using) in a cast iron skillet which as been placed in a pre-heated oven set at 450 to 475 degrees. Let the butter melt until it is sizzling. Remove the skillet from the oven and add the drained potatoes, tossing to coat all potatoes with butter. Return to the oven and bake, turning occasionally, until potatoes are very tender inside and browned as desired.

Once in a while, Mother would make Spoonbread instead of Baked or Fried Cornbread for us to eat with our evening meal. Here's her recipe:

SPOON CORNBREAD

Grease a baking dish and heat
Pour 1½ cups boiling water over 1 cup meal and 1 teaspoon shortening.
Beat one egg and add to corn meal mixture.
Add: **1 cup buttermilk**
       ¾ teaspoon salt
       ½ teaspoon (baking) soda
Bake at 350 degrees for 35 minutes.

The first plantings to go into the garden were the lettuce and spring onions. Daddy made a lettuce bed of wide boards. After the seeds were planted, lightly woven white fabric was placed over the bed with tiny nails. When some of the lettuce was big enough to eat, and some of the onions which had been planted from onion sets were big enough to eat, the fabric was pulled back just long enough to pick the lettuce and replaced so the rest of the lettuce could grow. Then, we had our first scalded, or wilted, lettuce—or as one of my former students once called this dish, "kilt lettuce"—for supper. The following is not the recipe that Mother used; in fact, I never saw her consulting a recipe when she made this dish. This is a recipe is a pretty close second to Mother's, however.

SCALDED (WILTED) LETTUCE

1 large bunch leaf lettuce, preferably homegrown
6 to 8 spring onions (green onions, scallions)
4 slices bacon or the approximate amount of a good quality salt pork OR about ¼ cup vegetable oil
2 tablespoons apple cider vinegar
3 tablespoons water
Salt to taste
1 tablespoon granulated sugar (more or less to taste)
Wash and dry the lettuce. Tear into small pieces if you have large leaves. Wash and slice the onions into thin rounds. Place lettuce and onions into a serving bowl. Fry the bacon until crisp or fry the salt pork until golden brown; remove from the skillet. To the grease in the skillet, add the vinegar, water, salt, and sugar. Bring to a boil. Immediately pour over the lettuce and onions. Toss. Adjust the seasoning.

Serve immediately. If you use the oil instead of the meat, heat the oil in a small saucepan and follow the remaining directions. You may want to crumble the bacon and add to the top of the salad.

You can leave out the meat seasoning or the oil; if you do, just bring the vinegar, water, salt and sugar to a boil and pour over the lettuce and onions.

One other note about Wilted Lettuce. In 1985, Marie and I went to Europe with a group of high school students including Linda, and some of her friends and a larger group of adults, including some retirees. One night Marie and I were eating supper in Naples, Italy with a couple from Idaho, the Carneys. When I tasted my salad, I said, "Oh, this reminds me of Mother's Wilted Lettuce." Mr. Carney said, "But I'll bet she didn't make hers with olive oil!" I responded, "No, she didn't!" This salad is delicious—even with olive oil—extra virgin olive oil, please.

Sometimes, Mother and Daddy planted a few early peas; then, we would have several meals that included them. I especially liked Mother's Creamed Peas. I don't have an exact recipe, but an easy way to make these follows:

CREAMED PEAS

Wash and hull the peas, put enough water on to boil to cover the peas, adding a bit of salt. When the water comes to a full boil, put the peas in and let them cook over medium heat until tender. You probably won't have much water left in the peas after cooking. If you have water left, turn the heat to low and let the liquid evaporate until you have no more than ¼ cup left in the peas.

While the peas are cooking, make a cream sauce: Stir 2 tablespoons all-purpose flour into 2 tablespoons butter which has been melted in a small saucepan. Combine well. Use a whisk if you have one. Then, slowly pour in 1 cup of milk. Stir the mixture constantly until it comes to a boil. Cook until nice and smooth and of the desired consistency you want. Add salt to taste. When the peas are done, add as much of the cream sauce as you like.

This is not the way Mother actually made this dish, but the results are essentially the same. Her way for this was a pinch of this and that and make some thickening, etc. Marie and I have talked about some of the disasters we have made because we tried to imitate Mother's "smidgin' of this," "pinch of that" method of cooking. And Marie suggested that I might want to put a disclaimer on some of our recipes given here—"Eat at your own risk" or some variation on that theme.

When the weather was just right, the other vegetables were planted—other types of onions, potatoes, cabbage, turnips, carrots, radishes, beets, corn, cucumbers, beans, and tomatoes. Daddy also raised strawberries. Mother sometimes made a fresh Strawberry Pie or Strawberry Shortcake instead of serving the simple dish of Strawberries and Cream recipe given previously. Here is Mother's recipe for

STRAWBERRY SHORTCAKE

1½ cups sifted flour
1½ teaspoons baking powder
½ teaspoon salt
1 tablespoon sugar
½ cup shortening
1 egg, beaten slightly
Milk to make soft dough—about 6 tablespoons
Soft butter

Turn out dough onto lightly floured dough board and knead 8 to 10 times. Divide dough in half. Roll out or pat each half into a circle. Make circles of equal size. Brush with soft butter. Bake in a 400 degree oven for 12 to 15 minutes. Let cool. Stack the layers on top of each other. Split each cake in half, horizontally. Spread sweetened strawberries (see the recipe for Strawberries and Cream) between all layers and on top of the shortcake. To serve: Cut in wedges and serve with cream or slightly sweetened whipped cream or vanilla ice cream.

NOTE: You can use this same basic recipe for other kinds of fruit. Fresh peaches are also really good!

In our back yard, we also had grapes and two apple trees; and, of course the sour cherries from "my" tree. Sometimes Daddy would raise pumpkins and Mother would make Fried Pumpkin Blossoms which were delicious. Reba once asked Mother to make more pumpkin blossoms. Mother said that if she that she made more, we wouldn't have pumpkins in the fall. Here's how to make this dish:

FRIED PUMPKIN BLOSSOMS

Pick the male pumpkin blossoms. Consult a botany book if you can't tell the difference between male and female flowers; or if you don't care

about having pumpkins in the fall, pick any of the blossoms. Wash them, take out the inside of the flower. Blot the blossoms on paper towels. Melt some shortening in a skillet. Dip the pumpkin blossoms into flour to which you have added a bit of salt. You may dip them into a beaten egg mixed with a little water and then dip them into the flour, if you want. Sometimes this method will keep the flour on the blossom a bit better. Then, fry the flour-coated blossoms in the shortening until golden brown and crisp. If you never have pumpkin blossoms, zucchini blossoms are also good. I have even used Day Lily blossoms but, please don't go out and pick the "wild" day lilies that grow at the edge of highways.

Another way to use the blossoms is to make Stuffed Pumpkin (or Zucchini or Day Lily) Blossoms. This is a recipe I experimented with, trying to remember a dish I had seen someone prepare on television:

STUFFED BLOSSOMS
Prepare the blossoms according to instructions given above. Make a mixture of fresh bread crumbs made from 4 - 6 slices of bread mixed with an egg. Add: A sprinkle of salt; a small clove of garlic, crushed; 2 tablespoons mild onion or shallot, minced; 2 tablespoons fresh, flat-leafed parsley, chopped; ¼ teaspoon dried basil or ½ teaspoon fresh basil, chopped; and, 2 teaspoons extra virgin olive oil or more to make a soft stuffing. Then, stir in shredded provolone, mozzarella, or Monterrey Jack cheese. Place about one tablespoon of the filling into each prepared blossom, folding the tops over after stuffing. Roll the stuffed blossoms in flour. Place in a greased rectangular baking dish. Pour melted butter over. Sprinkle with Italian Bread Crumbs (use the dried packaged kind) and bake covered in the oven at 350 to 375 degrees until for 10 minutes. Uncover and bake until they are nicely browned and the filling is hot and the cheese melted. These are yummy.

Like watermelon, I loved corn-on-the-cob and ate so much, Mother thought I would be sick. Daddy worked as a foreman at a lumber company. Often when the railroad cars, filled with the wood came in, they not only contained the wood, but sometimes additional "treasures" which the men could take home. One afternoon, Daddy came home with a large round platter edged in gold. In the center were painted three ears of corn. He said that was my plate since I liked corn so much.

To make ties for the tomato plants, Daddy brought home a big roll of worn out sandpaper from work. This sandpaper was soaked in a big bucket of water until any remaining sand was removed. Then, the fabric backing was dried and torn into strips to make the ties wide enough and long enough to prevent their cutting into tender tomato vines. When I got old enough, one of my jobs was to change the water on this sandpaper every day. This was done way out in the back of the garden where there was a water spigot next to the barn which bordered on an alley. The barn, which I thought then was just called a barn and never used as a real barn, had originally been used to keep Pet, the family's cow, when she was not put in the pasture at Blackley's Field. When it was time to stake the tomatoes, Daddy checked the stakes he had left from the years before and if he needed new ones, he made them at work.

While major emphasis was put on the vegetable garden, Mother's flower garden was not neglected. She raised all kinds of flowers, both annuals and perennials—pink and white peonies, iris, gladiolus, hyacinths, tulips, lilies, hydrangeas, sweet williams, four o'clocks, house leek, larkspur, dahlias, cannas, zinnias, cosmos, marigolds, scarlet sage, asters, crysanthemums, and others.

Sometimes, I got my own little square of garden to plant. I had radishes and carrots, and Mother gave me some of her remaining flower seeds to plant in my little garden. One spring or fall, Tunis took us hiking in the mountains, along what we know now as the Appalachian Trail, one leg of which is on top of Holston Mountains. During our walk, I saw a tiny bulb protruding out from the dirt on a clay bank. I took it home and planted it. The next spring, it bloomed—a jack-in-the-pulpit.

In addition to the outside plants, Mother had potted plants — several varieties of African violets, Christmas cactus, geraniums, surprise lilies, and her prized night-blooming cereus which had the most heavenly scent when it bloomed. We always waited with great anticipation for the night, or nights if there was more than one bud, the flower would bloom. It never bloomed until really late at night; and, I believe that some nights, we went on to bed and then got up about the time Mother thought it would open. That's how rare and beautiful it was!

Mother also had a rose garden. My favorite rose was a rambler with the prettiest buds I have ever seen on any rose and the smell was wonderful, not like ordinary roses. Mother said that it was an old-fashioned rose. When the flowers would begin to open, the cream-colored buds, inside, started faintly showing the palest shade of peach. Then, as the flowers opened even more, the cream still showed on the tips of the petals and down about an inch; but, from there down to the base of the flower, the peachy-pink color intensified. The stage I loved most was when the buds had barely begun to open. I tried to find a rose like this for years; I even wrote to a nursery that specialized in antique roses, but they didn't have it. Now, sometimes, I see one growing in the yard of a deserted or even occupied house, but I have not had the nerve to stop and ask for a cutting. With my not-so-green-Green Thumb, it would probably die, anyway. I told some of my students one time that the only things I could raise were things that could be neglected. One of them said, "Well, you don't have any children, then, do you?" I said, "I meant plants!" I don't think anybody could ever accuse me of neglecting our children; perhaps I could be accused of just the opposite.

Daddy built flower boxes to set on the front porch bannisters. Mother always put petunias in these. The Friday afternoon before every Mother's Day, Daddy always brought Mother two dozen pansy plants. This was his special present for her.

Of everything Mother and Daddy raised in the garden, he was most proud of his tomatoes. We had an abundance and they were the best on Carolina Hill. He and Mother shared the vegetables we didn't need with the neighbors, especially those who had no garden. After I grew up, every time I saw a former high school basketball coach who later lived in Barbara's house, he always talked about Mother and Daddy keeping them well fed.

Daddy's and Mother's idea of sharing was not limited to food from the garden. One winter, very early in the morning, when I was tiny and still sleeping in Mother's and Daddy's room in an iron cot on my little feather bed, I heard Mother and Daddy talking in the kitchen. Then, I heard another voice I didn't know. I got up and sleepily went to the kitchen. Daddy had asked the paper boy to come in to warm up and to have a cup of hot chocolate. I remember their talking later and saying that he was about to freeze. Evidently, Daddy had seen him another morning, maybe on the way to work, and they were concerned about him.

During the winter sometimes the milk delivered to our front porch would begin freezing before Mother and Daddy got up in the mornings at 5:30. Sometimes the milk had frozen so much, the expansion had started to push the cardboard stopper off the top of the round glass milk bottle. To Marie and me, this was great because we liked to eat that icy, slushy milk.

Mother and Daddy were not the only sharing people on Carolina Hill! One of the most caring, sharing, and dear persons was "Uncle Ben," a brother to Mr. Buckles. By the time I came along, Uncle Ben, as I remember, already had white hair. He raised beautiful roses. During the holidays, before so many children moved into the neighborhood or were born on the hill, Uncle Ben used to give the children gifts. He still did what he could when I was little. I remember one Easter weekend. We had been out on Saturday night, and when we got home, a grass nest was in the middle of our front porch. In it were beautifully colored eggs. Nobody ever claimed responsibility, but I still believe Uncle Ben did this.

The family who lived in Barbara's house for several years after "Coach" included a girl two or three years younger than I; her name, also, was Barbara. It was during their living there that I tasted some new foods. Her mother, Elizabeth Young, had some chives growing and even in the winter, she could be seen coming out to snip off some of the chives for use in their evening meal.

Barbara and I used to go to Fairmount School sometimes during the summer for their special activities. There we learned how to do screen painting. Other times, at home, we drew and colored extra clothes for our paper dolls or cut clothes out of catalogs. One of the things I remember most, I suppose, was Barbara's punishment when she had done something her mom thought she shouldn't have done. She had to sit in one of their Adirondack chairs in the back yard for awhile. That was unlike any punishment I ever got and I just couldn't understand how that could be punishment!

When I got punished, I usually got switched by Mother. I only remember three spankings, and that was enough, from Daddy. He used his hand to spank my bottom. Once, I had done something that I knew I would get switched for, and so while Mother was out hanging up clothes, I got into the cupboard where she kept the switch and broke the dried twig into tiny pieces. Then, I nonchalantly went walking around the garden paths under the cherry tree, spreading the tiny switch pieces so they wouldn't be in one place. When Mother discovered what it was I had done, sure enough, she went for that switch, but there was no stopping Mother—a fresh one was gathered. After that, I decided that I would break no more switches because a fresh one hurt worse than a dried-up wimpy one!

One Sunday, I went with the Young family on what turned out to be an adventure for me. On the way to the grandparents' house in Emory, Virginia, we stopped along the way to watch and count different species of birds and their numbers. In addition to being a teacher, a wife and mother, and a good cook, Mrs. Young was a member of the Audubon Society.

While the grown-ups and Barbara's older sister finished cooking the lunch, Barbara and I went to the Emory and Henry College campus which was across the road from her grandparents' house. We played on a pile of dirt near where a building was to be constructed until lunch time. Then, we went back to the house and sat down to lunch which included the usual green beans, potatoes, and other side dishes. We also were served two dishes I had never eaten before, broccoli and Swiss Steak. I know that Mrs. Young prepared the steak because before we left to go to Emory, she lifted the lid covering the skillet and showed me what she was cooking. I believe that the broccoli may have come from her parents' garden. When I make Swiss Steak now, I still think back to that lunch. Here is my recipe:

SWISS STEAK

1½ to 2 pounds round steak, about ½-inch thick, cut into serving pieces, and pounded with a mallet

All-purpose flour to coat the steak

Salt and pepper to taste

Butter, margarine, or shortening—enough to brown the steak (3 to 4 tablespoons, approximately)

1 can (1 pound) chopped tomatoes or 1 pint home-canned tomatoes

1 green pepper, washed, cored, seeded and cut into ½-inch squares

Water, as needed, to keep the steak from sticking to the skillet.

Wash, pat dry, and pound the steak with a mallet. Cut into serving pieces. Dredge in flour. Melt shortening in a heavy skillet. Add the flour-coated steak and brown well on both sides. Sprinkle both sides of the steak with salt and pepper after it browns. Add the tomatoes and about 1 cup of water. Bring to a boil on top of the stove and cover. Reduce the heat to medium or medium-low or place the covered skillet into a preheated 325 degree oven. Allow to simmer for 1½ to 2 hours, depending on the thickness of the steak, checking every few minutes to make sure you have sufficient liquid remaining. If you need to, reduce the heat a bit more. About 30 minutes before the meat is done, add the green pepper. Taste a bit of the steak with sauce. Correct seasoning if necessary. Let this cook until the meat is fork-tender. If you have not cooked this dish before, I suggest that to be on the safe side, allow a total of three hours cooking time.

To serve: Place the pieces of steak on a platter with the sauce poured over or pour the sauce into a small bowl or a gravy boat so that each person can spoon or pour the sauce, as desired, over the mashed potatoes which is a must to serve with the steak, we think.

After lunch, we went for a walk around the farm on hills high over Emory where I collected what I believed were beautiful flowers. They must have thought I was a bit weird, but Mrs. Young put those things in the car and we took them home. Of course, by the time we got home, they were nicely wilted. This trip, the walk, and the good food were reminiscent of other times, at Aunt Cindy's and the King College Woods. I came home a tired, happy, and contented girl.

Their family always went to the public library on Thursday nights, and I was invited to go along. Mrs. Young helped to reinforce the love of reading my family had started, a love that still endures. The family moved to Florida some time after that and Mrs. Young and Mother wrote to each other sometimes. The Young family now lives a few hours' drive away from Bristol and I still hear from Mrs. Young once in awhile.

In addition to all the vegetables and fruit we had, Mrs. Marion who lived on the opposite side of us, had a huge sweet cherry tree, a gooseberry bush which "Barb" stripped practically bare, raspberries, and a plum tree. We got to pick all the berries and plums on our side of the fence row. When the cherries became ripe, several of Mrs. Marion's relatives and neighbors were allowed to pick all they wanted. Mother canned the cherries in an old hot water canner with wire rack to hold the jars. Then, during the winter, we had cherry pies.

Sometimes, Mother made a Cherry Pudding using the fresh cherries. This is Mother's recipe:

CHERRY PUDDING

2 cups cherries
1 cup of sugar
Pour sugar over cherries and let stand while making batter.
Batter: 2 heaping tablespoons butter
           Cream with 1 cup sugar
           Add 1 cup milk and 2 cups of flour which have been
           sifted with 2 teaspoons baking powder and ½ teaspoon
           salt.
           Vanilla extract, about 1 teaspoon (optional)
Pour batter in greased baking dish. Then, pour cherries on top of batter. Pour 2 cups of boiling water over the batter.

Cook (bake) until golden brown at 250 to 300 degrees. Gradually turn up the heat. Note: I believe that adding a bit of vanilla extract makes this taste a bit better, but this was not listed in the recipe.

A sassafras tree with several smaller saplings also grew along the fence row. When Daddy cleaned along the fence in spring, he would dig up some of the sassafras roots. Mother then made hot sassafras tea which was drunk in the morning instead of hot chocolate or Ovaltine. I didn't like it very much then, but do like it now, especially iced. Of course I would like it, now, when some sources say that it is a carcinogen—or that at least too much of it is. In fact, some of the health food stores no longer stock it—not even the instant liquid mix. We drank the tea sweetened. I remember that Reba used to put cream into her tea and it became, to me, a disgusting pink color.

I suppose that sassafras tea was used as a kind of spring tonic as were the first fresh greens of the season. I believe that these were probably better-tasting tonics than the proverbial sulphur and molasses which some people say they had to endure in the spring. I think we were very lucky not to be forced to endure that spring ritual!

Another thing that Daddy got sometimes when he was cleaning out the fence row was a good case of poison ivy. This was something that he originally had not been concerned about and evidently he took no precautions. Once, he had a rash so severe that his face swelled and his eyes were puffy. To make matters worse, the medicine he had to use was really dark. When he came home from work one day, he looked like a stranger, not my Daddy.

Mrs. Marion, whose children were all grown, worked at Nickles Mfg. in Bristol where clothing was made. Sometimes she would bring pieces of material to Mother out of which she made us dresses. I particularly remember a light-green cotton dress which I loved, a blue and white windowpane checked one, and one with a turquoise color in it. Mother made the latter into a dress with a gathered three-tiered skirt.

Mother had a Singer treadle sewing machine which was self-contained in an oak cabinet. Iron legs supported the whole, with the treadle in the middle, near the floor. I never could sew on that thing or any other treadle sewing machine! Somehow, I was not coordinated enough to keep that treadle going the right way. When I made a few stitches going the right way, my rhythm would change or something and the machine would take out the few stitches I had made. When I got older, Daddy electrified the sewing machine and the treadle didn't have to be pushed anymore.

When the canning season came, the jars and lids were brought up from the cellar for inspection. Any jar that had the barest rough edge was discarded because it would not seal properly. At that time, zinc lids with white milk glass linings and red rubber rings were used to seal the canned vegetables and fruits. The lids were inspected and if the linings were the least bit loose, they were not used. I used the loose linings for extra doll dishes to go along with my green glass doll dishes. The sealing rings for these jars were never reused; new ones had to be bought every year.

The first apples to become ripe, the early apples or the yellow transparent, as they were called, were often fried and eaten along with the other breakfast foods: hot homemade biscuits, butter, bacon or sausage, gravy, and eggs. To make Fried Apples, this is what Mother did:

FRIED APPLES

Wash the apples, remove any blemishes on the skin, or any bruises in the fruit. Cut the apples in half, core them, and then slice into thin slices from the stem end of the apple to the blossom end. Do not peel them. Put 2 to 3 tablespoons butter into a skillet to melt; when the butter begins to sizzle, add the sliced apples. Add a sprinkle of sugar. Cook over medium-high heat, turning the apples gently until they are tender.

The heat was not high enough to really brown the apples, or to really fry them, but was just high enough to allow them to cook and get a nice glaze on them. I guess the reason that the apples were called fried is because they were done in a skillet. I never paid much attention to how Mother made this dish because I really didn't like fried apples.

Other kinds of apples were dried for use in fried apple pies or canned fresh to be used in ordinary pies during the winter. Mother made the dried apples by peeling, coring, and slicing the apples, cutting away any damage to the fruit as she did to any fruit or vegetable, and putting the prepared apples into water to rinse them. They were then drained and put on clean screens which were placed on supports and dried in the sun. They would be turned as they dried until dry enough for storing in small brown paper bags tied with white string.

One year, after we had moved into our house, when Lynette was a baby, I tried to dry some apples from our trees the same way Mother had dried her apples. I never could get them just right. I learned that it was easier for me to dry the apples at a very low temperature in my oven.

Some apples, winesaps, which Daddy usually bought, were made into apple butter. Mother also made applesauce which she canned. When many apples were being prepared for canning in one form or another, Mother clamped her iron apple peeler and corer onto our kitchen table and made quick work of a tedious job.

One year, the neighborhood women got together in our backyard near the alley and made apple butter. They used Mrs. Marion's apple butter kettle, which, at other times of the year, was kept outside, turned upside down, under her cherry tree. The finished apple butter was put into clean sterilized quart or half-gallon jars, sealed, and put on shelves in the cellar with the other canned goods, waiting for those cold winter mornings. I still have one of the old jar lids and a half-gallon jar. Mother's handwritten label on the lid still can be seen. Here is a recipe for Apple Butter. It is not Mother's recipe, but it is still tasty. At least my family likes it.

APPLE BUTTER

In a large, heavy pot, put
4 quarts apples—washed, peeled, and thinly sliced
Cook in water to cover until apples are tender. Run the cooked apples through a canning colander or sieve. Return to the pot and add 3 to 4 cups sugar. If you want, add the sugar when you are cooking the apples and you may not need to add as much. Also add ½ teaspoon ground cloves, ¼ teaspoon allspice (optional), and 1 teaspoon ground cinnamon (some people use several drops of cinnamon oil instead of the ground cinnamon). Cook, barely bubbling, stirring very often, until the mixture gets thick. Don't let this scorch! Test this after about an hour by putting a tad on a saucer. This will be done when the butter placed on the saucer has no water around the edge after it sits for a couple of minutes. Put into hot sterilized jars, leaving ½-inch head space.

One of my favorite dishes using "cooking apples" is Apple Dumplings. Here's the way I make them:

APPLE DUMPLINGS

Make one recipe of Basic Pastry (see Index) or double the recipe if you are serving more than 4 to 6 people.

4 to 6 of the smallest cooking apples you can find no more than 3 inches in diameter
Sugar syrup
Make the pastry, wrap in plastic wrap, refrigerate for at least 30 minutes.

Wash, core, and peel the apples. Place in a large bowl of cold water to which some lemon juice has been added to keep them from turning brown.

Make the sugar syrup: In a medium saucepan, combine 2 cups sugar, 2 cups water, ¼ heaping teaspoon ground cinnamon, ¼ teaspoon or less freshly grated nutmeg, ¼ cup butter. Bring the mixture to a boil. Reduce the heat immediately and cook for about 5 minutes. Add the butter. Stir to combine. Set aside but keep warm. Remove the pastry from the refrigerator. Divide in half. On a lightly floured board, roll the pastry to about ¼-inch thick (make as much of a rectangle as possible). Cut the pastry into individual squares large enough to cover each apple completely, with a little extra pastry to seal over the apples completely. You may have to hold one of the apples over the pastry to estimate the cutting lines, if you've never done something like this before. Form any scraps of pastry into a ball and return to the refrigerator to use in a few minutes. On the first batch of pastry squares you have cut, center an apple. Sprinkle with ¼ teaspoon sugar and about 3 dashes of powdered cinnamon (additional nutmeg can also be sprinkled on, if you like). Into the hole made from removing the core, place about ½ teaspoon butter. Brush the outer edges of each square lightly with cold water. To bundle the apples, bring each corner of the pastry up over the apple to the center. You should have something that looks like four wedges with points in the center with all edges meeting without having to pull at the pastry too much. Pinch together the four edges made by the pastry. Be sure they are well-sealed.

Place into a large greased rectangular baking dish or a 9 x 13-inch size baking pan. Leave some space between each dumpling.

Roll out the second half of the pastry and any leftover scraps. Repeat the process of centering the apples on the pastry, sprinkling with cinnamon, sugar, etc., making the bundles, and placing them in the baking dish or pan.

Preheat oven to 350 to 375 degrees depending on your oven and the type of baking dish/pan you use. Just before you put the dumplings into the oven, pour about three-fourths of the sugar syrup over them. Bake for about 25 minutes. Then, pour on the remaining sugar syrup. Return to the oven and bake an additional 5 to 10 minutes. Serve warm with heavy cream (as is), whipped cream, or vanilla ice cream. As always, I like mine plain.

When the big harvest of vegetables occurred in late summer, the onions were pulled up and dried in the shade to be hung from the ceiling or stored on shelves in the smokehouse at first and then in the barn, after Daddy tore the smokehouse down.

I remember that at the front of the smokehouse, there were small holes in the ground with a little bank of dirt piled around each one. When I was really little and still playing under the sweet shrub, not climbing the cherry tree, somebody told me that the holes were doodle bug holes. Whoever told me this, taught me a little ditty to get the doodle bug to come out of its hole. The ditty started, "Doodle bug, doodle bug, fly away home, Your house is on fire and your children all gone..." I don't remember the rest of the heartbreaking appeal. Anyway, after I learned this, I used to squat at that hole and say that chant over and over; and, that doodle bug never came out. So, I gave up. I have heard that if you call, "Doodle Bug, Doodle Bug, come up and get your buttermilk," the bug will come out. Perhaps "my" bug died of shock from the bad news.

The potatoes were dug from the garden and the dirt rubbed off, but they were not washed and scrubbed. They were stored in bushel baskets in the cellar. Sometimes additional potatoes were purchased.

Mother and Daddy, and maybe some of my sisters, liked Fried Cabbage. This is the way Mother made this dish:

FRIED CABBAGE

Chop coarsely or slice into thin slices 1 head of cabbage. In a medium saucepan, place a sufficient amount of water to cover the cabbage. Bring to a boil*, adding about ½ teaspoon salt. Add the cabbage and boil slowly until it is tender. Don't "cook it to death." It needs to have some "body" left to it. Drain off all remaining water. Taste for salt. Add more if needed, but don't overdo it especially if you are using salt pork for the next stage of the recipe. Immediately put the hot cooked cabbage into hot grease fried out of salt pork, or into hot melted butter. "Fry" for a few short minutes to glaze the cabbage. Serve hot.

*A general "rule of thumb" in cooking vegetables that I learned years ago is: If the vegetable grows above ground, bring water to boil before adding the vegetable; if the vegetable grows below ground (a root vegetable), start the cooking in cold water.

I never developed the liking for Fried Cabbage; I would much rather have had cabbage in other forms, kraut or slaw, then, I would eat my fill. Now I like Creamed Cabbage once in awhile. Here is a recipe:

CREAMED CABBAGE

1 small head cabbage, outer leaves removed
1 stalk celery, sliced (optional)
2 tablespoons butter
2 tablespoons flour
1 cup milk
Salt and pepper, to taste
Packaged dry bread crumbs. I use the ones with Italian

seasoning
Additional butter

Core the cabbage; cut in half. Wash really well. Bring water to boil in a medium saucepan, adding a sprinkle of salt. Cut the cabbage into slices about ¼-inch thick. Place in boiling water and cook until the cabbage is crisp-tender. Drain off the water.

In a large skillet, preferably non-stick, melt the 2 tablespoons butter. Add the sliced celery and cook for about 5 minutes. Stir in 2 tablespoons flour, blending well. Gradually add in 1 cup milk, whisking continuously. Stir and cook until the mixture is thickened. Season to taste. Add the cabbage, mixing it into the sauce gently. Spoon into baking dish that has been sprayed with non-stick cooking spray. Cover with bread crumbs. Dot with additional butter. Bake at 350 degrees for about 30 minutes until lightly browned and bubbly.

Serves about 6 people.

Mother first made kraut in large, wide-mouth stoneware crocks. The chopped cabbage and salt were added to the crock; she included the trimmed cabbage stalk. The mixture was covered with a dinner plate weighted down with a clean rock. Then, a clean white cloth was tied tightly to the crock with white string. The mixture was allowed to sit for a few days in the cellar until Mother began to check it every so often. She added more salt water when it was needed and knew the right time to can the kraut. Then, it would be put in jars for the winter. Marie and I loved to eat the stalk right from the jar when it was opened. In fact, we used to argue over who would get to eat it.

I disliked cooked turnips even more than I disliked cabbage. I did like raw turnips a bit, and sometimes would go to the garden, pull one up, wash it, sprinkle it with salt, and eat it for a snack. I did this with the carrots and radishes, too, without the salt. One summer, Mrs. Marion gave us some long white radishes. Oh! Were they hot!

The only way we had cooked carrots, except in soup, was when Mother made a kind of carrot pudding which contained sugar and nutmeg. She cooked the carrots, mashed them, added the sugar and nutmeg, and some milk and maybe an egg. This was then baked for a few minutes and I remember that Reba really liked it. I never really learned how Mother did this because I didn't like that pudding and I have never found her recipe. I'd take my carrots raw, thank you.

After a few years, Daddy quit raising corn because it took up too much space in the garden. It took too much space away from another place he could raise tomatoes, that is. He stopped raising cucumbers and pumpkins for the same reason. Mother still made different kinds of pickles, though—dill (using fresh grape leaves and dill from the garden), sweet, sour, bread-and-butter, and fourteen-day. Different sizes of cucumbers were used according to which type of pickles was being made—from the smaller ones for the dill and sweet to the large ones which were quartered for the fourteen-day pickles. Mother's recipe for Fourteen-Day Pickles and Bread and Butter Pickles follow:

MOTHER'S FOURTEEN-DAY PICKLES
2 gallons cucumbers, cut, or small whole cucumbers
Let stand 1 week in salt water (2 gallons boiling water, 1 cup salt.)
Pour over cucumbers
The 8th day, wash cucumbers and put back in the crock
Pour boiling water over them and let them stand 1 day
Drain again and pour boiling water (1 gallon) with 2 tablespoons alum dissolved in it over the cucumbers
Let stand 1 day.
Drain off alum water.
Make a syrup of vinegar and sugar enough to cover cucumbers (6 cups of vinegar and 6 cups of sugar)
Let stand 1 day
Drain (reserving the vinegar/sugar mixture)
Heat vinegar/sugar mixture and pour back over cucumbers
Let stand 3 days
Add 1 cup sugar each day
(Drain and) heat vinegar mixture again
Put pickles in jars
Pour vinegar over pickles and seal

MOTHER'S BREAD AND BUTTER PICKLES
1 gallon cucumbers
8 small onions
2 green peppers
½ cup salt
Slice cucumbers, peppers, and onions. Add salt. Let stand 3 hours. Make a syrup of 5 cups sugar, 1½ teaspoons turmeric, ½ teaspoon cloves (ground), 1 tablespoons prepared mustard, 1 teaspoon celery seed, 3 cups vinegar, 2 cups water. Pour over cucumbers. Bring to boiling point. Can in pint canning jars and seal.

NOTE: I believe that Mother left out the green peppers in this recipe. I never remember them being in her pickles.

The recipe I use for Our Bread and Butter Pickles is slightly different from Mother's recipe. The first time I ever canned anything was when we were expecting Linda. Some of the men who worked with Ralph brought him lots of fresh vegetables during the summer, among them, an abundance of cucumbers. I decided that I would try to make some pickles and some of the other kinds took a longer time. I call them "our" Bread and Butter Pickles because this is the only recipe I have ever used for these pickles and I love them!

OUR BREAD AND BUTTER PICKLES
Slice into thin slices: 1 gallon cucumbers and 8 small onions.
Add ½ cup salt. Mix salt into the cucumbers and onions. Cover well and let stand for 3 hours. Drain off the liquid.
Make a syrup of: 5 cups granulated sugar
                          3 cups apple cider vinegar
                          2 cups water
                          1 teaspoon turmeric
                          ½ teaspoon ground cloves
                          2 tablespoons mustard seed
                          1 teaspoon celery seed
Pour syrup over cucumbers and place over low heat.
Heat to scalding (almost to the boiling point), but do not boil.
Put into hot sterilized pint canning jars and seal.

Evidently, Grandma Vance made preserves from cucumbers. I found the following recipe in handwriting that matches the handwriting in some of her Bibles. Mother had kept this recipe in her box:

GRANDMA VANCE'S SWEET CUCUMBER
PICKLE PRESERVES
Take good-sized cucumbers and put in brine that will float an egg.
Let stand 2 weeks.
Take out of brine and slice ¼ inch thick.
Soak 24 hours in fresh water.
Change water 2 or 3 times.
Then boil in strong alum water ½ hour.
Then boil in strong ginger tea ½ hour.

Make a syrup of 3 lb. white sugar, 1 pt. vinegar, 1 pt. water.
Add desired amount of cinnamon, cloves, allspice.
Put in cucumbers and boil till clear and syrup is thick.

There was no indication of how much alum or how much water was required to make "strong alum water"; and, the directions for making "strong ginger tea" were not given, either. I suppose that people back then knew how to do that. If you would like to try these, you could experiment. I know that to make regular-strength ginger tea, ½ teaspoon to 1 teaspoon of ground ginger is added to a cup of boiling water; so maybe you can judge from that.

The beans we picked but did not eat during the season were canned in the hot water canner, according to the method given in the Ball Blue Book®, so we would have green beans all winter. Some of our other neighbors raised green beans, too.

One day, I was playing with Betty Jean, and when it was time for lunch, Mrs. Barker asked me to stay and have lunch. Mother said that I could. Mrs. Barker brought freshly-cooked green beans and hot cornbread to us in the backyard where we were playing. That tasted so good! Her green beans tasted a little bit different than Mother's did; maybe they were a different kind of green bean than what we had.

One afternoon, Mrs. Barker asked Mother if I could go for a ride with them. She had learned to drive, or maybe she already knew before that, and she and another lady, Betty Jean, and I set off in the car. First we had to stop by some repair shop to either pick something up or drop something off, and then Mrs. Barker headed down first one road and then another, out in the country somewhere. Sometimes, the two grown-ups would say to each other, "Where are we?" Then, they would discuss which road we should take. Somehow, I got the impression, even then, that she didn't know where in the world she was going. Eventually, they figured out where we were and we got home. When I got there, Mother said, "Where did you go?" I said, "I don't know." And, I never did figure out where we had been that day, but, it was fun.

Sometimes, when Mother had more green beans than she wanted to can the regular way, she made pickled beans. This is her recipe for Pickled Beans:

PICKLED BEANS
Cook beans 30 minutes to 1 hour.
Cool beans in the cooking water.

Then, pack beans in jars and add 1 rounding teaspoon salt to each quart.
Seal.
If water runs out, add salt water when the beans get through fermenting and reseal.

Mother also made "shuck beans." Green beans were broken as usual and then strung together with a needle and thread. The strung beans were hung on the back porch to dry. When dried sufficiently, enough for one meal was put into a brown paper bag and tied with string. The beans were soaked in water before cooking. Sometimes people made "leather britches." These were green beans left whole except for having the ends trimmed. They were strung like the shuck beans. When they dry, they look like tiny leather britches (long pants), hence the name.

The dried beans—Octobers usually—which we knew as soup beans were purchased at the store. Sometimes, Daddy raised cornfield beans which he planted with the corn and whose running tendrils and main vines were supported by the corn stalks. Morning glories sometimes grew beside the corn, but to Mother and Daddy, they were pesky things rather than things of beauty. The beans Daddy favored raising were half-runners.

Mother canned many tomatoes in pint and quart jars. We always had the tomatoes during the winter to eat with beans, etc. She also used the tomatoes in her wonderful vegetable soup. She also made tomato juice which was put into quart or half-gallon jars.

We also had canned beets sometimes, but we preferred Mother's Pickled Beets instead of the plain ones. Here is her recipe from the 1936 Ball Blue Book®:

PICKLED BEETS

Cook small beets until tender. Cold-dip, dip into ice water, and slip skins. Make a pickling syrup of 2 cups sugar, 2 cups water, 2 cups vinegar, 1 lemon, sliced thin, 1 tablespoon cinnamon, 1 teaspoon cloves and 1 teaspoon allspice. Cover beets with the mixture and simmer for 15 minutes. Seal in clean hot BALL® Jars. I never remember seeing Mother using the lemon; and our pickled beets never had lemon slices in them. She must have just left this ingredient out.

From an assortment of vegetables, chow-chow, a type of pickle relish with a distinctive flavor, was made. Mother canned this in pint jars. Her recipe follows:

CHOW-CHOW

Combine
1 quart chopped cabbage
3 cups chopped cauliflower
2 cups chopped onion
2 cups chopped green tomatoes
2 cups chopped green sweet peppers
2 cups chopped sweet red peppers
3 tablespoons salt

Make a syrup of
2½ cups vinegar
1½ cups sugar
2 teaspoons dry mustard
1 teaspoon turmeric
½ ground ginger
2 teaspoons celery seed
1 teaspoon mustard seed

Bring this mixture to a boil. Add the drained vegetables. Bring back to a boil and can in pint canning jars.

NOTE: I never remember Mother putting cauliflower in her Chow Chow. She just used more cabbage in place of the cauliflower.

The recipe I now use to make My Chow-Chow is a combination of several recipes I found. Once, I used one particular recipe and the result was so strong only a few people liked it. So, I started experimenting and here is the result:

MY CHOW-CHOW

1 quart celery, diced
1 head cauliflower, chopped finely or 1 head of cabbage,
   chopped or a combination of both
1 quart carrots, diced
1 sweet red pepper, seeded, and diced
1 sweet green pepper, seeded, and diced
1 quart corn, cut fresh—do not scrape out the milk
5 to 8 green tomatoes, cored, and chopped
1 cup onions, chopped

Pickling Mixture: 5 cups apple cider vinegar
1½ cups water
5 cups sugar
¼ cup salt

Blanch carrots in lightly salted water. Drain well. Combine the ingredients for the pickling mixture in a large stockpot. Add all the vegetables. Stir to combine. Over medium-high heat, bring the mixture to a boil and boil for 10 to 15 minutes. Pack tightly into hot sterilized pint canning jars and seal.

Grape jelly and grape juice were made from our grapes. Mother used a special strainer and a small cloth bag which she washed and saved year after year. The grapes were cooked and put by spoonfuls into the bag until it was just full enough to allow twisting it at the top. The juice was squeezed out by twisting the bag. This method allowed the juice to be extracted without the pulp, skins, and seeds. While a canning colander was used in making applesauce, this method did not make good clear grape juice.

The grape juice was put back into the kettle and sugar added; this mixture was cooked to the right consistency and them immediately poured into jars. Later, Mother used powdered pectin in the jelly and the process of jelly-making was quicker than waiting for the mixture to get just right. And, oh! The aroma that came from that kitchen!

Mother's strainer and jelly bag are still used in my kitchen. But, when I made Scuppernong Jelly last summer, I didn't get the jelly bag out. I just used several thicknesses of cheese cloth to strain the juice. Since I had a case of the Scuppernongs, it would have taken me forever to finish if I had used the little jelly bag.

The strawberries were used fresh for berries and cream, strawberry shortcake with real whipped cream and strawberry pies. Other strawberries were made into preserves and put into small jars and covered with melted paraffin, as was the grape jelly.

Daddy bought bushels of peaches to can for winter. They always had to be the freestone type because they tasted better, were bigger, and were easier to prepare. So, in addition to fresh peach cobbler and pie, we had peaches to eat during the year. I now look forward to having fresh peaches during the summer. Here is a recipe for Peach Cobbler:

PEACH COBBLER

6 to 8 large peaches
½ cup water
½ cup sugar
A dash of salt
1 tablespoon butter
A dash or two of cinnamon or nutmeg

To prepare the peaches: Wash. Bring water to a boil in a small saucepan. In a bowl, place cold water and about 8 ice cubes. When the water begins boiling, stick a peach onto the tines of a fork and hold the peach in the boiling water for about 1 minute. Immediately put the peach into the ice water. Repeat this procedure until all of the peaches have been put into the ice water. Pour the boiling water out. Slip the skins off the peaches, cut in half, remove the pit and discard. Slice each peach half into wedges, about four. To avoid the peaches turning dark, you may want to rest the slices in lemon water while you are preparing the remaining peaches. When all have been sliced, make the sugar syrup. Combine the water and sugar over medium heat, stirring until the sugar dissolves. Remove from the heat; add butter, the dash of salt, and cinnamon or nutmeg. Spray a baking dish (8 x 8 x 2-inches) or a small rectangular dish with non-stick cooking spray. Place the sliced peaches drained of the lemon juice, into the bottom of the dish. Pour the sugar syrup over the top.

Dough Topping: Make Baking Powder Biscuits (see Index) and add 1 tablespoon sugar. Roll the dough out thinner than you do biscuits. Cut into two-and-one-half inch squares. Place on top of the peach filling. Bake in a 375 to 400 degree oven for about 30 minutes. Serve with vanilla ice cream.

As we got old enough, we helped prepare the food for canning. I never could peel peaches as smoothly as Mother did until I got much older and learned that I could dip them in boiling water for a minute and then dip them in ice water before peeling. This made the skins practically slide off. When I first began to string beans for shuck beans, I think I shattered more beans than I actually threaded, but Mother just took the shattered beans and cooked them. I guess she thought I had to learn how to do this right and no waste was involved, or at least, not much. When I was young, sitting on the back porch in the little spinning chair or in one of my own little chairs helping to fix the beans, I thought that only little fingers got sore from breaking so many beans. I now know better.

The meat we had to eat when I was growing up, except for chicken, was purchased at a neighborhood grocery store, Monte Vista Grocery, which delivered the groceries, or Morton's, on Pennsylvania Avenue, where Daddy stopped on his way home from work on Fridays to buy things not purchased during the week.

The main meat day was Sunday. On week days, Mother would sometimes use the leftover meat from Sunday (if the meat was beef) to make soup, stew, or beef hash. In Mother's old recipe box, I found a booklet *Wartime Suggestions to help you get the most out of your Refrigerator* that was published by the Frigidaire Division of General Motors Corporation, Dayton, Ohio and Frigidaire Products of Canada, Ltd., Toronto, Ont. The booklet was published in 1943 to help people make the most of the food they bought and to give suggestions for using their refrigerators more efficiently. During this time, rationing, even of some food items, especially commercially canned foods, was occurring and metals used to manufacture such things as refrigerators were being diverted to military use. People had to be more creative to come up with ideas for meals using leftovers in many various ways. The booklet gives 140 suggestions for using all categories of leftover food. The first page of the booklet encourages the people to understand that their having to change some of the customary ways of doing things has a good and beneficial purpose by saying,

Because our fighting men must be properly fed, the supply of many foods is limited here at home. All of us are willing to make this sacrifice, because we know that the food we do without will help speed final victory…. Until Victory is won, our resources are pledged to the manufacture of more and better weapons for our armed forces. At the same time, we want to do everything possible to help refrigerator users solve their new food-keeping problems…. We hope the suggestions it (the booklet) contains will help you during this critical period.

One of the recipes contained in the booklet, Glorified Baked Hash, is similar to the dish Mother sometimes made from Sunday's leftover boiled beef. While the recipe given here contains a few more ingredients and was baked, the basics are what Mother did, except for the baking. Here is this old and probably much-used recipe:

GLORIFIED BAKED HASH
2 cups diced cooked potato

2 cups diced cooked meat (soup meat, beef, lamb, pork, veal or chicken)
2 tablespoons grated onion
1 teaspoon salt
⅛ teaspoon pepper
1 teaspoon Worcestershire sauce
1 tablespoon chopped parsley
½ cup Soup Stock or beef broth left from cooking the beef
½ cup water or leftover vegetable liquors or additional beef broth

Combine potato, meat, onion, salt, pepper, Worcestershire sauce and parsley. Add stock and water or vegetable liquors; mix well. Pour into greased casserole. Bake in a moderate oven at 350 degrees for 1 hour. Serves 4-6.

Mother combined the ingredients in a saucepan on top of the stove. She added some "thickening," about one tablespoon flour mixed with about ½ cup of the broth. This was cooked until the mixture was fairly thick. Instead of putting the potatoes into the hash, Mother always served this with mashed potatoes.

If we had fried chicken or chicken and dumplings on Sunday, there usually was no leftover chicken. During the week, in addition to perhaps something made from Sunday's leftover beef, we would have salmon cakes, liver, homemade scrapple, stuffed peppers, and meat loaf.

I have tried to make scrapple like Mother did, but of course it has never turned out like hers. I have learned to make a fairly good scrapple, though, some people think. You may want to try it.

SCRAPPLE

In a large heavy pot, cook a small 2 to 3 pound pork roast in salted water until the meat falls off the bone. Remove the meat from the broth and let cool. Measure the broth. You will need 5 to 6 cups. If you don't have enough, add some water. After the meat has cooled a bit, remove the fat, bones, and any gristle. Shred enough of the meat to make 2 or 3 cups.

You can use any left for pork barbecue sandwiches or a variation of Cuban sandwiches. Put the broth back into the pot. Bring to a boil. Add: 1 teaspoon salt, 2 to 3 tablespoons rubbed sage (or to taste), 1 teaspoon ground black pepper or to taste, and ½ teaspoon thyme leaves (optional).

Then, very slowly, pour in 1½ cups corn meal as you do when making Mush or Polenta. Cook, stirring constantly for about 5 minutes. Turn the heat down and cook about 20 more minutes, stirring often so the mixture doesn't stick to the bottom of the pan. When the mixture is really thick and getting harder to stir, stir in the shredded pork, combining well. Taste for seasoning. Add more if needed. Cover the pot and cook about 10 more minutes or until no moisture remains. Spoon into greased loaf pans and refrigerate. To serve, slice and fry in a small amount of shortening.

When Mother had an abundance of green peppers but had no ground beef on hand to stuff the peppers, she used potted meat instead. We thought that this variation was great! After I married, I thought of those stuffed peppers and substituted potted meat simply because I had started thinking about the ones Mother made. Mine turned out to be horrible! I don't know what Mother did to make hers taste so good.

The following is a very good recipe for Stuffed Peppers:

STUFFED PEPPERS
To serve four people
Two large green bell peppers, washed. Cut the peppers in half, vertically. Remove the stem parts, the seeds and ribs. Blanch for one minute in boiling salted water. Remove from water and drain on paper towels.
Stuffing:
1 cup pre-cooked rice, cooked with salted water
3 green onions, with some of the tops, thinly sliced
½ cup chopped yellow or white onion
¼ to ½ cup fresh flat-leaf parsley, finely chopped
½ pound lean ground beef (ground round, preferably)
2 tablespoons olive oil
½ teaspoon salt approximately
**A few grinds of freshly ground black pepper OR a couple of
  dashes of cayenne pepper**
1 egg, slightly beaten
**½ can, about 1 cup, chopped tomatoes with some of the juice,
  or the equivalent amount of skinned, cored, and seeded fresh
  tomatoes**

To assemble: In a rectangular or square baking dish, place peppers which have been stuffed with the beef-rice mixture. Pour the remain-

ing half of the tomatoes with juice around the peppers. Add about 1 cup of water. Drizzle more olive oil over the peppers and into the tomatoes surrounding the peppers. If you have used fresh tomatoes, pour 1 (8 oz.) can tomato sauce into the dish instead of the remaining canned tomatoes. You may want to add a sprinkle of salt if you use the sauce. Cover with aluminum foil and bake for 30 minutes in a 350 degree oven. Uncover; sprinkle with grated Parmesan cheese and return to the oven for an additional 30 minutes, adding more water to the dish if necessary to keep the peppers from scorching.

Mother would sometimes order "steak fish" from the grocery store because it was almost boneless. Fresh fish caught by Mrs. Marion's relatives were usually politely refused because they were too "boney." They probably were trout, and, if they were, boney or not, we missed some good fish! Catfish were never eaten, Mother said, "because they were scavengers and you didn't know what they had eaten!" I never had catfish until about 10 years ago when my husband and I ate at a restaurant in Fulton-Tupelo, Mississippi. The fish and the other food was wonderful. I fix catfish now, but mine never tastes as good as that Mississippi fish did. I just roll mine in seasoned cornmeal mixed with a little flour and salt to fry in a skillet or deep fryer. That restaurant had their own catfish pond and took the fish out fresh. I like to think that this is one of the differences.

One of our weekday meals might include pork chops; I never remember having them on Sunday. Once, a distant Crumley cousin arrived at our house, unannounced, on a weekday morning. She had come to get the family dates because she was working on the Crumley family genealogy. The cousin stayed and stayed and it got to be time for lunch. Marie remembers that Mother, evidently thinking that she couldn't give that cousin what we would have eaten, became frustrated. She had only three fresh pork chops to cook and she didn't think that was enough to fix for our visitor. Evidently Mother had cooked enough pork chops the night before, for us, and she had these left. Mother was always particular about what and how she cooked for company; but, she did not like surprises by little-known visitors.

Sometimes, people who worked with Daddy and lived on farms in the country, several of Mother's cousins included, would bring him fresh meat. They brought fresh tenderloin and backbone and ribs. I remember one squirrel and one rabbit, and some frog legs.

In the morning we usually smelled the bacon or sausage frying, biscuits browning in the oven, and fresh coffee making on the stove for breakfast. Sometimes we could smell the maple syrup warming on the stove which meant we were having pancakes that morning. One morning, I woke up to the most wonderful smell coming from the kitchen. But, this smell was so different! I went into the kitchen and asked what smelled so good. They said, "Brains!"

Mother and Daddy really liked brains scrambled with eggs; but, even though they smelled wonderful, I could not bring myself to the point of trying them and I doubt if they would have helped my mentality. I could barely stand to taste the squirrel and rabbit back then, much less brains! And, so I decided that at least for that morning I would just stick to shredded wheat or Cheerios for breakfast.

Sometimes the men who worked with Daddy brought him some chinquapins. These were a real treat and that little brown paper bag was soon empty. Chinquapins are a small variety of chestnut, but to me they did not taste anything like chestnuts. An area of Sullivan County near Bluff City is called Chinquapin Grove, probably because so many of these trees used to grow there. Few of the trees are left; some probably were lost because of development and others died, some people say because of a disease similar to the chestnut blight that killed so many trees years ago.

Saturdays and Sundays were special days at our house. On Saturday, besides our getting up early to clean the house from top to bottom, this was the day Mother began to cook or prepare the meat and desserts for Sunday dinner. At Betty Jean's and Herbert's house, they got ready to go to town.

This was when Bristol was known as "The Shopping Center of the Appalachians," and the downtown streets were always crowded. Sometimes, the sidewalks were so crowded, you could hardly walk. Often, on Saturdays, people would just park their cars along State Street and people watch. But, when I was very young, we rarely went to town on Saturdays. I guess Mother had her fill of going to town to take me to the doctor during the week. I was a puny little kid and had a lot of colds and sore throats. She took me to Dr. Rock who had his office over Bristol Drug Company, on the Virginia side of town. When we went to the drug store to get my medicine, I heard songs like, "Sentimental Journey," "Harbor Lights," and "Faraway Places," coming from the jukebox—songs that always made me a bit sad for some reason. Sometimes, while we were waiting for the bus to go home, Mother would take me Woolworth's or Kresses' and buy me a new coloring book or a new box of crayons. This was not something to be expected every time, though.

Often, Mother would buy a chicken, young fryer or a hen, from Mrs. Rowe who lived behind us on the next street, always asking ahead of time to be sure Mrs. Rowe would have one available. Mrs. Rowe raised chickens and sold the eggs and would also sell the chickens, to Mother, at least. Before Mother paid Mrs. Rowe for the chicken, they always weighed it either on Mrs. Rowe's scales or on Mother's little brass scale. Mrs. Rowe also sold Blair Products and Mother always bought the vanilla extract from her.

Daddy killed the chicken by chopping off its head with an axe on a chopping block near the barn. After the head was chopped off, I remember watching the bird flopping around. The first time I saw this, I told Daddy the chicken was not dead and he explained to me what was happening. After the chicken quit moving, the blood was allowed to drain some, and the chicken feathers plucked. Sometimes, if our pillows needed to be renewed, Mother would save clean feathers. Then, she would singe the chicken, scald it, and remove any remaining pin feathers.

Mother then cut the chicken into pieces. This used to fascinate me, and I would ask, "What's that?" over and over and over. Mother was so patient as she explained what she was doing, or why she cut the chicken at certain places, what part of the chicken it was, what its purpose was, and while answering all these questions, she kept cutting away at the bird. I guess the greatest curiosity I had was about the gizzard. When Mother cut it open, after telling me what it was, and I saw gravel inside, I started into another series of questions. I knew the pieces and parts of a chicken and what their purposes were long before I knew the pieces and parts of a human being!

If we were going to have Fried Chicken on Sunday, she put the chicken in a big bowl and covered it with salted water to keep it fresh. This was covered and refrigerated until Sunday morning when Mother took it out, rolled the chicken in flour and browned it in shortening, getting the cooking started before we went to church. After church, water was added and the chicken was steamed until it was tender. Gravy was made from the drippings left in the skillet, flour, milk, and salt. Mother rarely used black pepper. And, she never used a recipe for this. Here, in the best way I can explain, is the recipe for Mother's Fried Chicken:

MOTHER'S FRIED CHICKEN

I won't go through the process of cutting up the whole fresh chicken. It's easier, but not as economical sometimes, to just buy the chicken pieces your family likes.

Wash chicken pieces.

Place in a large bowl and cover with salted water. Refrigerate overnight (or for several hours). When ready to cook, drain the water off the chicken. Roll the chicken pieces in slightly salted flour OR put the flour in a brown paper bag (or plastic bag), adding a piece or two of chicken at a time, holding the bag opening closed and shaking it to coat the chicken.

In a cast iron or other heavy skillet, over medium heat, melt 3 to 4 tablespoons shortening or half shortening and half margarine. Place chicken pieces into the melted shortening. Fry over medium-high heat, turning it as it browns, until a dark golden brown. Remove the chicken pieces to a platter as they are browned. When all pieces are browned, return them to the skillet and pour in enough water to cover the chicken. Cover the skillet and bring the chicken to the boiling point. Reduce the heat and let simmer until fork-tender, until it is almost falling off the bone. This will take 30 to 45 minutes or more, depending on the size of the chicken pieces and the age of the bird. You may need to add more water during the cooking process. When the chicken gets done to your liking, remove to a platter and keep warm while you make the Chicken Gravy.

CHICKEN GRAVY

To the pan drippings, add ¼ cup of all-purpose flour. Stir the flour into the drippings, scraping the Bottom of the skillet to include any browned chicken bits. Let this cook, while you are stirring, until the mixture begins to bubble and flour begins to get a bit brown (but, please, don't scorch it). Then, add 2 cups of homogenized milk [Mother always used equal amounts (about 1 cup each) of evaporated milk and water mixed together, but when I have tried to do this, the gravy tastes too much like the evaporated milk]. Cook over medium-high heat, stirring constantly, until the gravy begins to boil. Add salt to taste. Reduce heat and let the gravy just bubble (don't boil it furiously), until it gets to the desired consistency. Taste and add more salt, if needed. [Mother never used black (or white) pepper, but you can, if you like]. If the gravy gets too thick, add a bit more milk.

You MUST serve this with hot homemade rolls or biscuits and of course, mashed potatoes, (and hopefully at least one green vegetable or salad).

When we had chicken and dumplings made from a nice fat hen, the chicken was cooked on Saturday afternoon, left in the big pot and refrigerated until the next day. Sometimes the hen had small eggs still inside. These were left attached and boiled with the chicken. Marie and I used to argue over who got the little bitty eggs to eat.

On Sunday, after church, the chicken in broth was heated and then the chicken was removed to a platter. The broth was thickened with flour and milk and brought to a boil. The dumplings were then dropped in and simmered until light and fluffy. Mother always made dumplings the way she made biscuits, with buttermilk. The dough was rolled out and cut into small squares for dumplings. When I was little, we always had chicken and dumplings for our holiday meals. We also had homemade sage dressing, mashed potatoes, and all the other vegetables. I hope when you try this recipe that you understand Mother never used a recipe. When I have tried to make chicken and dumplings, they never have tasted as good as hers, but this is about the closest approximation as I can get:

CHICKEN AND DUMPLINGS

Choose a nice fat hen. Wash the hen, inside and out. If there appears to be little fat, you will need to add some butter or margarine while you are cooking it. Cut the hen into individual serving pieces or buy the chicken already cut up and buy the pieces your family likes. Put the chicken into a large heavy pot—preferably one that is non-stick. Pour water over the hen to cover. Put on stove on high heat. Start bringing to a boil. As the chicken starts cooking, begin skimming the foam that gathers on top of the water. Continue skimming until no more foam appears. Add about 1 tablespoon salt for a whole big bird. Cover the pot and reduce the heat to medium or medium-low. Let the chicken simmer until it is very tender, adding more water as necessary to be sure you have plenty of broth, at least one quart, when finished. If the broth tastes too weak, and this may happen if you use only fryer chicken pieces, add either some butter or a can of chicken broth, or if you have made some chicken stock ahead, add some of it. When the chicken is done, remove with a slotted spoon; place on a large platter. Keep warm while you are finishing the Dumplings.

About fifteen minutes before the chicken is done, make Buttermilk Biscuits (one recipe is given below; for a different recipe, consult the Index) or you can use biscuit mix, but Mother never used this mix in her entire life. Roll out as directed in the recipe, and cut into squares about two or three inches in size. Don't waste the little edges you may have left from cutting the squares, just put them into the pot, too.

BUTTERMILK BISCUITS

Measure 2 cups sifted flour.
Add ½ teaspoon baking soda and ½ teaspoon salt.
Sift again.
Cut in 4 tablespoons shortening.
Add enough buttermilk, about ¾ cup, to make a very stiff dough.
Turn out onto floured board.
Knead slightly.
Roll ½-inch thick.
Cut with biscuit cutter
Bake in hot oven 450 to 475 degrees for about 15 minutes.

To finish the dumplings:

In a small bowl or a measuring cup, mix together about ¼ cup flour and 1 cup of milk. Pour this mixture into the boiling broth, stirring constantly. Cook for about two minutes. Check the gravy for salt; if you need more, add a bit now. Bring broth to a rolling boil; add the dumplings, one at a time. Adding the dumplings should not stop the pot from boiling. After all dumplings have been put into the gravy, reduce the heat a bit, but keep the pot bubbling steadily. Cover and let this cook about 15 minutes. Remove the cover and gently push the dumplings into the gravy a bit. Reduce the heat to low-medium and immediately return the cover. Let the dumplings just steam on the lower heat for another 10 minutes or so, or until they are done inside. If you plan to have this for lunch, also plan on taking an afternoon nap.

When I was very young, we had a Hoosier cupboard in the kitchen with a bin for flour on the left side. Under the flour bin with attached sifter, Mother always kept a large light-green enamel bowl. This was Mother's bread bowl; this was the only use the bowl had. To make biscuits or dumplings, Mother sifted the flour into the bowl and then made a well in the center of the flour. Into the well, she added the correct amount of salt, baking soda, and shortening; then, she would add the buttermilk. This was then mixed into the flour with her light hand until the mixture was just right to roll on the bird's-eye maple dough board that Daddy made. The remaining flour was put back in its place to be ready for the next day. The flour was never wet and was never wasted!

After Daddy remodeled the kitchen, the cupboard was sold, but, Mother continued throughout her life, to put the excess flour left in the bowl back into the built-in cabinets to be ready for the next time. I still use that bowl, but it is no longer used exclusively for bread-making. When I make biscuits, I stir the mixture with a fork or spoon, for I have never had the light hand Mother had and usually need to measure the flour to get the right consistency. Mother just seemed to know the right amount by the feel. Mother's dough board and rolling pin have helped me prepare many kinds of breads and pastries for my own family.

Mother rarely consulted recipes when she cooked our everyday meals. If she did measure anything, she always used an actual teaspoon or a serving spoon instead of measuring spoons. For cup measurements, she used a white tea cup with an old design containing flowers outlined in black with touches of dark pink and light blue. This cup was a remaining piece of a set of dishes Mother and Daddy had used in earlier years. Even after she began using the measuring spoons, Mother could still be seen using the teaspoons and serving spoons. In fact, when making gravy, or thickening for soup and other dishes, she never used measuring spoons.

Sometimes, we would have boiled beef or a boiled pork roast on Sunday. These were cooked on Saturday because they cooked for several hours and were reheated in their broth on Sunday. One of the things I remember most during the fall, especially, was when Mother boiled a picnic ham for Sunday. The smell made my mouth water and I could just taste that ham!

Many times these memories are associated with the leaves changing colors, the smell of neighbors burning leaves, and the sounds of the University of Tennessee's football games my sisters were listening to on the radio. If the ham was for dinner on Sunday, it was served the usual assortment of vegetables, salads, and bread. Sometimes, the ham was taken on picnics and served with potato salad, deviled eggs and all the other trimmings.

One of the cakes that Mother made during the fall and winter was a spice cake with sea foam icing. Here is Mother's recipe:

RAISIN SPICE CAKE
Sometimes Mother left the raisins out

2 eggs
1 cup milk
1½ cups sugar
3 cups (all-purpose) flour
1 teaspoon baking powder
1 teaspoon ground cinnamon
1 teaspoon ground (or freshly grated) nutmeg
½ teaspoon allspice
⅛ teaspoon salt
½ cup butter
1 cup raisins

Beat eggs together. Add milk and sugar. Sift together remaining dry ingredients and turn in on top of liquids. Stir until barely mixed. Add butter which has been melted and stir about 50 strokes. Turn into greased layer pans. Bake in a moderate oven 350 degrees for about 30 minutes.

SEA FOAM ICING

2 egg whites unbeaten
1½ cups brown sugar firmly packed
¼ teaspoon cream of tartar
5 tablespoons water
1 teaspoon vanilla
¾ cup broken pecan meats

Place ingredients, except flavoring and pecans, in top of double boiler. Cook over rapidly boiling water for 7 minutes, beating continuously with a Dover egg beater. Remove from fire, add flavoring, and spread between layers and on sides and top of cooled cake. Sprinkle pecan meats thickly on top.

NOTE: Some of the Dover egg beaters made in the late 1890s were made of cast iron. I'm sure your mixer will work just as well!

Desserts for Sunday and salads, if we were having congealed salad, were also made on Saturday. The congealed salads were always served on individual salad plates lined with a crisp lettuce leaf; a tiny dollop of mayonnaise always topping the salad. Sometimes we had half a canned pear or peach or a fresh tomato slice topped with cottage cheese. These were also placed on the lettuce-lined salad plates and topped with that inevitable tiny dollop of mayonnaise.

Most cakes and pies were made from scratch. By the time I came along, Mother had started using filling mix to make the cream pies and lemon pies that she topped with meringue. Fruit pies and cobblers were made during the week and usually were not served on Sundays. Mother always made Seven-Minute Frosting for the white cakes, including the fresh coconut cake.

Sundays were usually the company days at our house. Uncle Cloyd and Aunt Blanche, and their children when they were younger, came maybe twice a year. Some of my sisters' boyfriends, some of them later to become their husbands, were there almost every Sunday and sometimes during the week. My friends came home from church with me often and spent the rest of the day until church on Sunday nights. We took turns going to each other's houses. I couldn't go to anybody's house again to eat until they had come to my house.

One of my friends and her immediate family always ate at her grandparents' house on Sunday. All of her aunts, uncles, and cousins did, too. I saw one of her uncles not long ago and I mentioned that I remembered his daddy always serving everybody. He would carve the meat and put a portion on each plate and the plates had a special order in which they were served and then passed to the people sitting at the table. I said that I had never seen anybody do that. The uncle said, "Well, the only time he did it was when we had company!"

The preachers came to eat with us several times during the year. Usually our minister and his wife, and the children if they had children at home, were invited at least once during the year. The visiting preachers who came to hold revivals in the spring and fall, along with our own minister, ate with us once during the revivals. Despite some peoples' ideas that all Baptists and especially all Baptist ministers are very stiff, stern, and strict, most of the time, the dining room was filled with talk and laughter. If this had been just the immediate family, Daddy would have sent us away from the table for laughing; he didn't cotton too much to laughter at the table—at least when we were growing up.

One minister who was a frequent visitor when I was very young is remembered much better by my sisters. His name was Haven Lowe and he was full of funny stories. His stories should have been written down because his sense of humor did not quit!

Mother often made lemonade for company, especially during the summer. I suppose it was always a treat for her when she was young. The lemonade was served, sometimes, in what I called the rose glasses. The glasses had roses with green leaves painted on the outside. These glasses were used only for company as were the scalloped and gold-edged good plates.

One Sunday when Haven was there, he was telling one of his funny stories when Reba got tickled at the same time she was taking a sip of lemonade. She laughed and choked at the same time. Haven, sitting beside her, responded by putting his hand under her mouth, and saying, "Spit it out in Mommy's hand; spit it out in Mommy's hand!" That made Reba worse and spit it out she did!

Marie remembered that once we had an Cherokee Indian minister speak at the church. He was very tall, big-built, and soft-spoken. Marie said that Mother was worried that she wouldn't have any food that he liked to eat. She evidently thought that he ate food different from ours. I asked Marie what we had. She doesn't remember everything, but said that one of the things Mother finally decided on was corn. This was an appropriate choice, but I really doubt if anyone considered the symbolism and importance many native people and their ancestors attached to corn.

When Mother had boiled beef, Daddy used to save a bite of his beef to eat with his cake for dessert. I always thought this was stranger than his eating sugar rather than salt sprinkled on fresh sliced tomatoes. He also poured his coffee out of the cup into the saucer and drank the coffee from the saucer. Everybody used to think he did this so the coffee would cool; but, I read much later that this was a German custom.

When we had company and Daddy wanted another helping of a certain food or another cup of coffee, he would say, "Dilla, pass _____ (the person's name) some more dumplings" (or whatever he wanted); or, "Dilla, pour _____ (the person's name) another cup of coffee." Now, some of my brothers-in-law and my husband say the same thing and we accuse them of "pulling an Oscar." I suppose this was Daddy's way of being a generous host without bringing attention to himself or to his needing or wanting another helping.

After the lunch dishes were finished, if we had company, all of us usually gathered in the living room where we were often called upon to entertain. I use the word "entertain" here very loosely. Reba, Marie and I were the only ones still at home. So, Reba played the piano and we all sang. Once when a minister and his wife were visiting from Kentucky while the church was searching for a new minister Mother told them that I was recovering from a cold and that my voice was still hoarse, perhaps her way of explaining why we may have sounded a bit different than usual, or maybe we sounded awful that day.

I suppose next to food, our house was most often filled with music, often of our own making. When I was very young, often after supper during the week, the quartet would come to practice. This quartet was composed of Uncle Johnnie Vance, J.C., who was Uncle Johnnie's youngest son, Uncle Clyde, and Reba who also played the piano. Reba said, "Mother didn't sing bass then," referring to when we would sing while doing the supper dishes at night and when Mother would sing the bass part—quite well, incidentally. Daddy never could sing, but we often heard him humming while he was working around the house.

The quartet sang at different churches and for different occasions. I remember Uncle Clyde's wonderful booming bass voice. J.C., Reba, and two other people about their ages also sang on a radio program on WOPI, "The Radio Voice of the Appalachians," every Saturday morning. The opening song for this program was "Marvelous Grace." When I was little, Uncle Johnnie was the song leader at our church, where Reba played the piano and Marie sang in the choir.

At the closing exercise of what would be our last year of attending Bible School, which was held after our regular school was out for the summer, Patsy, Carol, Jane, and I sang "Now The Day is Over," a capella. After this, we had several "singing engagements," as Carol called them. When our preacher held a revival at some of the country churches near Bristol, he wanted us to come sing, and we did. Sometimes, we even sang some quartet songs, with me playing the piano. The people seemed to love those songs. Sometimes when we sang "Now The Day Is Over," as we got to the part which says, "… guard the sailors tossing…," we got tickled and could hardly sing. We had met some sailors—one from New York and one from Louisiana— through an older sister of another of our friends. The reason we got so tickled when we were singing that song was that one of those sailors said that he loved to hear Farrin Young sing. I didn't even know who Farrin Young was because we didn't listen to hillbilly music! That sailor further said, "If God had made anything better than hillbilly music, it would have died and gone to heaven!"

When we became too old to go to Bible School, some of us taught the younger children. One day, I missed a day of teaching. Patsy was getting married and I was her attendant. This was a secret to most people. Larry, Patsy's boyfriend, borrowed a car from one of his friends and we went over the mountain to a small town where they were married—where else but in a Baptist church. These days, Larry, jokingly says that I was the one who got him into a whole lot of trouble. Today, they have children and several grandchildren.

Sometimes I stayed for choir practice on Wednesday night after prayer meeting so I could walk home with my sisters. Even then, it was not very safe for a girl to walk alone at night—especially on the main highway which ran by the church. One night, one of the older girls who attended our church was walking home by herself and a car full of guys pulled up, stopped, and asked, "Do you want a ride?" The girl, in all her wisdom, asked, "Do you have any gas?" The unanimous response from the car was, "Yes!" She then said, "Well, step on it!"

During choir practice when the choir director was having the sections sing their part, separately, Marie and I often would hum the part—whether tenor or bass, keeping our mouths closed. Both of us were altos, but if the bass part was not really low, we could manage it. The choir director would say, "That sounds better! Now, let's put it all together." After a bit of the song, he would stop and say to the tenor or bass section, "You didn't sound as well then as when you sang your part without the others. What happened?" Marie and I would get tickled. We don't know if the choir director ever knew what we were doing or not.

When Uncle Cloyd and Aunt Blanche came to see us, whether they came for lunch on Sunday, or just came to visit on Sunday afternoons, we always had fun. They were the nicest, kindest, and funniest people! Perhaps this was why Uncle Cloyd's nickname was "Happy." They were wonderful storytellers and it amazed us that they could be telling stories on opposite sides of the room and still be listening to the other one's story. If one began to tell the story wrong, the other one would correct it from across the room. Reba used to laugh until she literally cried! Sometimes when Uncle Cloyd was telling a story, we would get so tickled at one line, he would have to kind of hesitate, saying, "And, ah ..." until we kind of settled down; and, if his "And, ah..." didn't work, he would kind of laugh, and then wait a bit more until he could go on with the rest of the story he was telling. Sometimes I think he got a bigger kick out of watching us laugh than he did out of the stories he was trying to tell amidst our laughter!

One of the stories Uncle Cloyd told was about an old bachelor who lived out in Hickory Tree. One day, he decided he wanted some rice and went to the store and bought a bag of it. He took it home and put all of it in a pot with some water to cook. He couldn't wait to taste that rice! Then, he noticed that the rice was coming over the top of the pot, so he got out another pan to transfer some of the rice. Boy, he couldn't wait until it was done! But he noticed more rice was coming out of the pots. So, he got another pan, and then another, and then another. This process continued until the old man had every pan in his house filled to overflowing with rice!

Uncle Cloyd may have told this story when they were talking about learning to cook or how difficult it was to cook well, I don't remember.

I do remember a discussion on cake baking once to which Daddy's comment was, "Well, it doesn't take much to make a cake—just a bowl and a big spoon to stir it up!" For a while after that, when we had cake and someone commented on it, the response was, "Well, it was just stirred up with a big spoon."

If we didn't have company on Sunday, sometimes we went riding in one of our sister's boyfriend's car in the country or to another town. Marie and I always liked to get back home by 5 o'clock so we could listen to the mystery shows that were on the radio. And, we'll never forget that eery sound and the deep serious voice asking, "What ...lies beyond that creaking door? ... "Only The Shadow knows."

After church on Sunday night, we gathered in the kitchen where we laughed, talked, and had a snack. My favorite snack was a chunk of cooking cheese, as Mother called it, and a slice of bread. Bread, especially fresh French bread, and cheese is still one of my favorite snacks.

During the winters, we had more soup beans than green beans during the week. On Mondays, Mother always did the washing as did all the other neighbors. The housekeeping skills of the women were partially judged by the whiteness of the wash and the time the clothes were hung on the lines outside. If a woman did not get the wash hung by 10 o'clock, she was considered to be somewhat lazy. When I was very little, Mother sometimes put the beans—or whatever we were having for supper—on to cook while the laundry was being done or when she had something to do which required more attention than closely watching the stove.

The first washing I remember was done with an electric washing machine with a double roller though which the wet clothes were pressed to wring out the excess water. At first, I was not allowed to help wring the clothes because I think Mother had heard horror stories about children getting their arms pulled into the rollers and having their arms crushed. Mother had two big galvanized wash tubs which were positioned behind the wringer. The tubs contained clear water and were used for doing two rinsings. When whites were being done, the second was used for blueing. Blueing was a mixture Mother bought in a bottle which, mixed with the correct proportion of water, made a solution which made white clothes "whiter." The leftover blueing water was poured on the blue hydrangea to intensify the blue color of the flowers. After all this process, the colored clothes were washed while the whites were being hung on the clothes lines which were strung on both sides of our walk going out the middle of our backyard toward the barn. The lines were attached to iron poles which Daddy had embedded in concrete in the ground so they would be extra sturdy.

In the winter, when the weather was not suitable for drying outside, clothes were dried on lines hung in the kitchen, so that by midday, walking through the kitchen was like walking through a wet maze. When the clothes were dry by the end of the day, they were taken down, sprinkled with water, rolled up, and put into a sheet-lined clean bushel basket and covered with a folded white sheet, ready to be ironed on Tuesday. The lines in the kitchen were removed from their little nails, rolled up, and put in a drawer to be ready for the next cloudy or cold wash day.

For supper, we would have the beans—if that is what Mother started that morning—cornbread, fried potatoes, and either home-canned tomatoes, mustard greens, or kraut. This meal, I learned was not just traditional with my family.

When Barbara, my lifelong friend, and I worked for the federal government, one of the first landladies we had was originally from West Virginia. We lived with her for a few months and sometimes baby sat her little boy and girl. Her husband had been killed in a boating accident on the Potomac a year or so before. Once when we were sharing our common home experiences, she decided she would cook all of us a home-style meal. We invited some of our friends who worked in D.C. who were also from Southern Appalachia. We had the traditional beans, greens, fried potatoes, and cornbread, and so many other additional dishes that our landlady remembered from her home, that the table which seated about ten of us was full to overflowing. This was one of the most memorable home-cooked meals I had in D.C.

Another was when Lila, "my D.C. mom," invited us to her home to have an Italian meal and to meet her family. Lila helped train me when I first went to work for the government and she was the one who I asked many times, "What do you think?"

The fried potato stories Barbara and I have could practically fill another written chapter, and our food-related experiences, a book. When Barbara went to D.C., the only things she knew how to cook were made-from-a-mix biscuits and fried potatoes. I had never heard of biscuit mix then because Mother always made biscuits from scratch. Almost every night, Barbara and I had fried potatoes for supper, and we could always tell who fixed them by the way the potatoes were cut. Her mother had always cut the potatoes in cubes; Mother always sliced them, so that's the way we cut them. At least we had some variety! Thank goodness we did buy a balanced meal for lunch!

Barbara said, "I think Sandy and I grew up with our heads in a poke!" She continued, "All we knew was Mother worked in the kitchen! We never watched to see how the food was prepared or anything; we just knew mother worked in the kitchen and food appeared on the table in the dining room."

To purchase the potatoes and other groceries, Barbara and I rode the streeetcar which ran about three blocks from our house. On paydays every two weeks when we were clearing $107.14, which supposedly was "good money" in those days, we went to a supermarket which was at least four blocks from the street car; this was an up-and-down hill walk. The trip to the market was a piece of cake compared to the return trip because we always had at least two full grocery bags each plus a carton of soft drinks and a big bag of potatoes. One of us would carry the drinks and the other one carried the potatoes; and, sometimes, we would switch items while we were walking. As we trudged, loaded down with all these simple necessities, we often had to stop to rest, to shift the weight in the bags, or just stop to laugh. We often have thought and talked about those days and the images they now bring back.

One afternoon while we were waiting for the streetcar after our trek to the grocery store, Barbara was starving. She said, "I'm going to fix a sandwich," and proceeded to get the bread, the mayonnaise, and the bologna out of the grocery bag and place them on the large boulder against which we used to lean to rest after this leg of our ordeal. Never mind the fact that the streetcar was due any second, Barbara was hungry! I asked how she was going to get the mayonnaise on her bread, and she was about to demonstrate, when lo and behold, here came the streetcar around the bend! We began throwing things back into the bags, and of course the weight was shifted again! What a sight!

Some of the situations we got into remind me of the "Laverne and Shirley" television series without their accents, our course—our accents were sufficient. We didn't have much sense, but we had plenty of potatoes!

After the streetcar was discontinued, Barbara bought an old black Lincoln from one of our friends at church. We called the car Beezlebomb, my variation of Beelzebub. The first Christmas Barbara had the car, we and another friend at the time started home about midday in what appeared to be a light snow. We found out that the windshield wipers didn't work; so, we rigged up strings to the wiper blades that were pulled from inside. On top of this, the heater didn't work, and we were freezing!

The roads kept getting worse and worse, and one of the worst stretches we had to face was what people called Christiansburg Mountain. The road was steep and resplendent with curves. Since I didn't know how to drive, I was in the back seat—as far into that seat as I could get! When we started up that mountain, just as we were headed into yet another sharp curve, I looked out, and blurted out, "Oh, my gosh, look at that!" Behind us, I saw what resembled a demolition derby; tractor-trailers, cars of all varieties, and people were going in all directions. I turned toward the front of the car and Barbara had turned to look back, too. I yelled, "Not you!" She made that curve with no problem.

When we got to Wytheville, usually a speed trap area, the highway patrol was stopping people and advising them to get a motel room and wait it out. But, Barbara was determined she could make it with Beezlebomb. So, we called home and kept plodding along. A trip that normally took no more than eight or nine hours with meal stops took us sixteen hours.

The car had electric windows. When the button was pushed to lower or raise the window, the front seat moved forward, then backward, and then the window would move. This created many surprised looks on people's faces especially at the drive-in restaurants in Bethesda and many funny stories. The most important thing is that this car was instrumental in Barbara's future.

One night after a snow, of course, we were headed out to go somewhere. We had gone about three blocks from our apartment in The Clara Barton House and were at the streetcar tracks when the car got stuck. No matter what Barbara tried, Beezle just sat there spinning his wheels. Then, a knock-knock-knock came on Barbara's window. The button was pushed, and after the usual seat-moving ritual, the window opened. Peering into the window was a very much surprised but smiling handsome face —one Barbara had been noticing for weeks after we passed his apartment one day, about a block from our own apartment. It was Bert. He helped get the car on the way and began coming over to see her and the rest is history.

Our landladies and the owners of the Clara Barton House were three sisters, the Frank sisters. One, Miss Henrietta, had been the Dean of Women at the State University of Iowa, as she said. So, you can be well-assured that we were under proper supervision. They reviewed our dates, whether the dates were formally introduced to them or not. The house had sufficient windows which allowed such reviews. Later, they would give us their collective analysis without our asking.

Miss Henrietta walked with a cane much of the time, and when she wanted to have a discussion with us, serious or otherwise, she would tap her cane on the floor. When we were "summoned," we would go scampering up the back staircase outside of our kitchen which led to the center hall on the main level of the house. They, evidently, had noticed that I had been receiving some mail from a certain male. Someone who lived in the house, whoever got home from work first or one of the landladies, would walk to the Glen Echo Post Office and collect all the mail for house occupants and place it on a table in the central main floor hall. Everyone who lived in that small village went to the Post Office to collect mail; there was no house-to-house delivery. One evening when I was visiting in their sitting room, I told the sisters that a guy was coming the next night to have supper with us. They told me to bring him up and introduce him.

The next afternoon after work, on the antique sideboard in our apartment, there was a huge creamy-white magnolia blossom still attached to the dark waxy green leaves from one of the trees on the house grounds floating in an antique bowl filled with water. We thought "What in the world?!" After supper, I took the guy upstairs to meet the landladies, as I had been told to do. After the introductions and a little small talk, one of the sisters said, "I know what you all need... a _____." I've forgotten what she called it, but after they bustled around in their kitchen, two rooms beyond the sitting room, and brought the drinks in to us, they turned out to be Root Beer Floats. If you've never had one, here's what you do; into a large glass, preferably frosted in the freezer, pour some cold root beer. Then, add a scoop or two of vanilla ice cream. After we drank their special drink, I took the visitor on a tour of the rest of the house that was open. The next day, the sisters could hardly wait to find out "how it went." And, they were so disappointed to learn that this guy was not my "special guy." And the magnolia? They had wanted to do something special for the occasion. We were very lucky. They cared about us.

The house grounds at Clara's house were like a park. Some days after work, I went out to my "thinking ledge," a large boulder which protruded out from the side yard and overlooked the canal. This was my quiet time, something which Barb and some of my other friends did not quite understand, at that time.

The house was built with lumber from the barracks built to house people in the aftermath of the Johnstown, Pennsylvania flood. When the barracks were demolished, the lumber was given to Clara in payment for her coming to help the townspeople during those terrible times. The wood was floated down the Chesapeake & Ohio Canal which ran down at the bottom of the hill behind the house. In the house itself, were Clara's pianoforte, a painting of her cat, and several pieces of furniture and other gifts given to Clara by foreign heads of state for her help in their countries. The main floor hallway was lined with book shelves containing Clara's books.

The room I liked best, the "Red Cross" room, was a suspended room at the front of the house, which appeared to literally be suspended from the rafters. (It had no visible means of support). The centers of the two windows in this room had small red glass window panes in the shape of a cross. This room housed Clara's bed and some of her other belongings, including her slipper stool—a wooden box with hollow interior and upholstered lid that she used to hold her shoes. The house has been designated as a National Historic Site and is now operated as a museum.

Our apartment was called "The Terrace Apartment." In our terms, it was in the basement along with Clara's canoe. The first meal Barb and I really tried to cook in our "new apartment" was Sunday lunch after we had moved in on Saturday. We had a new cast iron skillet and we were going to do ham, candied sweet potatoes, and green beans. We were doing an easy version of Candied Sweet Potatoes, of course; we didn't own a cookbook then. This is what we used to do to make this dish:

CANDIED SWEET POTATOES

Open a can of sweet potatoes. Drain off some of the water. Add the potatoes and the remaining water in the can to a skillet. Add 1 to 2 tablespoons butter. Let the potatoes simmer until the majority of the water has evaporated. Sprinkle brown sugar over. Add another tablespoon of butter. Toss the potatoes to coat them and let them cook until the brown sugar-butter mixture forms a glaze and syrup around the potatoes. You may have to add more butter and sugar, depending on your preference.

When we tried to cook on the little two-eyed contraption of an electric cook top that was in the apartment, we couldn't get it to heat. And, we were hungry! So, in desperation, we put the skillet with ham on the top of the oil heater used to heat our apartment; the sweet potatoes and green beans were put into saucepans. We thought we had it made. Then, when we started to eat our wonderful meal, everything tasted of oil fumes! Our "celebration lunch" was ruined. We were reminded later that to use the cook top, we had to plug it in each time we used it and that we were to disconnect it when we were through cooking.

Just about every Saturday morning, one of Barb's friends from work came by the apartment and we all went to the Bethesda Farmer's Market. There, we bought homemade breads, jellies, and a special and different treat—to us at least. These cookies were called Chinese Chews. For many years I tried to find a cookie recipe or to create one that was like these cookies; the closest I came to them was a recipe for Date Nut Bars. I don't even remember who gave me this recipe, but here it is:

DATE NUT BARS

¾ cup shortening
1½ cups sugar
3 cups flour
1 cup buttermilk
1 teaspoon salt
1 teaspoon baking powder
½ teaspoon baking soda
1 cup dates, chopped
1 cup chopped pecans
Confectioners sugar

Cream shortening and sugar. Add buttermilk, baking powder and baking soda which have been mixed together. Sift flour and salt together. Then add dates and pecans. Bake 20 minutes in 350 degree

*oven. Cut into squares or bars and roll in confectioners sugar while
they are hot.*

Several years after I was married, I finally found the real recipe in the
1959 *Farm Journal's Country Cookbook.* So, for Barbara, especially, here
is the recipe for:

CHINESE CHEWS

1 cup sugar
¾ cup sifted flour
1 teaspoon baking powder
¼ teaspoon salt
1 cup chopped pitted dates
1 cup chopped nuts
2 eggs, beaten
   *Sift sugar, flour, baking powder and salt into bowl. Stir in dates and
nuts. Add eggs; mix thoroughly. Spread in greased 15½ x 10½ x 1-inch
pan. Bake in a 375-degree oven for 15 to 20 minutes. Cut into squares
while warm. Roll in confectioners sugar. Makes about 6 dozen.*
   *NOTE: These, as well as the Date Nut Bars, keep really well if you
send "care packages" to college students or others who are away from
home.*

When Barbara's sister and some of her friends moved into the apartment, we still got a summons every so often to come upstairs, and we still
had potatoes, but at least we didn't have to lug them for blocks. We had
Beezlebomb. Once at the grocery store check out while we were waiting
with multiple bags of potatoes, Barbara's sister said, "Do you think we
have enough potatoes?" The cashier looked at her like she was crazy.
Another time, all of us were packed into Beezlebomb making our way
home after work when someone said, "Who's fixing the potatoes tonight?"
It was as if everybody gasped, and then, we all broke into laughter. We then
realized that every night we had been eating fried potatoes with whatever
else we had, so we began changing our diet somewhat.
   One Saturday, I walked to the D.G.S., District Grocery Store, in Glen
Echo and bought a beef roast for one of our Sunday meals. From the leftovers, I made soup on Monday trying to make it like Mother did. I cooked
diced potatoes and onions in the broth and then added a can of tomatoes,
some corn, peas, and carrots. It turned out pretty well. Bert happened to
come over later and Barbara gave him some of this soup. He started eat-

ing it and said it was good. Then, he asked her if she had made the soup and she said, "Yes." Twenty-five years later, she confessed to Bert and to me that she had taken credit for that soup, trying to impress Bert. We kidded her saying that he married her under false pretenses.

Today, Barbara lives in Kansas and neither she nor I fix fried potatoes with any frequency or regularity, not even when we do see each other, except in a dish called Hoppel Poppel that I started making years ago. Sometimes this dish is called Miner's Breakfast. Barb and Bert have this for breakfast on Saturday mornings. And, sometimes, Bert does the cooking.

HOPPEL POPPEL (MINER'S BREAKFAST)
This amount may serve four to six people, depending on the appetites
4 potatoes, peeled, parboiled, and sliced (or just saute them until tender in butter or margarine)
8 eggs
8 slices bacon
1 to 2 onions, chopped
Salt and pepper, to taste

Cut bacon in small pieces. Fry over medium-low heat until crisp. Remove from skillet. In bacon grease, saute onions until translucent. Scramble eggs into this mixture, adding bacon and potatoes.

Sometimes, I have used the small canned whole potatoes and sliced them instead of cooking potatoes. The canned are easier, but the flavor is just not the same. Also, instead of scrambling the eggs in the bacon grease, I sometimes scramble them in margarine and then, just add the other ingredients.

Barb and Bert have made this a low-fat/low cholesterol recipe by using a soft vegetable spread instead of the margarine or butter, the veggie lean strips that are similar to bacon, and egg substitute. Barb sometimes tops her serving with shredded cheese, but Bert is more careful after open heart surgery. Barb says that this variation still has the same good flavor.

Another variation: This variation is good for a buffet breakfast or brunch. Place in a chafing dish or casserole with warmer underneath to serve. Cook grits and put in the bottom of a casserole. Saute some chopped sweet red and green pepper and add to the egg mixture, along with cubed and cooked new red potatoes, and the sauteed onions. Scramble the eggs with these additions. Place on top of the grits. Top with strips of bacon or crumble the bacon and sprinkle over the top.

Going back to more simple days and foods, sometimes when Mother was rushed for time, had been quilting, or didn't feel like cooking a big meal, she made mush. She put water on to boil and added salt. When this came to a full boil, she ever so carefully stirred in cornmeal, in a small steady stream. She stirred the mixture until it reached the right consistency. We ate the mush with lots of country butter. Sometimes if we asked what we were going to have for supper that night, Mother would say, "Mush. Eat it and hush." We didn't think that was funny then, but we do now.

In the second grade, my teacher, Miss Tilson, was talking about food one day and asked how many of us had ever eaten mush. I started to raise my hand when I noticed no one else was raising theirs, so I didn't either. The teacher then went on to talk about how good mush was. Of course, what we have always called mush has been known as polenta in Italy for years. And, on the restaurant menus in our country today, if a dish were called "Mush with Fried Dry Land Fish," it would never sell. Call it "Polenta with Sauteed Morels," and it's a winner. But, at home, to us, mush was just something we ate sometimes—nothing special.

The following is a recipe for Mush that can be gussied up, if you want, with extra ingredients.

MUSH

Into 5 cups of boiling water, stir in 1 teaspoon salt. Gradually sprinkle in about 1½ cups cornmeal as you are continually stirring the mixture. A whisk works really well here to remove any lumps that like to form. As the mixture begins to thicken, begin stirring with a long-handled spoon as this tends to bubble and spatter. Cook, uncovered, stirring for about 5 minutes. Then, turn the heat to low, cover the pot, and let the mush continue cooking for about 30 minutes, stirring occasionally.

Remove from the heat, taste for salt, and adjust if necessary. Serve with butter.

Suggested additions to gussie it up:
1. *½ cup grated or shredded cheese (Parmesan or your favorite)*
2. *Morels or other fresh mushrooms sauteed in vegetable or olive oil. A touch of nutmeg, a tiny bit of garlic, and some parsley could be added I suppose; but if you are using morels, I don't see why you would want to hide their wonderful flavor.*
3. *Use both of the above suggestions and make a light cream sauce to bind the two together . If you use the suggestions, above, the first two can be stirred into the cooked mush or they may placed*

on as a topping. I would not stir a cream sauce into the mush, but would use it only as a topping. However, just plain old mush is good!

When I was very young, Daddy bought butter from a Mr. Hunt who had a farm on the Bluff City Highway. On Saturdays, since we had no car, he would ride the bus to the Hunts' to get the butter. Sometimes I got to go along. I remember once that Marie, about 12 years old, went, too; and, one of Mr. Hunt's sons gave her some lilacs which were growing around their house. I felt left out, but I was just a little kid.

After a while, the Hunts quit making butter and then we began to have margarine. The margarine was white but it came with a little packet of coloring which Mother mixed with the white mixture to make it look like butter. She then molded the fake butter in her round butter mold with the acorn and oak leaf design which I still have. Sometimes I have taken half a pound of margarine or butter and molded it in that butter mold just to have for special meals.

Often some of my friends in school would talk about what they had for supper, or dinner, some had started calling it, the night before. One of my best school friends at that time was cared for much of the time by a maid who also did the cooking for the family. My friend talked about having asparagus sometimes and also about cauliflower with cheese sauce. These were foods I had never eaten. I kept trying to get Mother to cook these, but she liked cabbage rather than cauliflower and didn't like asparagus then, at all.

Asparagus grew in our side yard next to a tamarisk tree which I called the fuzzy tree because of its pink fuzzy blossoms. Mother never cooked the young shoots of asparagus; instead, she let them grow until they became feathery and then used the fronds in cut-flower arrangements that she arranged in vases and put on the piano or the mantel in the living room. Finally, one spring night, she did cook some of the young asparagus shoots. I did not like the taste at all nor did anyone else in the family; and I never asked Mother to cook asparagus again. Tastes change. Now, most of us love asparagus. Marie began bringing an asparagus casserole to family meals when we started sharing the cooking responsibilities with Mother. Here is her recipe:

MARIE'S ASPARAGUS AU GRATIN
2 tablespoons butter
2 tablespoons all-purpose flour

1 cup milk
½ teaspoon salt
1 cup grated Cheddar cheese
1 cup soft buttered bread crumbs
1 (#2) can asparagus spears, drained
2 hard-boiled eggs, sliced

Melt butter; stir in flour; blend in well. Slowly stir in milk. Add salt. Cook until thickened, stirring constantly. Add cheese. Stir until melted. Place half of the crumbs into a casserole dish. Top with asparagus and sliced eggs. Cover with cheese sauce. Top with remaining crumbs. Bake at 350 degrees for 45 minutes. Makes 4 servings.

My family especially likes asparagus for a very late breakfast-brunch-early lunch when I serve it with Eggs Benedict. When I can get good fresh asparagus, I like to steam it peeling the lower stems with a potato peeler and discarding the tough woody parts, but one of our daughters still prefers the canned asparagus. My Eggs Benedict are a lazy variety of the real thing, but here is my version:

LAZY WOMAN'S EGGS BENEDICT

1 package English Muffins
2 eggs for each person you are serving
1 slice of cooked, smoked, cured ham for each person you are
    serving (Or, if you want to be more traditional in this recipe, use
    two slices of Canadian Bacon)

To serve four-to-six people, prepare 2 packages of hollandaise sauce mix. I substitute water for the milk called for on the package directions and add some lemon juice. Keep the sauce warm.

Saute the ham slices in a very small amount of margarine in a large skillet; mainly, you just want to heat and not overly brown the ham or Canadian Bacon. Remove from the skillet and keep warm.

Poach the eggs in simmering, but not boiling water, to which you have added 1 tablespoon vinegar and a sprinkle of salt. If you do this in a medium-sized saucepan, you should be able to poach two eggs at a time. When the eggs reach the degree of doneness you desire (you don't want them to be fully cooked like a "boiled egg"), remove from the water and place in a rectangular baking dish to which you have added a tiny bit of warm water to keep the eggs from sticking to the dish. Keep warm in a very low oven while you prepare the remaining eggs.

Split the English Muffins and put them into the toaster just long enough to get them well heated but you don't want to really "toast" them. If you don't have a toaster, wrap the split muffins in aluminum foil and put in the warm oven to heat. Keep the muffins warm until all are finished.

To assemble: On an individual plate, place the two muffin halves split side up. Place the slice of ham over the muffins (the ham will cover both muffin halves); then, top with two poached eggs—a poached egg on each muffin half. Spoon on the desired amount of Hollandaise Sauce.

For a really full meal, serve these with asparagus spears, Hash Brown Casserole, and mixed fruit.

If Mother and Daddy didn't like foods or thought the ingredients were not good or good for us, we never had them at home. These foods included hot dogs and bologna. I was in the sixth grade, I believe, before I ever ate a hot dog. One of my school friends and I went Christmas shopping in town and went to Bunting's Drug Store, the oldest in Tennessee, where the best hot dogs in the world were sold. Bunting's was the place to go in Bristol and one of the meeting places for older elementary, junior high, and some of the high school kids.

Bunting's was torn down in the 1970s, as was the block of buildings surrounding it and many of the buildings behind it which fronted on Shelby Street. This was done despite many peoples' efforts to save that little bit of history. This institution was replaced by yet another asphalt parking lot.

The same large city block, or double block, had included Hooks & English Eye, Ear, Nose and Throat Hospital where I had my tonsils out, and the old Bristol, Tennessee Fire Station. Crossing Shelby Street to the side of the hospital were some of the oldest little houses in Bristol. The street sloped down a hill. These four or five little houses were built like row houses and each had an individual roof. Because the houses followed the slope of the small hill, from the top of the hill, they looked like stair steps, reminding me of pictures I had seen of little slate-roofed cottages in Europe.

They called this, "Urban Renewal." Later a modern drug store without the history, charm, character, and home we found in Bunting's was built on the same site, but nothing could replace Bunting's.

The first time I ever went to Bunting's was on a Sunday afternoon when I was about five years old. One of Thelma's friends had a little sister who was my age. The friend got her family's car and she and Thelma took their little sisters to Bunting's to get a chocolate nut sundae—my first, but surely not my last!

When I got old enough to go to town with my friends, sometimes the smell of fresh bread baking wafted over the downtown area. Hecht's Bakery, the maker of Sunbeam Bread, was one block away from State Street. That bread smelled so wonderful and it made us want some of it slathered with butter. The building is still standing but the bakery is no longer in operation here, another unique thing about our little area lost.

People in the South, no matter what part of the South, are sometimes stereotyped as eaters of grits and fried green tomatoes. I never remember having either at home. Thelma and Reba said that they had fried green tomatoes, maybe before I was born. Marie barely remembers that they had them some, but she says, "I didn't like them." It was in my first year of college, I believe, that I first tasted grits and many years later before I ever ate fried green tomatoes. Now, I love them both. Just about the only way my husband will eat grits for breakfast is with sugar—like a cereal. One of our favorite ways to have grits is in a casserole that Marie began bringing to our family dinners. She had gotten the recipe from someone in her husband's family, the Maiden family. This is the recipe:

GARLIC GRITS

4 cups boiling water
1 slight teaspoon salt
1 cup quick grits
Let cook until it starts thickening.
Remove from stove and stir in ½ cup milk with 2 eggs beaten in the milk. Add 1 stick of margarine and 1 roll of garlic cheese, diced.
Bake at 350 degrees until golden and bubbly, about 30 - 40 minutes. Makes 6 - 8 servings
You may substitute a fresh garlic clove, crushed, and 1 to 2 cups of shredded sharp Cheddar cheese for the garlic cheese.

Another food we never had was black-eyed peas. Mother and Daddy didn't like their taste. The first time I ever tasted black-eyed peas was the summer before my sophomore year in high school. Some of my friends and I were at Ridgecrest Assembly in North Carolina for Foreign Missions Week. The cottage we stayed in during the week was run by the Holston Association and we took meals like in a college dining hall —except it wasn't cafeteria style. One day, we had black-eyed peas with whatever else we had and on the first bite of those things, I thought I was going to faint dead away in the floor. Mercy! Now, I may fix them for New Year's Day, but I add so many other ingredients —vinegar, garlic, olive oil, onions, and herbs—that the flavor which is very strong to me is disguised. Sometimes this disguised version of black-eyed peas is called Southern Caviar or Texas Caviar. Here is a recipe I use:

SOUTHERN CAVIAR

2 (16 oz.) cans black-eyed peas with no meat seasoning included
¾ cup extra virgin olive oil
¼ cup red or white wine vinegar (or just regular apple cider
   vinegar)
¼ to ½ cup finely chopped onion
¼ cup chopped flat-leafed Italian parsley
½ teaspoon salt
1 large clove garlic, mashed and chopped (If you have one of
   those fancy garlic crushers, use it.)
Freshly ground black pepper to taste

Drain and rinse the black-eyed peas. Add the chopped onion and parsley. Whisk together the olive oil, vinegar, salt, garlic, and freshly ground black pepper. Pour over the black-eyed pea mixture and toss. Cover and refrigerate for at least 24 hours. Before serving, taste and correct seasonings. This will keep in your refrigerator for at least one week.

One New Year's Day, Barb was in town visiting and came over to have supper with us. I made Hoppin' John, a "traditional dish" for the day. Barb loved it, but Ralph and I could barely eat enough to say that we had consumed our "good luck" or "prosperity" food (I always get these two classifications mixed up)! This is easy to make and perhaps you will like it:

HOPPIN' JOHN

6 slices bacon, fried and crumbled, reserve about 2 tablespoons
 of the grease
1 large onion, chopped
1 cup pre-cooked rice, cooked in salted water
½ cup water
1 can black-eyed peas, drained and rinsed
¼ chopped flat-leafed parsley
Salt and cayenne pepper, to taste

Hot sauce, optional, to taste

In a large skillet, fry, drain on paper towels, and crumble the bacon. Set aside. In about 2 tablespoons of the bacon grease, saute the chopped onion until translucent. Into the same skillet, put the pre-cooked rice, the water, and the drained and rinsed peas. Season to taste. Spoon into a Pam-sprayed baking dish and cover. Place into a 350 degree oven until hot.

On Wednesday nights at home, Reba began to cook our suppers. She wanted to practice cooking for when she got married and she wanted to learn to cook new things. Since all businesses closed on Wednesday afternoons during those years, it was a good day for her to cook. I remember especially two new things she made. She did something called barbecued hamburgers. The meat for hamburgers was mixed with green pepper and onions and other things probably, maybe Worcestershire sauce, and then broiled rather than fried.

The other new dish she cooked was shrimp. She purchased the shrimp at a market called Mick & Mack. The shrimp were wonderful we thought. However, in the middle of the night, Mother became very ill. Evidently, she was allergic to the shrimp, as were Uncle Cloyd and some of his children, we learned later. Reba kept cooking, but we never had shrimp at home again.

On Saturday nights Reba started a tradition of our having regular hamburgers with the trimmings and sometimes we had french fries. This was easy and quick to fix and was a bit different from the weekly meals.

Once when Mother was staying with Thelma after one of her children was born, Marie and I had to cook the suppers. One night, we cooked some kind of meat—pork chops, probably—and tried to make gravy like Mother did. We kept adding flour because it just didn't look thick enough. Then, when the gravy began to cook and thicken, it could be cut! It probably would have made good mortar, but it surely wasn't gravy!

As Daddy and Reba came though the front door after work, we threw out our wonderful gravy. We also had tried to make mashed potatoes and reasoned that if the potatoes were cut very finely, they would cook quicker. I think we shredded them on the hand-held grater/shredder. We ended up with almost a soup with some crunchy potatoes intermingled. Our family put up with our messes and we all finally learned to cook a decent meal.

When we were younger, the Saturday afternoon before Easter was always set aside for dyeing eggs. Mother would buy an extra supply of eggs from Mrs. Rowe so we would have plenty. After we went to bed that night, Mother would arrange the Easter baskets to be ready for us the next morning. She always included special candy and sometimes someone in the family had bought feathery chickens or paper mache rabbits to be included in the basket, but, we never had the tradition of believing in the Easter Bunny.

On Sunday mornings, Mother would come up the hall and yell into each bedroom, "How many eggs do you want? How do you want them?" This was the only time during the year these questions were asked, and we never had more than one egg at a sitting any other time—unless we counted the deviled eggs. Some symbolism may have been attached to the number of eggs eaten on Easter, I don't know. It must have been more than just the symbolism of life that the egg represents; or, maybe this was just something Grandma used to do when Mother was growing up.

The hen had been cooked ready to make chicken and dumplings; potatoes were cut and put into water ready to be cooked; rolls were left to raise; the salads and desserts had been made. We always had cake and boiled custard on Easter. Sometimes Mother got fancy with the white cake and made each layer a different color, pink, yellow, green, by putting a tad of food coloring into the batter. Then, the cake looked like the colors of spring. After church, the green beans and other things would be cooked or finished and the pickles and other things would be put on the table.

After breakfast, we all got ready to go to church. We sisters always had something new to wear and I was very proud until one Sunday I walked into the Sunday School room and one of the little girls had on her old clothes. I felt terrible! I remember that I left the room and took off my hat, I suppose thinking that would make my new clothes less conspicuous.

The little girl's clothes were scrubbed clean and ironed to perfection. Her hair was perfect and her shoes were shined until they almost sparkled. The girl and her family lived just outside of the Bristol city limits; the house was at least an eighth of a mile walk from the road, and maybe more. Her father was very ill, one of the first people I had known to have cancer. Several other children were in the family. I believe that seeing her that day made me really understand the real meaning of Spring and Easter and made me realize that I needed to be more aware of other people. I was 11.

During certain days of the year, especially July 4 and Labor Day, we had family picnics. We would all load up into my sisters husbands' or boyfriends' cars and go to the mountains, to the lake, or to a park for the afternoon. We always had fried chicken and/or ham, deviled eggs, potato salad, vegetables, bread, usually rolls, desserts, and sometimes cantaloupe.

The first picnic I ever remember was when Hobart took Mother, Marie, and me, and maybe everybody else, too, to the foot of Holston Mountain, the mountain we used to look out and see every morning from our house. A tablecloth was spread on the grassy ground and we sat on the edges of the cloth while the food was put in the middle of the cloth. This was one time I don't remember the food! I just remember the vivid green of the grass and trees and riding in Hobart's boxy black car.

Watermelon, which was messier to eat than cantaloupe, was reserved for Sunday afternoons during the summer. Daddy always liked the dark green rather than the striped melons. He would thump the watermelons until he found one he thought was just right and then would ask to plug the melon, or have someone who worked there plug it. Daddy bought many of the watermelons at Bristol Coal & Ice in Bristol, Virginia, which sometimes gave their customers ice picks with wooden handles, advertising their company on the handle. These picks were and still are useful. While the original purpose of the picks was to chip off chunks of ice from a large block, I have used that pick for many other things such as sewing and other craft projects.

A long sharp knife was used to cut approximately a two-inch square in the center of the melon. The plug was then removed to check the quality and ripeness of the fruit. If it was perfect, Daddy would buy it. The watermelon was kept in the refrigerator until mid-to-late Sunday afternoon when we would all gather around the kitchen table to cut it. We ate as much as we could hold and the remaining melon was put back into the refrigerator. Sometimes I ate some after church and I always wanted it for breakfast the next morning. Mother always said, "It will make you sick," but, it never did.

In late summer when paw paws ripened, we walked to Uncle Johnnie's on Virginia Avenue and filled bags with this sweet, unusual fruit. I can barely eat one now, but then, they were special. When Lynette was very young, she found some seeds, left by a previous family, at the corner of our house. She asked, "If I plant them, will they grow?" I told her they might and that she could try. We now have several paw paw trees growing. None are nearly as big as Uncle Johnnie's and the trees do not bear the vast amount of fruit, but they are still special. She planted lots of the "whirly-birds" from maple trees, too. We now have several large maples growing in our backyard because of her interest and curiosity.

When fall and winter came, Sunday dinners at home consisted more of the boiled beef, pork roasts, and cubed steak than we usually had during the warmer months. The beef or pork broth was used to boil the potatoes and then the broth, unthickened, was used as gravy. And, the thought of that broth ladled over fresh hot homemade biscuits still makes my mouth water!

These meats were usually special Sunday dishes; they were rarely served during the week unless company was invited. Likewise, the meats served during the week were not considered appropriate for Sunday meals. I remember that once after I was married and doing volunteer work, one of the other volunteers said she was baking a meat loaf for supper. I thought, "How strange to have meat loaf on Sunday!" I suppose it tastes the same any day, but it was not one of the traditions at home.

I believe that Mother got tired of what she considered the "same old food." Why else would she have saved different recipes and why else would she try cooking something she had never done before simply because the recipe looked like it was good? An example of this is the Cheese Souffle she made one night for supper. She baked it in the medium-size, straight-sided blue earthenware bowl that she used to bake the "usual" Macaroni and Cheese. When Mother took the souffle out the oven, it was so puffed and pretty. Then, in just a few minutes, the "poof" went out, and she thought that her recipe had failed. Here is the recipe she used from a 1940s magazine judging from the pictures on the reverse side.

CHEESE SOUFFLE

1. Melt 4 tablespoons of butter or margarine in the top of a double boiler. Add 4 tablespoons of flour, 1 teaspoon of salt and a dash of cayenne. Add 1½ cups of milk, blending it in well. Cook over hot water, stirring constantly.

2. When the sauce is thick and smooth add ½-lb. cheese of your choice, sliced.

3. Stir the sauce until the cheese is melted. Remove from the heat and add 6 beaten egg yolks, stirring constantly. Cool slightly.

4. Carefully fold this cheese sauce into 6 egg whites beaten stiff but not dry. Cut and fold the mixture throughly but lightly so that it is well blended.

5. Pour into an ungreased 2-quart casserole. Now to make your souffle puff up with a "top hat" as it bakes, do this: Run the tip of a tea-spoon around in the mixture 1 inch from the edge of the casserole, mak-ing a slight 'track' or depression.

6. Bake 1¼ hours in a slow steady oven—300 degrees. Serve at once.

I don't remember how this tasted, but I remember how disappointed Mother was when the "top hat" started falling down. To our way of think-ing, though, any dish that includes cheese has to be good!

To make Macaroni and Cheese, Mother didn't do anything fancy. She simply

MACARONI AND CHEESE

Boil the amount of macaroni needed to serve the family (2 cups macaroni will make 4 to 6 servings) in salted water. Then, she drained off the water, added some milk and a little bit of cheese (always "cooking" cheese—today known as Longhorn, Colby, or Cheddar) and butter. Then, into the blue earthenware bowl that had been greased, she put a layer of macaroni, a layer of cheese, and another layer of macaroni. For the top, she cut thin slices of the cheese and placed them, evenly spaced. She sometimes sprinkled on a little bit of black pepper or paprika. Then, she baked the casserole for about half an hour at 350 degrees until it was bubbly and the cheese on top was slightly toasted.

In some of the area's produce markets today, the owners will have a big wheel of red wax-wrapped cheese; the taste of this cheese is like the cheese Mother used in her cooking.

When I make Macaroni and Cheese these days, I usually make a light cheese sauce (cream or white sauce with Sharp Cheddar—and sometimes a little American, or other mild cheese— added), and a little bit of dry mustard. Then, I layer the macaroni and then some more cheese. I do this until the casserole is almost full. Then, I pour on some of the cheese sauce and add some sliced or shredded Cheddar to the top, sprinkle with pepper, and sometimes I add packaged dry bread crumbs.

At Halloween, Daddy would bring a pumpkin home if he had not raised pumpkins. The pumpkin was carved on the kitchen table with layers of newspaper placed over the oilcloth tablecloth. The top was cut out of the pumpkin, then we scooped the seeds out with our hands. Sometimes Mother saved the seeds and toasted them in the oven for snacks. The face of the jack-o-lantern was drawn on the pumpkin with a pencil which was sharpened with a paring knife before we ever got a real pencil sharpener. The eyes and nose of the jack-o-lantern were always triangles; the mouth, made into a wide grin, always contained squared-off teeth. Never was there a deviation from this set pattern.

At first, we used a candle in the jack-o-lantern. Then, after one of the neighborhood kids kept stealing everybody's pumpkins, Daddy got the idea to put his extension cord with the light bulb attached inside the pumpkin instead of the candle. I think that the first year this was done, the pumpkin was still stolen. Then, the next year, Daddy hid down behind the bannister and watched. When the hand started to reach down into the pumpkin to remove the light, Daddy grabbed the wrist. Tommy's screams probably echoed for blocks! We never had another pumpkin stolen!

Sometimes during the fall and winter, Mr. Rowe would come out to the house after supper and sit at the kitchen table talking with Daddy. One night when he was visiting, Marie and I had just been sharing part of a Turkish Taffy candy bar which was the new rage then. The remainder of the candy, wrapped in its wrapper was still on the table. Mr. Rowe kept looking at it. I asked him, finally, if he wanted some. He said he would take a little. So, Daddy broke off a piece for him.

After a little while, Mr. Rowe started making strange faces; then, he kept twisting his tongue inside his jaw. Finally, he tried to open his mouth and twist his tongue at the same time. The candy had started softening! Then, his teeth stuck together. He tried to get them unstuck and his dental plates started moving—first the upper one would come down, and he would try again. Then, the lower one would come up. When Marie and I saw this, we got so tickled, we voluntarily left the table and got out of the room that time before we exploded! We couldn't hold back the laughter any longer!

Mr. Rowe finally left and Daddy scolded us for giving him the candy. I think he believed that we had done it as a prank— and who better than Daddy to recognize a prank. We never even thought of Mr. Rowe's having dentures, much less thinking about the taffy's effects on their proper functioning!

During the fall and winter, when visitors were not expected for meals, Mother set up her large quilting frame in the dining room. We first learned the process of tacking in which we used embroidery or other heavy thread to hold the top, batting, and lining together. Then, as we got older, we were allowed to make some stitches. Mother said that the stitches had to be very small to be good quilting. Marie and I used to look at the quilts on our bed when we were little and remember where the different materials had originated. Some of the older quilts even had some material from Grandma's things that I didn't remember.

Mother still made quilts later in her life, on a small portable frame, but she said that her stitches were getting too big. I used to take leftover material from making our children's clothes and some of my clothes to her. When a top was finished, I bought the lining material and the batting then Mother and I put the different layers together ready for quilting. Mother made several new quilts for me in the patterns I wanted. The quilts were still being stored at her house when she died.

Thanksgiving at our house meant that all the family would be coming to eat. Of course, this was not too unusual because many times, everybody would be there on Sunday. The only difference in our Thanksgiving meal and the regular Sunday meals was that we had more dishes than usual. For dessert, we had pumpkin pies and walnut cake. Sometimes there were other desserts, too, but these were the traditional ones.

Preparation for Christmas began a week before the celebration. Daddy would bring a tree home, sometimes a pine, sometimes a cedar. One year, the tree had a bird's nest in it and I got to keep it. Mother kept it for years, just as she kept the perfect fern fossil I had found in a piece of coal that was in the basement ready to be thrown into the furnace. We didn't know then, and for years afterwards, that some people believe that having a bird's nest in a Christmas tree is good luck.

In addition to the tree that Daddy brought in, Reba brought other greenery home from town. People used to stand along the sidewalks on State Street and sell holly, bittersweet, mistletoe, and other greenery. Greenery and candles were placed on top of the piano and on the mantel. Before Daddy put the furnace in, we always had a warm fire going in the living room fireplace. We always had a Christmas program at church and the Sunday morning before Christmas, every person who attended church that day was given a "treat bag." The little brown paper bag contained an orange or apple, some nuts, and some candy. Then, we waited for the big night when Santa would come.

One Christmas Eve, Mother took Marie and me next door. This was out of the ordinary and I couldn't figure out why she did this. I kept looking out the window and Mother kept trying to get me to sit down and stay away from the window. Then, a few years later, I learned why. They had stored our toys in the Buckles' upstairs so Daddy and some of the rest of the family had to go retrieve them. This was the year I got my little table and chairs. Santa seemed always to visit our house earlier than he did other houses. We always had Santa come and we also opened our presents on Christmas Eve. On Christmas morning, we just played or helped with lunch.

Sometimes for our Christmas meal, Mother would make a fruitcake, but not very often. All of us liked the Walnut Cake much better than any fruitcake! I did find one recipe for fruitcake among Mother's collection and here it is:

INEXPENSIVE FRUITCAKE
3 eggs
1 cup sugar

½ cup butter
1 teaspoon soda dissolved in 2 tablespoons water
1 cup watermelon preserves
1 cup cherry preserves
1 cup applesauce
1 cup spiced grapes
2 cups ground cherries
1 cup raisins, seeded or seedless
1 cup black walnuts
½ teaspoon cloves
½ teaspoon allspice
1 teaspoon nutmeg
1 teaspoon cinnamon
3 cups flour
pinch of salt
1 teaspoon vanilla extract
½ teaspoon lemon flavoring
1 teaspoon mixed fruit flavor if you have it.

Bake 2 hours. The directions that were left out probably were: Grease large tube pans. Line the bottom of the pans with brown paper. Grease the brown paper. Pack the fruitcake mixture into the pans. Bake at moderate heat about 325 degrees.

Mother's recipe for Cherry Preserves is a simple one:

CHERRY PRESERVES

Into a medium saucepan, place 2 cups cherries and 1 cup of sugar. Turn the heat on to medium and when all the sugar is melted, increase the heat and boil for 15 minutes stirring constantly. Put in sterilized jars and seal. Unless you process these in a pressure canner, I would refrigerate them until you use them.

This is Mother's recipe for Spiced Grapes:

SPICED GRAPES

2½ quarts stemmed Concord grapes
5 cups sugar
2 teaspoons ground cinnamon
½ teaspoon ground cloves

½ teaspoon ground allspice
1 cup vinegar

Separate pulp from skins of grapes. Cook pulp until soft; press through a sieve or food mill to remove seeds. Combine skins and pulp with remaining ingredients. Cook almost to the jellying point. Stir frequently to prevent sticking. Pour, boiling hot, into sterilized jars. Adjust caps. Makes about 5 pints.

Mother also made mincemeat pies, sometimes making her own mincemeat. She liked her own much better than the canned or jarred mincemeat. She said that the kind you could buy was "too strong." Here is Mother's recipe for Mincemeat:

MINCEMEAT

2 pounds lean beef
1 pound butter
4 pounds tart apples
3 pounds currants
2 pounds raisins
6 cups sugar
1 teaspoon each nutmeg, cinnamon, cloves, and allspice
½ teaspoon mace
Juice and grated rind of 2 oranges
Juice and grated rind of 2 lemons
½ pound citron
1 tablespoon salt

Stew beef in small amount of water until done. Chop fine. Add all other ingredients, chopped. I believe that this is when Mother got her meat grinder out. She ran the ingredients through the grinder—probably so she wouldn't have so much chopping to do. Cook for one hour. Seal in sterilized jars. Makes 12 pints. If you make this these days, I suggest that you process in a pressure canner—20 minutes at 10 pounds pressure— or freeze.

The main dish for Christmas, as on other holidays, was chicken and dumplings with all the trimmings, including homemade sage dressing made with bread. I never saw Mother's recipe for her dressing. She must have just memorized what Grandma or Grandpa had done. When I asked her how she did it, she said her usual... "Well, you just take you bread, eggs, salt, onions, sage, etc..." In other words, just throw everything in and keep adjusting the seasonings until you get it right. We had our usual assortment of vegetables, salads, pickles, etc., and may have had some other traditional things, but I don't remember them. When I got older, we began having Cranberry Sauce. I never remember having ham for Christmas until I was grown.

On Christmas afternoon, Daddy, the other men in the family, and some of my sisters, too would play Rook until it was time to heat up the lunch leftovers for supper. Sometimes we played Monopoly and Chinese Checkers. If we had gotten a book for Christmas, which was often the case, many Christmas afternoons found some of us absorbed in those books. Many of these books were purchased at Kemble-Cochran, our favorite book store, which thankfully is still in operation.

One year during the week before Christmas, I was trying to learn what was in my wrapped presents under the tree. I finally figured one out—it was a book—a gift from Marie. I kept wanting to open it since I had guessed what it was. I was such a nag that they did let me open it just to shut me up. It was a fairy tale book and it kept me out of the grown-ups' hair for awhile, anyway. This was the only present I ever opened early and I never thought then about my ruining Marie's surprise for me.

Sometimes my sisters' friends would visit during Christmas. I remember one girl who told me that if I swallowed a tangerine seed, it would sprout and start growing out my ears. Reba had a date one night and they were in the living room where I was with my new doll. Reba's date kept trying to get me to leave the room and I wouldn't. He finally offered me a quarter to leave, but I stayed. I don't remember what ever made me leave. Maybe Reba threatened me.

At least once during the winter, on a Sunday afternoon, we went to visit Aunt Cindy and Uncle Bob. While the grown-ups talked, we looked at pictures of places we had never even heard of through Aunt Cindy's stereoscopes. She had two, so Marie and I didn't have to take turns. Marie and I also remember sitting around the fireplace in the living room and Aunt Cindy passing around baskets full of fresh crispy apples from their trees. Aunt Cindy always put several knives into the baskets in case we wanted to peel our apples before eating them. I have always loved baskets. Maybe they remind me of the good times I had growing up.

When I was a junior in high school, Daddy sold the house Marie and I were born in, and we moved to a new, smaller house Daddy had built on Georgia Avenue. Although we were still near the old neighborhood and we still had a garden, home to me was never the same. Many tears were shed when we left our old house. Once when Mother was talking about Daddy after his death, she said that somehow he never seemed to be really satisfied by any place after they left Lenoir City and that she didn't know why. I believe that he missed his home, just as we did.

After we moved to the new house, I decided to make some brownies one day. We had a box of brownie mix, something new that had come out, and Mother said just to use it. I had always made them from scratch, and, making these was an experience! The directions on the box said to mix with a mixer or by hand. I thought, "What?" Mother was busy ironing and I didn't bother asking her about it. We didn't have a mixer at that time, so I used my hand. What a mess! I kept trying to get that goo off my hand, and I finally asked, "Mother, how am I going to get this stuff off my hand?" She looked around and said, "What in the world?" Then, she just started dying laughing. Finally she asked me why I did that. I told her what the directions said and she replied, "Well, when it says mix by hand, you don't use your hand, you use a spoon!" So much for that home economics class, huh? But, the brownies came out fine, even though I got lots of laughs over them. I didn't really make homemade brownies, but I made handmade ones!

This is one of the made-from-scratch brownie recipes we have used often. During my first year of college at Mars Hill, Mother kept me well-supplied with "care packages" of brownies or cookies and she always included enough for me to share generously with my friends. Sometimes when she and Daddy came over the mountain for visits, we would go on picnics and I would take any leftovers back to the dorm. Mother even started making her potato salad a little "stiffer" than usual, making it into balls, and rolling the balls in cracker crumbs just so I would have a convenient way to take potato salad back to the dorm without having to keep a dish and wash it. She always made extra fried chicken for me to take back, too. And, when I came home on weekends, I usually took food back with me. Some Sunday evenings, Spilman 214 was the most popular room on the floor. The girls practically fought over Mother's food! Mother usually doubled the recipe given here:

BROWNIES
⅔ cup sifted all-purpose flour
½ teaspoon baking powder
¼ teaspoon salt
⅓ cup shortening
2 squares unsweetened chocolate
1 cup sugar
2 eggs, well beaten

½ cup broken nut meats—walnut or pecan
1 teaspoon vanilla
Set oven at 350 degrees. Grease an 8 x 8 x 2-inch pan. Sift flour once, measure, add baking powder and salt; and sift again. Melt shortening and chocolate over hot water. Add sugar gradually to eggs, beating thoroughly. Add chocolate mixture and blend. Add flour and mix well; then mix in nuts and vanilla. Spread in greased pan. Bake in preheated oven 25 minutes, or until done. Cool in pan, then cut in squares. Makes about 2 dozen brownies.

I believe that my family and I came by our love of good food and of cooking honestly. We had the examples set by Mother and Daddy and by other family members who appreciated both the food, the cooking, and the sharing. When Mother died in 1984, Thelma and Marie told me to take her recipe box. Some of the recipes are from the early to mid-1920s or earlier through the early 1980s. Included in this collection are clippings from magazines, newspapers, product labels and special recipes written by hand on white paper. On some, Mother had made a note, "Try this," or, "Fix this for Sunday." Some of the handwitten recipes include recipes for some of the old canning recipes. One recipe is for Mrs. Honaker's Rolls. Evidently, Mother had eaten some of her rolls somewhere and thought they were better than the ones she made.

Mrs. Honaker was a lady who attended our church. She always sang in the choir. Her daughter, Betty, played the clarinet in the high school band. Sometimes, she and Reba played a duet for the offertory at church on Sunday mornings. Some Sunday afternoons, Betty came to the house, when we still lived on the Hill, and they practiced. They would be playing along and Betty's clarinet would let out this wild squeak. We all would get tickled and sometimes Betty got so tickled, she couldn't play. Other times, she would try to keep playing and she would be shaking from laughing and still playing and then, another squeak. It was hilarious! Then, everything would stop. Everybody would settle down and the playing would begin again. Sometimes on the very first note, everybody burst out laughing again, just thinking about the other times. Finally, everything would be okay. In church, the clarinet may have squeaked once or twice, but nothing like the wild ones in our living room!

When Betty came to practice, she stayed and had Sunday supper with us before we went to church. During her summer break from college one year, she went to Ridgecrest as our counselor. She probably needed a different kind of counselor after spending a week with us. The next spring, she invited Carol and me to come to Carson-Newman for the weekend. So, we went and had a great time! We were just sophomores in high school and we thought we were something special because we got to spend a weekend on a college campus!

Evidently, Mother had called Mrs. Honaker to get this roll recipe. The phone number, "1843-W" was at the top of the page. Our number was "921-W" during the early years when the operator took the number you wanted to call by saying, "Number please." Then, the operator would connect us to the person we were calling. Most of the times, everybody had "party lines" and sometimes people used to pick up their phones just to hear some gossip. When I talked with Betty after I found this recipe, I asked her if she remembered their old phone number; she tried to remember, and then I gave her the number I had. She said, "That was it!" Then, we talked about the recipe. She said that her mother took those rolls to every lunch or dinner meeting anybody ever had at the church, she thought. Everybody loved them! Here's the recipe:

MRS. HONAKER'S ROLLS
1 cup warm sweet milk
1 cup warm water
2 tablespoons sugar
1 teaspoon salt
1 cake fresh yeast (today, I would substitute 1 envelope active dry yeast)
2 tablespoons shortening
Enough flour to make a soft dough.

Mix all ingredients together. Put in a bowl. Let rise until double in bulk. Work down (knead) real good. Roll out thin and cut out like biscuits. Grease with butter and put on top of each other. Bake at the same temperature used for other rolls—about 400 degrees for 15 - 20 minutes, or until golden brown.

Another roll Mother recipe made once in awhile was one that Carol's mother made when I ate lunch sometimes at their house on Sundays. I kept talking about these rolls and so Mother asked her for the recipe. Here it is:

REFRIGERATOR ROLLS
I called them Potato Rolls
1 cake yeast or 1 package granular yeast mixed with ½ cup

lukewarm potato water (water in which sliced or diced potatoes have been boiled)
¾ cup shortening
½ cup sugar
1 teaspoon salt
1 cup mashed potatoes
1 cup scalded milk, cooled until lukewarm
2 egg whites, unbeaten
Enough flour to make a stiff dough (4 cups or more)

Combine ingredients in a large bowl. Beat well. Grease top of the dough. Cover. Leave in refrigerator overnight or for several days. Knead on lightly floured board. Roll out and cut with a biscuit cutter. Dip into melted butter. Fold over to make "pocket book" rolls. Let rise in baking pan for about an hour. Bake at 400 degrees for about 20 minutes.

The collecting of recipes, and of cookbooks in my case, still continues in the family, just as sharing recipes and meals with each other continues. In the late 1980s, some our second cousins in the Greene family decided that we should start meeting together and having what other people might call a reunion. We started saying that "the cousins" were going to meet. Sometimes the meetings were held at individual homes; other times, we would meet in a local restaurant. When we met in the homes, we all brought food to share and some of us always ate too much. Several of the cousins have died since we began having these get-togethers and are missed very much.

Chapter 8
Family Comfort Foods, Memories, and Stories

Knowing that the love of good food was a common thread in the family, judging from the foods we have shared, when I asked some of them about their comfort foods—the foods that make them feel better when they are a bit down, homesick, or foods that they loved to eat—or would love to eat—that remind them of being at home, they also shared some of their memories of growing up, their food-associated memories, and stories they remembered about other family members, neighbors, and friends.

When I asked Thelma what her comfort foods were, she first said, "I don't have any." Then, she said, "Biscuits and gravy for breakfast, but now you can't eat that every morning." Some of us have hypertension and/or high cholesterol levels and are supposed to watch our diets. Several of us also have a friend, "Arthur"—ritis, that is, which is affected by some foods. Biscuits and gravy were almost always a part of our breakfasts when we were home. Of course, we probably got more good exercise, too, because we walked to many of the places we had to go or wanted to go. Thelma's husband, Henry, said that his Mother made Cold Water Pie when he was little. He said, "That's my comfort food." The pie is similar to a butterscotch or caramel pie and here is the recipe:

MRS. TAYLOR'S COLD WATER PIE
Makes 2 pies
2 cups brown sugar (press this firmly into the cup to get the right amount)
2 cups cold water
¼ cup flour
Stir sugar into flour. Add water
Add: 3 egg yolks
½ cup butter

1 teaspoon vanilla extract

Cook in a double boiler over simmering water or cook in a saucepan directly over the stove eye, but watch carefully to make sure it doesn't scorch until the mixture thickens, stirring the mixture until it is done.

Pour into a baked pie crust (See Index). Cover with meringue, recipe below.

Place in oven until meringue browns to your liking.

MERINGUE

Beat 3 egg whites until stiff. Add sugar 2 tablespoons, or to taste and ½ teaspoon cream of tartar

Henry was born and raised near Lebanon, Virginia. He said that they lived 'way up in the mountains and one of the houses they lived in was haunted. When they first moved in, they noticed several deadbolt latches on the front door, but didn't think too much about it ... until after the door was locked at night. The door would mysteriously open, no matter how often or how many times the door was closed and locked. And, too, things in the house would move around.

Lamp chimneys could be heard falling off a shelf upstairs and rolling across the floor. When someone went to pick them up to put them back on the shelf, the chimneys were on the shelf and none were broken.

When Henry's older brother was going out at night, one night as he came close to the house, he saw all the lights in the house burning. Thinking that the family was still up or that something was wrong, he walked into the house only to find everybody asleep with the lights off. After this happened several times, he became afraid to go out at night. As if this weren't enough, when visitors spent the night, they could feel "somebody" patting them during the night, as if "tucking them in." But, when they looked up, nobody was there, but the patting continued. It scared one visitor so much that he declared that he would never spend another minute in that house!

The final straw came one night when Henry's daddy had gone fishing or hunting. When darkness came, the family began to hear a woman scream. The screaming continued all night while Henry's mother tried to keep herself and the children calm. When their daddy returned, he said that he would never leave them alone again. And, the family moved from the house. Even though no one was ever hurt, living there was just too eery.

Thelma and Henry are keeping some of the family traditions alive by raising a big garden every year, supplying us and others with homegrown zucchini, yellow squash, cucumbers, tomatoes, and green beans. They raise different varieties of beans including a "giant pink tip."

After his retirement, Henry was given seeds of this bean by a farmer for whom he had done some lawnmower repair. The man who lived up in the Virginia countryside somewhere had planted pink tip beans near his cornfield beans. The two beans cross-pollinated, the man believed, and the "giant pink tip" resulted. Thelma and Henry save seeds from one year to the next for a good crop of these beans which Henry believes may be the only ones of their kind grown today. The man who gave Henry the seed died and his son does not garden.

When the beans and tomatoes come in, just about any day will find Thelma canning one or the other. She cans hundreds of quarts of food each year. And, the food tastes so good in the winter time!

Another of their comfort foods during the winter is soup beans eaten with the canned tomatoes and cornbread. Instead of using salt pork to cook in the beans, margarine is now used. Their favorite soup is Potato-Tomato Soup, a soup Mother made up. One day, when Thelma, Reba, Marie, and I were still living at home, Mother made potato soup as she usually did and then added some onion and some canned tomatoes. The result was wonderful! This is always eaten with cornbread.

MOTHER'S POTATO-TOMATO SOUP
We don't have a real recipe for this, but this is an approximation
4 medium potatoes, peeled and cubed
1 medium onion, diced
Water to cover
Salt and pepper to taste
1 can (16 oz.) tomatoes, chopped, OR
 1 pint home-canned tomatoes, chopped
¼ cup flour
1 to 1½ cups milk
2 to 3 tablespoons butter or margarine
Put prepared potatoes in medium saucepan. Add cold water to cover. Add a bit of salt. Bring to boil. Turn heat down and cover the pan. Cook at a slow boil for about 15 minutes. Add the chopped onion. Continue cooking until the potatoes are really tender and the water starts looking a little bit milky. Whisk the flour and milk together, removing any lumps. Slowly stir into the potatoes (do not drain the potatoes of water before doing this). Cook over medium heat until the mixture starts to thicken. Add the tomatoes and heat through. If the soup

is still not as thick as you would like it, take about ½ cup of the liquid out of the soup and stir 1 to 2 tablespoons of flour into it. Return to the other soup and simmer for about 5 minutes. Add a dollop of butter. Taste and adjust seasoning.

Keep warm until you are ready to serve it with cornbread. This will probably make 4 - 6 servings, depending on the appetites.

Following are two recipes that are very popular at Thelma's and Henry's house. In fact, the spaghetti sauce is popular at Reba's house, also. Thelma said that the recipe originally came from the Red, White and Blue Barbecue which was a popular restaurant in Bristol years ago. One of Thelma's friends had the recipe and passed it on to Thelma. Thelma then gave the recipe to Reba and to Mother. Here it is:

ITALIAN SPAGHETTI
The amounts given here will serve 2 to 4 people,
depending on their appetites

½ pound ground beef/ground round
¼ cup onion, cut up
1 small can Franco-American sauce with meat
1 small can (8 oz.) tomato sauce
Chili powder, red pepper, garlic salt to taste
2 bay leaves
Butter

Put some butter in saucepan. Put in onion and brown. Then put in ground beef and brown. Pour in the sauce with meat and tomato sauce. Add the bay leaves, chili powder, red pepper and garlic salt to taste. Simmer 30 minutes to 1 hour. When done, take out bay leaves.

Cook ½ box spaghetti in salted water. Put out on dish and pour sauce mixture around spaghetti.

Franco-American sauce is awfully hard or impossible to find here today. Thelma began substituting another sauce with meat and even has to have that specially ordered through a nearby neighborhood market. You may have to buy today's variety of Italian tomato sauce with meat.

When Thelma and Henry invite the family to their house for a meal, we are often served a very good beef roast. Thelma says that the credit goes to Susan, their daughter, who gave her the recipe. Thelma just cooks her roast a little longer than Susan does. It is very tender and would be awfully good to use for roast beef sandwiches. Here's the recipe:

TAYLOR BEEF ROAST

1 eye of round roast (size according to the number of people you are serving)

Sprinkle roast with some garlic salt and pepper.

Place on heavy-duty aluminum foil. Sprinkle a package of onion soup mix over the roast. Fold the aluminum foil over the roast to enclose, leaving a small opening. Pour a little bit of water into the opening and then close the foil package tightly. Place in a pan and roast at 325 degrees for 30 minutes to 1 hour per pound. Thelma says that she cooks her closer to one hour per pound. The roast comes out perfectly done and tender.

One of the recipes that Thelma makes is a family favorite. Mother really liked this:

THELMA'S BLUEBERRY DELIGHT

14 whole graham crackers
1 pkg. (6-serving size) instant vanilla pudding
1 cup (8 oz.) prepared whipped topping
1 can (21 oz.) blueberry pie filling

Line the bottom of a 9-inch square pan with whole Graham Crackers, breaking them to fit the pan. Prepare the pudding and let stand 5 minutes. Then, blend whipped topping into the pudding. Spread half the pudding over the crackers. Then, add another layer of crackers. Top with remaining pudding. Then, put in the remaining layer of crackers. Spread the pie filling over the top of the crackers.

Chill 3 hours. Makes 9 servings.

A favorite family dessert that Thelma often brings to our get-togethers is her peanut butter pie. We call it Thelma's Peanut Butter Pie. Here is the recipe:

THELMA'S PEANUT BUTTER PIE

3 to 4 ounces cream cheese
1 cup confectioners sugar
½ cup peanut butter
1 large carton (12 oz.) whipped topping
1 Graham Cracker crust

Mix cream cheese and confectioners sugar. Add peanut butter. Stir in one-half of whipped topping. Pour into crust and top with the remaining whipped topping. Refrigerate for several hour or overnight.

Thelma and Henry celebrated their golden anniversary not so long ago at a reception given by their children and their spouses: their son, Steve, and his wife, Cheryl; their daughter, Susan, and her husband, Ted. After the reception, the immediate family was invited to an informal supper at Thelma's and Henry's house. One of the dishes we had was a great chicken salad Cheryl had made. Several of us asked for the recipe and she willingly "obliged," as Daddy used to say. This is Cheryl's recipe:

WILD CHICKEN SALAD
1 (6 oz.) package wild and long grain rice
1 cup mayonnaise
½ cup sour cream
1 cup pecans, chopped
2 tablespoons white onion, chopped
⅛ teaspoon salt
⅛ teaspoon pepper
3 (5 oz.) cans chunk white chicken in water
Cook rice as directed and cool.
Add remaining ingredients and stir well. Cover tightly and refrigerate until ready to serve—at least 48 hours for best flavor.

Marie's response to "What are your comfort foods?" was: "Chocolate doesn't count, does it?" Then, a giggle. Her next response was, "Chicken and dumplings." Other favorite foods mentioned were beans and cornbread, country ham, Mother's pot roast, and "Oh! Her pies!" Marie favored Mother's meringue pies over the fruit pies. And, although she liked them all, chocolate probably was her favorite.

Mother did not use a special recipe for her meringue pies. She used pudding and pie filling, the kind you cook. She made a basic pie crust which she baked blind. Then, when the filling and crust were cooled a bit, she added the meringue. That, too, was just a basic recipe; but, the taste of her pies was not just basic, it was special.

Sometimes, not often, Daddy would buy some "good country ham." Mother sizzled the ham in an iron skillet, added a bit of water, and the resulting gravy was called "sop."

Mother's pot roast that Marie and her family liked was something I learned to cook when I lived and worked in D.C. A friend cooked short ribs and later a roast using "my mother's recipe." After I moved back home, I showed Mother how to make it. So, either way you look at it, it's Mother's Pot Roast.

MOTHER'S POT ROAST

Purchase a two-to-three pound pot roast or chuck roast, or one large enough to feed your crowd. A solid cut such as eye of round or top roast will not work well in this recipe. Wash the meat. Dry with paper towels.

If desired, lard the lean portions of meat with bits of uncooked bacon by making a few holes in the meat an inch-to-two inches apart with a sharp, narrow-blade knife and inserting the bits of uncooked bacon.

Dredge the roast in flour, patting it in well. In heavy Dutch Oven or other heavy pot, melt about 4 tablespoons shortening. When the shortening melts, add the roast. Slowly brown on all sides. Try to get each side as brown as you like before turning.

After all sides and edges of the roast are brown, add 1 finely chopped onion. Sprinkle with garlic powder or 1 crushed garlic clove, salt, and pepper to taste. Don't be stingy with the garlic.

Cover the roast with water. Bring to boil. Cover the pot. Place in a 350 degree oven for 3 - 4 hours, or until the meat is so tender it almost falls apart OR simmer on top of the stove. Important: Occasionally, baste the meat, remove excess grease, check to see if it needs more seasoning, and add more water when needed. You don't want this to get completely dry.

If desired, fresh potatoes and carrots may be added about an hour before the roast is done.

To serve, place the roast on a platter and surround with the vegetables. If desired, serve with the pan drippings which have had as much of the grease removed as possible.

Jim, Marie's husband, likes most foods. So, he fits in quite well with this family! When he was little, he had a pony named Tony that he used to ride in Abingdon, Virginia, where his family lived, and sometimes he would ride Tony to the Esso Service Station to get a coke. The cokes and other snacks were kept inside. At that time, you just didn't put your money into a slot, push a button, and retrieve your purchase. Jim rode Tony inside to get their cokes. Yes, Tony had to have a coke, too. Mr. Nunley would yell, "Dub, get that horse out of here!" I guess Jim was not about to leave his pony outside!

One of his favorite memories was when his daddy used to come to Bristol on Saturdays. He would buy fish. And, they would have fish for breakfast on Sunday mornings. Jim loved that!

Marie is a wonder at making luscious desserts. But, she also makes some other wonderful food. One of our favorite appetizers is Cheese Puffs. Marie started bringing these to family meals at Daddy's and Mother's for the whole gang of us to snack on before the big dinners. They are habit forming. Here's the recipe:

MARIE'S CHEESE PUFFS

1 cup shredded cheddar cheese
3 tablespoons soft butter
½ cup all-purpose flour
1 teaspoon paprika
½ teaspoon Worcestershire sauce
Dash of cayenne
Dash of salt
24 medium green olives stuffed with pimientos

Cream the cheese and butter together. Blend in the other ingredients. Mold a small amount of dough around an olive and repeat with the remaining olives. Place on an ungreased cookie sheet and bake at 400 degrees for 12 minutes or until golden brown.

Once when we were at Marie's and Jim's for a meal, Marie had made a wonderful chicken dish. She served this with a fruit salad, green beans, rice, homemade rolls, and a homemade dessert. Here's chicken recipe Marie made:

HOT CHICKEN SALAD

3 cups diced cooked chicken
2 cups diced celery
1 cup sliced (or slivered) almonds
1 small jar pimientos, drained
Salt and pepper to taste
1 teaspoon lemon juice
1 teaspoon minced onion
1½ cup mayonnaise
½ cup chicken broth
Topping: 1 cup grated cheddar cheese

Crushed potato chips

Mix all ingredients together, except the topping ingredients. Place in a rectangular baking dish that has been sprayed with a non-stick cooking spray.

Cover the top with grated cheese. Top with crushed potato chips. Bake 10 minutes at 450 degrees.

One of the really good fruit salads Marie makes is just packed full of healthy fresh fruit and is really good during the summer when cantaloupes are at their best:

PINA COLADA FRUIT SALAD

Dressing: **1 cup unflavored yogurt**
1 jar (2 oz.) crystallized ginger
½ can (6 oz.) frozen pineapple juice concentrate, thawed
Salad: **1 pineapple, cut into chunks (or 2 cans pineapple chunks, drained)**
1 cantaloupe, cut into chunks
3 navel oranges, sectioned
3 kiwi fruit, peeled and cut into slices
1 cup shredded coconut, toasted

Prepare Dressing: Combine yogurt, ginger, and juice concentrate in blender. Blend until smooth. Pour into a bowl. Cover with plastic wrap and refrigerate until needed.

Combine fruit except coconut in serving bowl. Cover tightly with plastic wrap and refrigerate. Just before serving, combine fruit and dressing. Sprinkle on the toasted coconut.

During the summer when the zucchini is in full production and every few days Thelma and Henry share their bountiful supply, we make all kinds of salads, casseroles, breads. Sometimes, I make Stuffed Zucchini "Boats."

STUFFED ZUCCHINI BOATS

To make the "boats," you can use the same basic ingredients listed for Stuffed Blossoms (see Index), adding some finely chopped, unpeeled zucchini. To prepare the zucchini, cut in half lengthwise and scoop out the center leaving a ½-inch shell or "boat." Blanch the zucchini in boiling slightly salted water for one minute. Drain, turned upside down, on paper towels.

When the "boats" have cooled, stuff with the bread crumb mixture and bake uncovered for about 30 minutes at 350 degrees. During the last 5 minutes of baking, you may sprinkle with additional cheese Parmesan.

One way Marie uses the zucchini is to make the following casserole:

ZUCCHINI CASSEROLE

3 cups zucchini, cubed finely
1 green pepper, chopped
1 onion, chopped
3 tablespoons margarine
1 pint tomatoes (fresh tomatoes, peeled, and seeded OR canned
  tomatoes that have had most of the juice squeezed out)
1 tablespoon flour
2 tablespoons sugar
1 teaspoon salt
Cheddar cheese

Cook vegetables in margarine until tender. Mix together the flour, sugar, and salt. Add to the vegetable mixture, blending well. Place in a greased baking dish. Cover with grated cheddar cheese. Sprinkle with plain bread crumbs. Bake at 350 degrees until cheese is melted and bread crumbs are browned.

One of the cakes that Marie makes has become a family favorite. We like to have it when the "cousins," whether the Greene and/or the Vance cousins get together during the year. This is so moist because of the fruit and we rationalize our eating perhaps more than we should by talking about all the healthy fruit it has in it.

HUMMINGBIRD CAKE

3 cups all-purpose flour
1 teaspoon baking soda
1 teaspoon cinnamon
2 cups sugar
1 teaspoon salt
1 cup vegetable oil
1½ teaspoon vanilla extract
1 (8 oz.) can crushed pineapple with juice
3 eggs

2 cups diced bananas
1 cup chopped pecans

Mix dry ingredients together. Add the remaining ingredients; mix well, but do not beat. Spoon into a tube pan or a 9 x 13-inch baking pan that has been sprayed with non-stick cooking spray. Bake at 350 degrees for 1 hour and 20 minutes.

FROSTING FOR HUMMINGBIRD CAKE

Mix together: 8 oz. cream cheese that has been softened and 1½ cups confectioners sugar. Blend thoroughly. Then, fold in 8 oz. Cool Whip or your favorite whipped topping.

And, with all the chocolate-lovers in this family, no big meal is really complete without at least some taste of chocolate! Marie uses that comforting ingredient in two different forms in this recipe:

ROCKY ROAD CAKE

1 cup rolled oats or regular oatmeal
½ cup margarine
1¾ cups boiling water

Combine the above ingredients and set aside for 10 minutes.
In another bowl, combine:

1 cup brown sugar
¾ cup white sugar
2 eggs, beaten
1½ cups all-purpose flour
1 teaspoon baking powder
2 tablespoons cocoa
½ teaspoon salt
1 cup chocolate chips, divided ½ cup in the batter and
  ½ cup reserved for the topping
½ chopped pecans
1 cup miniature marshmallows

Spray a 9 x 13-inch baking with non-stick spray. Combine the oat mixture with the chocolate chip mixture. Put into pan. Place the ½ cup reserved chocolate chips on top. Bake at 350 degrees for 40 minutes.

Reba did not hesitate to say that chicken and dumplings was her comfort food. She went on to describe the rich creamy gravy and the fluffy, light dumplings done just right. She liked them so well that she used to eat them for breakfast on Monday morning if we had leftovers from Sunday. I remember that I used to think that they would be disgusting to eat for breakfast and I would stick with my shredded wheat. Then, one Monday morning, I tried the dumplings. And, they tasted just as good or better then than they had on Sunday at lunch.

Reba also mentioned beans, cornbread, fried potatoes, and greens as comfort foods. She said, "When we were growing up, beans were a staple. I guess that's why people say, 'You're full of beans'!" She said that when she and her husband and son lived in Chattanooga, one year at tax time, the local gasoline dealers got together and had a symbolic meal of pinto beans, cornbread, and something else, "because they said, 'the IRS has taken all our money'!" These foods are also comfort foods to Reba's own family.

One of the foods I remember that she really liked when I was very little, which she didn't mention as a comfort food, was toasted biscuits. When Mother had made extra biscuits or when we had some left from the night before, Mother toasted biscuits using her long two-pronged iron toasting fork, probably made by one of our ancestors since several of them were blacksmiths. This was before we had an electric stove. Mother would split the biscuits, spread the inside with butter and place one biscuit half on each tine of the fork. She lifted the eye off the right round iron burner on the stove and then held the biscuit directly to the fire until it was toasty brown and the butter sizzling. These were sooo good eaten plain or with homemade apple butter or preserves. Reba now has the fork since those toasted biscuits always seemed more special to her.

Another breakfast food that I remember that she liked very much was Buckwheat Pancakes. This is the recipe Mother kept in her little box:

BUCKWHEAT PANCAKES
Make night before to be served in the morning
2 cups buckwheat flour
1 cup plain flour
3 teaspoons salt
⅓ cup sugar
½ cake yeast (I believe I would use the granular yeast—½ of the package)
4 cups warm water
½ cup bacon drippings (I would substitute oil—vegetable or

even peanut oil)

Sift together both kinds of flour. Add salt and sugar. Dissolve yeast in warm water. Add to other ingredients, then add bacon drippings or oil. Put in refrigerator overnight. Next morning, add a pinch of baking soda before frying. Fry as you do other pancakes—on a griddle or in a frying pan. Serve with maple syrup.

Although Reba doesn't have the memories Marie and I have of Aunt Cindy's, she said that once when our family had a meal there, Aunt Cindy had made a cooked tomato dish...tomatoes and okra, tomato pudding, I don't remember what it was, but I thought, "Oooh, yuk, hot tomatoes??"

When Grandpa Vance was ill, Reba used to live with him and Grandma some, or at least stay with them during the day. "This was so I could go next door and use the telephone if Grandma needed the doctor to come, or something," Reba said. While Reba was staying there, Grandma taught Reba to make those favored Fried Peas. Reba said, "You put the fresh peas in the frying pan with butter and just cook until the peas are done, but not browned. It doesn't take very long." Since Lorena heard about these Fried Peas, she tried to do them and she said that they seemed a little hard to her. So, you may want to parboil the peas in slightly salted water for about 5 minutes, drain them, and then add them to the butter in the frying pan. Don't overdo the salt if you are using salted butter to fry the peas.

When Grandpa was really ill, toward the end of his life, several of the grandchildren stayed with them to help. Thelma said that she stayed at night and that when Grandpa got worse, Hobart, Raymond and George took turns sitting with him at night.

Hobart is no longer with us; but, during some of our telephone conversations when we both got older, he told me some stories that were reviewed with Grandpa when people came to visit with him. Hobart said that one night, A.V. and Collis, two of Grandpa's nephews came to visit. They talked about when they used to go spend part of the summer with Grandpa and Grandma when they lived in the country in Bluff City. Grandma Vance saved wood ashes to make soap and A.V. and Collis stripped off all their clothes and jumped into Grandma's ash pile.

Another story they retold Grandpa was that they had seen him in the watermelon patch pricing some of the melons, probably the ones he was going to take to sell next, by scratching the price in the skin. A.V. and Collis went out later and scratched a price on all the watermelons in the whole patch with the smallest ones being the most expensive and the largest ones the least expensive.

Hobart said that Grandpa Vance "had a shot gun that would kill anything," so Grandpa said. A.V. and Collis had heard him talking about it and so somehow, they got it and tried it out. "They killed a bunch of chickens—every chicken they could hit—way up the creek." When A.V. and Collis were visiting Grandpa, they told him, "Yea, you bragged about how far your gun could shoot and we tried it out one day." I asked Hobart what Grandpa did. Hobart said,"He just laughed."

I never got a chance to ask Hobart about his comfort foods, but we talked about food some during our conversations. I don't remember how the subject came up; maybe I was getting supper ready one night when he called. I do remember that he got a good laugh when I told him that one time I was fixing a chicken dish that called for lemon juice. I didn't have any lemons or lemon juice and so I substituted lime juice, and the dish was horrible!

Once when he was visiting with Mother and Daddy when our children were very young, I prepared some food and took down to their house so Mother could visit more and not have to do all the cooking. Hobart liked everything that I took. Here are the recipes:

GREEN BEAN CASSEROLE
This is the old standby that many people make now, but when I took it to Mother's, it had not become popular.

2 (1 lb.) cans french style green beans
1 can cream of mushroom soup
1 can french-fried onion rings

Mix together the beans and soup. Make one layer of the mixture in a casserole dish. Add a layer of the onion rings. Add the rest of the bean mixture. Layer the remaining onion rings on top. Dot with butter.
Bake at 350 degrees until bubbly.

FRUIT STUDDED LOG
2 (3 oz.) packages cream cheese, softened
¾ cup sugar
2 tablespoons lemon juice
2 cups sour cream
2 drops red food coloring (optional)
1 (1 lb. 14 oz.) can fruit for salads, drained
⅓ cup coarsely chopped maraschino cherries
⅓ cup coarsely chopped pecans

2½ cups miniature marshmallows

Combine cheese, sugar, lemon juice and sour cream; beat until light and fluffy. Add coloring and blend. Stir in fruits, pecans, marshmallows. Spoon into two cleaned and dried one-pound coffee cans. Cover and freeze for 8 hours. To serve: Remove from the freezer and let stand 5 minutes. Decorate with fresh mint. Let stand for 10 minutes before slicing. Makes 14 to 16 servings.

SWEDISH MEAT BALLS

Meat Balls: 1 pound ground beef round, sirloin, or chuck
2 slices white bread
¼ cup milk, or a little more
1 small onion, minced or grated
1 egg
¼ teaspoon ground cloves
¼ teaspoon ground allspice
4 tablespoons butter
2 tablespoons fresh, flat leaf parsley, chopped (optional)

Gravy: 2 tablespoons flour
1 can beef broth
1 teaspoon Worcestershire sauce (optional)
Salt and pepper, to taste

Meat Balls: Soak bread in milk for 5 or 10 minutes. Whip together with a fork or whisk or mix with your hands until the mixture has a batter-like consistency. Add meat, onion, egg, and other ingredients. Form into small balls no more than1-to-1½-inches in diameter. In a large skillet preferably non-stick, melt butter. Add the meat balls and brown, a few at a time if you need to, until all are browned on all sides. Remove from the skillet.

Gravy: To the drippings left in the skillet, add the flour. Then, slowly add the beef broth and other ingredients. Cook over Low heat, stirring until as thick as you like. Taste for seasoning.

Place meat balls back in gravy. Serve immediately or refrigerate overnight or freeze for later use. When ready to serve, heat for about 15 minutes. If frozen, thaw in microwave and finish on the stove.

Swedish Meat Balls are traditionally served with Brown Beans, not our Southern Appalachian version of Brown Beans, but their own version. This is a recipe I have taken along with the Meat Balls when my students have had international meals. Both are always popular.

SWEDISH BROWN BEANS
This is my short-cut recipe.
4 (1 pound) cans pinto beans or light red kidney beans without meat seasoning
Add 1 cup corn syrup
¼ cup cider vinegar
1 teaspoon or less salt

Cook on medium-low heat for 45 minutes or until sauce has thickened. Taste and adjust seasonings. You may want to add a bit more syrup or vinegar to suit your taste.

Hobart sent Mother two recipes that I know about. She kept both, just as he had written them. The first one was sent to Mother when we still lived on Carolina Avenue. Hobart lived in California at this time; and, the recipe he sent was for banana bread. Although this was not a comfort food to him, or to us, and on the surface it looks like an ordinary recipe, it is a very unusual recipe—at least the way he wrote it to Mother.

HAITI BANANA BREAD
1 cup sugar
½ cup butter (or margarine or shortening)
2 eggs
3 or 4 bananas
2 cups flour
3 tablespoons sour milk
1 teaspoon soda (baking soda)
½ teaspoon baking powder
¼ teaspoon salt

Peel bananas carefully. Save peel to line the baking pan placing in pan as desired. Be sure the outside skin is next to the inside of the pan—that is the part that was next to the banana will be next to the cake. Bake 1 hour in loaf pan.

The general directions that he left out: Mash the bananas; cream together the sugar and butter; add the bananas to the sugar/butter mixture. Mix flour, soda, baking powder, and salt together, and add to the banana mixture, mixing alternately with the sour milk. Bake at 325 to 350 degrees for the time Hobart gave, above, or until the center is done.

When Mother got this recipe, she thought it was strange to use the banana peels, but knew that Hobart would ask if she had tried his recipe. So, she made it, according to his directions. The bread was very moist and yummy. A few days later, she either got another note from Hobart or he called her and told her that using the banana peels was not part of the real recipe. Hobart had pulled another good practical joke!

The second recipe Hobart sent to Mother was worked out by him later, when he lived in Denver. It was for his version of potato soup. One year, the club I sponsored at the college where I teach published a cookbook as a fund-raiser and I had his soup recipe put in the cookbook. The sponsor of another club at the time tried this soup and said that of all the recipes in that book, this was her favorite. Her club made this soup later and sold it at a bake-sale, fund-raiser. And, the soup didn't last very long! It is delicious! This is the recipe, as Hobart wrote it to Mother:

HOBART'S POTATO SOUP
3 medium potatoes—cubed to about ⅜ to ½ inch
1 medium or large onion, chopped fine
½ average carrot, sliced very thin
3 chicken bouillon cubes
1 tablespoon parsley flakes
3½ cups of water
1 tablespoon salt
¾ inch chunk of butter
Black pepper—I pile it on
1 small can evaporated milk
Throw it all into a pot, except the milk.
Barely bubble, covered, until potatoes are done. Turn heat down. Add milk and keep "just hot" for about 30 minutes. Eat with GUSTO!

One night when we talking on the phone, Hobart gave me his cornbread recipe. He said that this one was made with the real stuff, and none of this adding flour. He said that he had worked and worked with this until he got it to his liking. It is very good!

HOBART'S CORNBREAD
Preheat the oven to 425 degrees.
2⅓ cups cornmeal

1 teaspoon salt
½ teaspoon soda (baking soda)
2 large eggs, beaten
1¾ cups buttermilk
2 tablespoons vegetable oil

Mix all ingredients together except oil.

Heat oil in cast iron skillet as the oven preheats. Let the oil get almost to the smoking point. Remove skillet from oven. Pour oil into cornbread batter. Mix in quickly. Immediately pour batter into prepared skillet. Bake at 425 degrees until it is nicely browned and the center is done.

NOTE: To make Fried Cornbread, increase the amount of milk to bring the mixture to batter-like consistency. Use about ¼ to ⅓ cup of batter for each piece of cornbread. Fry in shortening until dark golden brown on each side. Mother always used a bowl- shaped very large serving spoon to ladle out the batter and I still do the same thing, with the same spoon, sometimes.

If you have some of the cornbread left over, as we usually do, you may want to make Marie's Cornbread Salad.

MARIE'S CORNBREAD SALAD

2½ cold cornbread
1 cup chopped green pepper
1 medium onion, chopped
1 cup shredded sharp Cheddar or Colby cheese
½ teaspoon celery seed
2 medium tomatoes, seeded and chopped
½ -to-1 cup mayonnaise or use the dressing mixture below

DRESSING FOR CORNBREAD SALAD

¼ cup cucumber dressing
2 teaspoons sugar
2 teaspoons prepared mustard
½ teaspoon salt
½ teaspoon black pepper

Whisk together.

To assemble:

If you are serving the same day: Gently combine the ingredients, cover tightly and refrigerate until serving.

If you want to make this to serve the following day: Layer the corn-bread, vegetables, and cheese. Drizzle half the dressing over. Sprinkle with half of the celery seed. Make another layer of cornbread, vegeta-bles, and cheese; top with the remaining dressing. Sprinkle with the remaining ¼ teaspoon celery seed. Cover tightly and refrigerate. About an hour before serving, remove from the refrigerator and toss gently to combine all ingredients. Return to the refrigerator until serving time.

Tunis, Reba's husband, said that one of the things he remembers having when he was little was coffee with cream and sugar and bread. "I thought that was so good, but I didn't know any better, then." He also mentioned beans, cornbread and greens as being good. "And," he said,"ice cream always makes me feel good!"

A special time at their house was in February or March. His parents started cutting the hams, and they would have their first ham of the sea-son with biscuits and gravy. When he was in school, he said that his mother used to send fried apple pies with him for his lunch. He said, "I used to sit in the back of the room because I thought that was kind of 'low food,' but that was good food!"

Here is a recipe for Fried Apple Pies:

FRIED APPLE PIES

Double the recipe for Basic Pie Crust (see Index) and refrigerate. Or, make your favorite biscuit recipe and roll the dough very thin.

1/2 pound of dried apples, washed, soaked in fresh water for at least 1 hour.

Drain off the soaking water.

Cook the apples in fresh water to cover, adding sugar, powdered cin-namon, powdered cloves to taste, and a dash or two of salt. (The amount of sugar used will depend on the variety of apples and your own taste). When apples are tender, remove from the heat and let cool. Adjust seasoning.

Divide the pie crust into fourths. Working with one portion at a time, roll out to the thinness of pie crust. Cut into at least four-inch circles. (Some people use a saucer as a guide). Place about 3 tablespoons of the cooled apples on each of the circles. Brush the edge of each circle with water. Fold the dough over the apples and press the edges of the dough together; then, go around the sealed edge with the tines of a fork to make sure it is well-sealed.

Heat an iron skillet preferably over medium heat and add about 2 tablespoons of Crisco. When the shortening melts, add as many of the pies as your skillet will hold. Fry until golden brown. Drain on paper towels. Continue until all pies are fried. If you get tired or run out of crust before you do apples, the apples can be refrigerated or frozen for another time. These are good warm or cooled.

At some point during our conversation, Tunis said, "Hot chocolate on a cool night is the best thing, and when out camping, a good cup of coffee!" Ralph and I will agree with Tunis about the good cup of coffee on a camping trip! We took an unforgettable camping trip with Reba, Tunis, and their grandson, Justin. Before going over the Alpine Loop, an old prospectors' trail that is still accessible only to four-wheel-drive vehicles, we camped in the Colorado Rockies at about 10,000 feet elevation. The temperature in late June was like a late fall evening-morning in the Southern Appalachians. I was the only one who took jeans and a sweat shirt and extra jackets and ponchos—no wonder we didn't have room to pack our little tent. Justin thought the ponchos were "cool." He also had his first experience at chopping wood and going to the well to get water. We had hot coffee after supper and before turning in, and of course to warm up our bones in the morning. Now, if we could just get the hang of baking the bread without making charcoal, our camping breakfasts would be perfect!

When Reba and Tunis lived in Chattanooga, we visited with them several times during the year. We always had some kind of adventure when we went to their house—from whitewater rafting to rushing from the Choo-Choo downtown, back to the top of the mountain one New Year's Eve to bring in the New Year, again. We celebrated in two different time zones.

Ralph and Tunis used to go hunting in the fall. They got up in the wee hours of the morning and put on all this garb and played the part of the big white hunters. Then, they trekked out into the wild. We never ate venison afterwards. One morning Ralph said that he saw what he believed was a deer, but then he thought that it could be a person, so he didn't pull the trigger. In a minute or two, he heard a rifle shot farther down the mountain. Somebody else had gotten "Ralph's deer." Later, he confessed that if that deer had stopped, turned around and looked him in the eye, he couldn't have pulled that trigger anyway.

One of the days we were out whitewater rafting, our raft got stuck on big rocks because the river was down quite a bit in the middle of that summer. After all it couldn't have been because the right hand—Tunis—didn't know what the left hand—Ralph—was doing, and vise versa. When we got stuck one more time, Tunis got out of the raft and was using the oar to help get us off the rock. The raft broke loose and began to float merrily down the river with the rest of us in it while Tunis stood in the middle of the river upstream still holding the oar. Mother loved that story! She said, "Well, I've heard of being up the creek without a paddle, but I've never heard of being up the river with a paddle and no boat!"

We ate so much good food at Reba's and Tunis's house, it is hard to decide which have been our favorites. The utmost favorite, I believe, is Reba's Squash Casserole that she began bringing up here for our family meals. It is expected at our house every Thanksgiving. One year I didn't fix it and I was asked, "Where's the squash casserole? We can't have Thanksgiving without casserole!" I almost had a revolt on my hands and so now, it is as important to make this as it is to have the turkey and cranberry sauce. Since I feel like it's not Thanksgiving without the dressing, I have included the recipe Reba gave me for her dressing. Here are the recipes:

REBA'S SQUASH CASSEROLE

1½ pounds yellow summer or crookneck squash *cooked until tender*
OR 2 packages (10 oz.) frozen squash cooked according to package directions
1 can cream of celery soup
1 16 oz. carton sour cream
1 cup or one small can water chestnuts, chopped fine
1 small jar chopped pimientos
2 medium, or 1 large, onion, finely chopped
1 stick margarine or butter, melted
1 small package stuffing mix

In a large rectangular baking dish, place half of the dry stuffing mix. Drain the cooked squash of water. Place into a large mixing bowl. Add the sour cream, water chestnuts, pimientos, onions, and melted margarine.

Mix together. Taste for salt and adjust if necessary. Place the squash mixture over the stuffing in the baking dish. Sprinkle the remaining half- package of stuffing over the top. Bake at 350 degrees for 30 minutes. This may be frozen before baking. Allow extra time for baking if you prefer to prepare it ahead of time and freeze it.

CORNBREAD DRESSING

4 cups bread crumbs from fresh or day-old bread; do not use the

packaged crumbs
4 cups cornbread that has been made with eggs
½ cup chopped onion
1 cup chopped celery including some of the leaves
Salt and pepper, to taste
1 teaspoon rubbed sage, or a bit more to taste
3 cups chicken broth
⅓ cup butter, melted
1 cup milk
Mix all the ingredients together and bake in greased pans at 350 degrees for one hour.

One of the chicken dishes Reba's family likes is her Barbecued Chicken. Here's the recipe:

BARBECUED CHICKEN

2 tablespoons salad oil
2 (3 pounds each) ready-to-cook broiler-fryers, quartered
Start heating the oven to 350 degrees. In hot salad oil in skillet, brown chicken well on all sides. Remove to shallow baking pan.
The Sauce: 3 cups tomato juice
½ cup vinegar
1 tablespoon sugar
4 sliced medium onions
3 tablespoons Worcestershire sauce
½ cup catsup
4 teaspoons prepared mustard
1 teaspoon pepper
2 teaspoons salt

In saucepan, combine all sauce ingredients and heat. Pour over the chicken. Bake chicken uncovered, 1 hour or until tender, basting often with sauce to keep chicken moist. If sauce is too thick, stir in a little water.
NOTE: For "no mess," use skinless, boneless pieces of chicken, instead of the quartered broiler-fryers.

One year during our Christmas Break, we went to visit, and Reba had made a wonderful snack. These can be served on a buffet table when having a reception and they are very good to counteract the sweets that are usually in abundance around Christmas time. We could eat them by the handfuls!

REBA'S COCKTAIL PECANS

2 tablespoons butter or margarine
½ teaspoon seasoned salt
1 or 2 dashed Tabasco sauce
1 pound pecan halves
3 tablespoons Worcestershire sauce

Put butter, seasoned salt, and hot sauce in a 12 x 8 x 2-inch baking dish. Place in a 300 degree oven until butter melts. Stir to blend. Add pecans, stirring until all are butter-coasted. Bake for 20 minutes, stirring occasionally. Sprinkle with Worcestershire sauce, stir again and continue baking another 15 minutes, or until crisp. Cool. Store in an airtight container. They may be frozen for later use.

Reba began bringing a dessert to family meals at Mother's, especially on special days we celebrated during the spring and summer. She could make the dessert in Chattanooga, pop it into their cooler, and tote it up here where it was soon devoured. When you make this, it surely will not last very long! This is another of those desserts that you can rationalize eating by saying that it's healthy with all that fruit, but whether people will believe you or not is another matter. Here's the recipe:

BANANA SPLIT CAKE

Mix together:
¾ stick margarine, melted
2 cups graham cracker crumbs
Line bottom of long pan or rectangular baking dish with the above mixture.
Blend together:
2 sticks margarine, melted
2 eggs
2 cups confectioners sugar
Mix these three ingredients for 10 minutes. Then pour on top of graham cracker crust in dish.
Slice 3 bananas *and layer on top of the filling.*
On top of bananas, add one **No. 2 can crushed pineapple,** *drained.*
On top of pineapple, layer **one 9 oz. carton whipped topping.**

Sprinkle chopped pecans on top of whipped topping, and add Maraschino cherries (with stems attached) in approximately the center of each serving. Cut into squares to serve.

After staying up late at night when we visited with Reba and Tunis, few of us got up very early in the mornings. Sometimes we went out for a big late breakfast-early lunch that lasted us until suppertime, and other times, Reba made a special breakfast-brunch for us. Following is another of the good dishes she makes:

REBA'S SAUSAGE CASSEROLE
2 pounds sausage, one hot and one mild or both the same kind
6 cups crisp rice cereal
2 small onions, chopped
2 cups cooked long-grain rice
2 sticks sharp cheddar cheese, cubed
4 eggs, slightly beaten
2 cans cream of celery soup
¼ cup milk
Brown sausage and chopped onion and drain well. Add rice. In a large rectangular baking dish, arrange in layers: sausage mixture, cereal, cubed cheese. Mix eggs, soup and milk and pour on top. Bake at 350 degrees for 40 minutes.

When they were living in Chattanooga or on Signal Mountain, Reba sent Mother a recipe for blackberry pie filling. They had found blackberries one day on one of their adventures and Reba had come up with this recipe that she shared. Here's her recipe:

BLACKBERRY PIE FILLING
3 cups blackberries
1 cup sugar
2 tablespoons orange juice
2 tablespoons flour
Pinch of nutmeg
1 tablespoon butter

Reba didn't include the pie crust recipe or the baking directions, so here's my way of finishing the pie: Combine mixture and place in pie shell; you can use the Basic Pastry recipe (see Index). Cover with plain or lattice top. Bake at 400 to 450 degrees for 15 minutes. Reduce the temperature to 350 degrees and continue to bake 25 to 30 minutes longer.

The first cousin who seems almost like a sister sometimes is Lucretia, the younger daughter of Uncle Cloyd and Aunt Blanche O'Dell Vance. She likes food as much as the rest of us do, is a wonderful cook, and we talk and laugh for hours at a sitting. When asked, she said that her comfort food was, "Lettuce—that's about all I can eat!" Then, we laughed. Then she said, "Biscuits and gravy, but now I fix creamed chipped beef instead." Later, she also mentioned a tomato dish Aunt Blanche made, Tomato Pudding also known as Scalloped Tomatoes. Here's the recipe:

TOMATO PUDDING (SCALLOPED TOMATOES)
In a baking dish, put a layer of cold biscuits cut in half, then a layer of canned tomatoes. Sprinkle with sugar. Make additional layers of the cut biscuits, tomatoes, and sugar until you have a sufficient amount to serve the number expected for the meal. Bake at 350 for about 30 minutes. Serve warm.

Young Aunt Blanche and Uncle Cloyd

Lucretia said that she also loved wilted lettuce, fried okra, and carrots. She said that her late husband's (Sherman Gilmer) comfort food was chicken and dumplings. She said that after she and Sherman were married, they spent a weekend with her Grandpa O'Dell. She said, "He told me, 'You cook fried chicken the way that I like it, but don't tell your mother!'"

Lucretia remembers that they had a turkey once and a turtle once. She said that Uncle Cloyd hung that turkey between the clothes lines and it looked so funny hanging there with its wings and feet out. Uncle Cloyd used to buy fresh fish at Travis Seafood, which Lucretia believes was in the alley between Piedmont and Moore Streets in Bristol, Virginia.

When I told her that we remembered sitting around the table at their house for a meal, we knew the table was full, but that none of us could remember what we had to eat because we were having so much fun. She started telling me what we probably had: country fried steak, beef roast, or fried chicken; macaroni and cheese; congealed salad; mashed potatoes; homemade rolls; green beans; corn; slaw; tomatoes; cucumbers and onions in vinegar; baked apples; and, for dessert, caramel cake and peaches, or devil's food cake.

When she got to the caramel cake, I remembered that! The cake itself was always a white homemade cake, as was the caramel icing; and, the peaches were home canned.

Aunt Blanche was a wonderful cook, but it was like Reba said, "I was just so happy to be at their house!" That's why we forgot all the food. Lucretia said, "Daddy always paid attention to young people and he loved you all." We loved him, too!

The every day meals Aunt Blanche cooked sometimes included Spanish rice, meat loaf, rice and beef, or other casseroles, and always jams and jellies. Deviled eggs were a special dish for them and Aunt Blanche made a dish called Roman Holiday. Here is Aunt Blanche's recipe:

ROMAN HOLIDAY

¼ cup shortening
1 onion, chopped
2 cups cooked spaghetti
1 pound hamburger
1 teaspoon salt
⅛ teaspoon pepper
1½ cups canned tomatoes
¾ cup grated cheese

Fry onion in shortening. Add meat and seasonings. Cook 5 minutes. In a baking dish, make layers of spaghetti, meat mixture, spaghetti. Pour tomatoes over the top. Sprinkle with grated cheese. Cover the dish. Bake at 350 degrees for 35 minutes. Remove the cover and bake 10 minutes longer.

Lucretia also remembers her mother's Swiss Steak and remembers that for Easter, they had pickled eggs in beet juice. Aunt Blanche always made cream gravy with country ham instead of red-eye gravy. Another dish that she made was Liver Pudding. Some people like this more than scrapple. I even have seen some recipes that call for using Liver Pudding as a base for scrapple. I believe that both of these dishes probably are of German ancestry. This is Aunt Blanche's recipe:

LIVER PUDDING
Boil liver in salt water until tender
Mash fine.
Add a cup of broth in which liver was cooked.
Bring to boil; stir in corn meal.
Salt to taste.
Add ½ teaspoon black pepper, 2 tablespoons sage, and red pepper to taste
   Eat cold or slice and fry in fat.

Aunt Blanche sold cottage cheese and maybe some of her embroidery at the Farmer's Market which Lucretia said was between Piedmont and Moore Streets in Bristol, Virginia. She also sold the butter to Hagy's Grocery on Russell Street. Before Lucretia and Sherman knew each other, his mother, Mrs. Gilmer, bought the butter Lucretia's mother made. Sherman's family lived near Hagy's Grocery at that time. Aunt Blanche used the money she earned from these sales to help pay for their daughters' piano lessons and other extras.

At their house, everything was shared. Lucretia said that even a small coke was shared five ways. Their family lived on a farm on the Blountville Highway outside of Bristol. The house still sits back from the highway, but it is now surrounded by businesses or other houses, and the open fields have disappeared. The children helped especially in the garden and Lucretia said that Claude, Jr., said that while they were picking the potato bugs off the potato plants and putting the bugs into kerosene, he used to look at the cars come and go on the highway and wonder where they had been and he was determined not to have a garden.

When I was very young, after lunch at their house, I used to go out to one of the sheds and get a jar of marbles that had been Claude's. We called him Junior, then; and, even today, I catch myself calling him that instead of Claude. I took the marbles inside and played with them on the hearth in the living room while the adults talked.

Lucretia remembers that her mother called shuck beans "hay beans." She also remembers having a meal at cousins Stevie and Bessie Greene's house once and that they had homemade loaf bread. "It was coarse like salt rising bread and it had some cornmeal in it." I found the following old hand-written recipe among Mother's collection. I don't know whether this is a recipe that was passed down in the Greene family or not, but it does have some cornmeal as an ingredient. If the use of lard, the wording, and the lack of baking instructions are any indication, this recipe predates peoples' use of electric ovens... probably by many years. Here's the recipe:

SALT RISING BREAD

Scald 1 tablespoon meal at night. In the morning, add 1 quart of warm water, 1 teaspoon salt, 1 tablespoon sugar, enough flour to make batter. Set in warm water. Let raise. Then add lard and mix with flour to make a soft dough. Put in pan. Let raise and bake.

NOTE: Since this recipe uses 1 quart of liquid, you can pretty well be sure that this makes more than one loaf (9 x 5 x 3-inch size. Have at least 3 of this size handy. The approximate baking temperature is about 400 degrees until the top is brown and the loaf sounds hollow when tapped. If the top begins to brown too soon into the baking time, reduce the heat a bit and cover with aluminum foil. Since salt rising bread is dense, this may take longer to bake than regular yeast bread, so estimate baking time to be between 1 to 1½ hours.

School days at Blountville were remembered and especially one student's lunch. Lucretia said that the mother had cut circles out of sandwich bread and put sausage between two of the bread circles. This reminded me of some of the girls' lunches at my school. Their sandwiches always had the crusts trimmed away. Mother's response to that was: "That's a waste of bread!"

Aunt Blanche was nine years old when her mother died. Mr. O'Dell took Aunt Blanche and her brother and moved in with his parents. Aunt Blanche learned to cook from her grandmother who cooked dandelion and poke greens, chicken and dumplings, and many other foods. Lucretia still uses her great-grandmother's recipe for boiled custard which Aunt Blanche served with fresh coconut cake at Christmas.

MARGARETTE CRUMLEY O'DELL'S BOILED CUSTARD
1 quart milk
3 eggs
3 tablespoons sugar
¹⁄₁₆ teaspoon salt
½ teaspoon lemon flavor

Heat milk in double boiler to boiling point. Beat eggs and sugar together. Add eggs and sugar to milk, stirring constantly. Add salt. Keep over fire until thick enough to coat spoon when inserted. Do not boil. Remove from fire and add flavor. Chill before serving. May be sprinkled with a dash of nutmeg.

NOTE: Mother's recipe for Boiled Custard is essentially the same as this recipe except Mother used vanilla extract in place of the lemon flavoring.

When Lucretia and her brother and sister were still at home, some of the canned cherries in the basement had "gone bad," resulting in "cherry wine." Lucretia said, "Claude, Jr. asked daddy, 'Is that the kind of wine it talks about in the Bible?' And, that killed the wine at our house!"

The first foods Claude, Jr. mentioned as comfort foods were fried fish and country fried steak for breakfast. I remember that Uncle Cloyd and Aunt Blanche loved to go fishing and they, too, loved to have fish for breakfast. They used to go out in the mornings to the river and fish at their special fishing place. They did this often after Uncle Cloyd retired, although Aunt Blanche was confined to a wheelchair by that time. She sat in that chair and fished right along with Uncle Cloyd and they had a ball!

Among other foods Claude, Jr. mentioned as favorites were fried peas and his mother's boiled and fried cabbage, kraut, kraut and wieners, greens, and apple float. He also mentioned scalloped tomatoes (tomato pudding), rice pudding, creamed rice (rice cooked in milk instead of water), bread pudding, and fresh berries with cream.

Several of their family's traditional recipes follow:

AUNT BLANCHE'S APPLESAUCE CAKE
Sift together into large bowl:

1¾ cups all-purpose flour
1 teaspoon baking soda
½ teaspoon salt
1 cup sugar
½ teaspoon cloves
½ teaspoon allspice
1 teaspoon cinnamon
   Add:
½ cup shortening
1 cup sweetened applesauce
   Mix. Then, beat 2 minutes.
   Add:
1 egg
½ cup raisins
½ cup nuts.
   Beat 1 minute.
   Bake in 8-inch pans at 375 degrees for 50 minutes or in a loaf pan at 350 degrees for 1 hour and 15 minutes.

AUNT BLANCHE'S SAUERKRAUT

Pack chopped cabbage in mason jars. Add 1 teaspoon sugar and 1 teaspoon salt per quart. Fill jars with boiling water. Seal. Allow to stand several weeks until fermentation is complete. If liquid lowers in jars, add brine water. After fermentation is complete, process jars in boiling water 15 minutes for pints; 20 minutes for quarts.

AUNT BLANCHE'S MOLASSES POUND CAKE
1 cup all-purpose flour
1 cup whole wheat flour
1 teaspoon baking soda
½ teaspoon salt
1 teaspoon powdered ginger
1 teaspoon powdered cinnamon
½ teaspoon powdered cloves
1 teaspoon vanilla extract
½ cup white sugar
¾ cup molasses
½ cup vegetable oil
2 eggs

2 teaspoons vinegar mixed with 1 cup hot water (Let cool
  before mixing)
Orange Glaze (recipe below)
*Mix all ingredients and beat well. Pour into greased and floured
tube (bundt) pan. Bake at 350 degrees for 35 to 40 minutes.*

ORANGE GLAZE

1 cup confectioners sugar
2 to 4 ounces orange juice
Mix ingredients to desired flavor. Pour glaze over cooled cake.

CHRISTMAS FRUIT SALAD

Large can of crushed pineapple
2 cups diced oranges
Sugar to taste
3 bananas, diced
2 cups diced fresh apples
Mix above ingredients a day or two before serving.

LUCRETIA'S CHOCOLATE APPLESAUCE CAKE

1¼ cups sugar
½ cup cooking oil
¼ cup cocoa
2 cups all-purpose flour
1½ teaspoon baking soda
¼ teaspoon salt
1½ cups applesauce
1 tablespoon hot water
1 teaspoon vanilla extract
*Mix sugar and cooking oil. Add applesauce, hot water, and vanilla.
Sift flour, baking soda, cocoa, and salt. Add to the applesauce mixture.
Bake slowly at 325 degrees for 1 hour.*

Lucretia and Claude both remember Grandpa and Grandma Vance well
since Claude lived with them so he could go to Fairmount School. Uncle
Johnnie's children also went to Fairmount, as did all of us... at different
times.

Ralph's grandfather, Henry Jones O'Dell, was a brick mason and he built Fairmount School as well as some of the other elementary schools in Bristol. Some of his sons, including Carl, Ralph's dad, helped their father. Henry was also the Stonemason Supervisor for what used to be called Bristol Municipal Stadium which was built adjacent to Bristol, Tennessee High School, as a WPA project. The stadium is now called the "Stone Castle" because it looks like a medieval castle with round turrets at each corner and is where Ralph played football for Tennessee High and where later, our daughters marched in the band.

Claude said that Grandma Vance really treated him well. He remembers her making vegetable soup for him at lunch. He also remembers having banana pudding for dessert. "Grandma had two kinds of tea—sassafras and spicewood." Claude said, "She made the spicewood tea from twigs of the trees which grew along the creek."

He said that Grandpa's grape arbor went from just outside the back door of the house all the way to the barn at the back of the lot, and that he used to love to eat those grapes. Claude thought the barn was interesting and that it used to house buggies, horses, harnesses, and other equipment. He wasn't around Grandpa Vance as much as Grandma because Grandpa was at work most of the time.

Claude also remembers going to visit my family when they lived in Virginia during the Depression. In the summer, he always wore white ducks and a white shirt on Sundays. When they went to visit my family, and to eat lunch, he and Hobart would play on a big high bank of dirt across the road from the house, making tracks for rolling their toy cars and trucks. After lunch, they would go outside and play some more. He said that two pecan trees, he believes they were, grew in the front yard. Other boys from the neighborhood or cousins who were playing chose sides for teams and had a game of throwing pecans from two pecan trees that grew in the front yard at

Aunt Blanche, Uncle Cloyd, and Their Children—Note Claude's White Ducks

each other. Claude continued, "Those things hurt, too!" He said that his mother used to fuss because the nuts stained his clothes and they were hard to clean. I can just hear Aunt Blanche blustering now!

After our family moved to Carolina Avenue, Claude didn't play that much with Hobart, since he was a few years younger, and by that time Hobart was doing other things with the Buckles boys, Jim and Charlie, across the street.

Grandpa Vance is remembered by Lucretia as being somewhat of a food critic. When her family went to Grandpa's and Grandma's for a meal, they always had roast beef and Grandpa had to taste it to make sure it was to his liking. Lucretia said, "He always did the grocery shopping. He called Jello 'shimmy pudding' and bought natural peanut butter that was so stiff, if you tried to spread it on the bread, the bread crumbled, and when you ate it, you almost choked to death!" He also wrapped apples in newspaper and stored them in the basement. Lucretia said, "He had a good orchard."

The first comfort food mentioned by Raymond, Uncle Johnnie's second son, was, "Mother's fried apple pies!" He said that he might get his wife, Pauline who we call Polly, to make them once every two years…"I guess they're kind of messy to make." They take a lot of time, too… At least they take *me* a long time. Raymond also mentioned his Grandma Harr's tomato gravy. He said that they had tried to make it, but "things just don't taste like they used to."

Other foods Raymond remembers eating when he was growing up, but not together in the same meal, were pickled beans, cornbread and gravy, and fried sweet potatoes. Referring to the fried sweet potatoes, he said, "You don't have those anymore; I guess they're kind of messy to fix, too; they kind of stick." He also liked fried potatoes and fried potato cakes made from leftover mashed potatoes, peas with dumplings, and scalded lettuce and onions, "made with fat back and other things." Here's a simple recipe for Potato Cakes that perhaps will tempt you want to make extra mashed potatoes, just so you will have some leftovers:

POTATO CAKES

Two cups of leftover mashed potatoes may make enough cakes to serve two people, so you can adjust the amount to feed the number of people you are serving. Be aware that when your family hears that you are making these, they may come and snitch one at a time, very sneakily sometimes, off the plate on which you have placed the completed cakes to keep warm. Other times, they may ask for one (at a time) very politely. So, plan to make plenty of them!

To the amount of cold leftover mashed potatoes needed to feed your crowd, add a bit of all-purpose flour and mix together. The amount of flour will depend on the amount of potatoes you have. If the potatoes are really stiff, add a tablespoon or two of milk. You need to have a mixture that will hold together well when formed into a patty. (If the potatoes have too much moisture already, you will need to add more flour). Form the potatoes into patties 3 to 4 inches in diameter. Put into plain flour that you have put on a saucer or plate. Turn to coat both sides of the potato cakes. In a large skillet over medium heat, melt about half a stick of margarine. When the margarine melts and begins to sizzle, add some of the potato cakes. Don't crowd the skillet. Sprinkle with additional salt or seasoned salt, and/or pepper, to taste (since the potatoes have been salted previously when cooked, you will need very little salt). Fry the patties until they are dark golden brown on both sides, adding more margarine as needed to allow them to "fry." Keep the heat at medium or medium-low and stand over these and watch them like a hawk since they tend to start browning quicker than expected.

You may want to add some grated cheese and/or some chopped chives to the mixture before frying, but most of us like them just plain. You can serve these with some sour cream and chopped chives to put on the top, but we usually don't do that, either.

When I asked Raymond about desserts, he said, "The only desserts there are, are banana pudding and pineapple upside down cake, aren't they?" The recipes following, for Banana Pudding and Pineapple Upside Down Cake, are from Mother's collection:

BANANA PUDDING

2 cups scalded milk
2 egg yolks (reserve whites)
⅓ cup sugar
1 tablespoon cornstarch
¼ teaspoon salt
Vanilla wafers
Bananas

Mix sugar, cornstarch, and salt in top of double boiler. Add scalded milk.

Cook a few minutes in double boiler and add egg yolks. Mix well. Keep over boiling water, stirring often, until the mixture will coat a spoon without immediately running off. In an oven-proof serving bowl, make a layer of vanilla wafers and then a layer of bananas sliced hor-

izontally. Pour some of the custard over. Make another layer of wafers and bananas. Top with the rest of the custard. Make meringue using the two reserved egg whites mixed with 4 tablespoons sugar. Beat the egg whites until they form stiff peaks. Spoon onto the top of the pudding and put into a moderate oven (350 degrees) and bake until lightly golden brown. Let cool to room temperature. Refrigerate if you are serving the next day.

PINEAPPLE UPSIDE DOWN CAKE

⅔ **cup vegetable shortening**
½ **teaspoon salt**
2 teaspoons vanilla extract
1 cup sugar
2 eggs beaten
3 teaspoons baking powder
2½ **cups sifted all-purpose flour**
1 cup pineapple juice drained off the canned pineapple
1 cup brown sugar
8 or 10 slices of pineapple

Mix shortening with sugar; then add beaten eggs. Sift flour, salt, and baking powder together. Add the flour mixture to shortening/sugar alternately with pineapple juice. Stir in vanilla extract. Grease 9 x 15-inch pan. Sprinkle with brown sugar. Place pineapple slices on sugar. Pour batter over top. Bake at 350 to 375 degrees for about 30 minutes or until the center tests done. While still warm, turn out onto a large platter, fruit side up.

Raymond also liked Grandma Vance's fried peas and her chicken and dumplings. He said, "She picked off the white meat and put it in the gravy." He said that he could eat cornbread everyday. "But," he said, "soup beans was the best food ... and bean dumplings. I've even eaten bean sandwiches!"

He said that Uncle Johnnie liked to eat the meat Aunt Ida cooked with the beans. Our Daddy did, too; and, when I was very little, I tried it some just to try to be like Daddy, but I soon decided I did not like that jelly-like consistency, and Daddy got it all after that!

When Raymond went to the doctor for a check up a few years ago, the doctor said, "Have you always overeaten?" Raymond responded, "Oh, yes! Ever since I was three or four!"

I asked Raymond if they ever did anything special with the paw paws they had. He said they just ate them as they were and he said, "You could have eaten them all day and still not have eaten much." Raymond said that Aunt Ida's recipes have been lost. She always kept them in the rack of the bottom door of her Hoosier cupboard. After she died and some of the furniture was sold, he realized that they had failed to remove her recipes before the cupboard was gone.

During the summer, one dish that Raymond and Polly like are her Stuffed Peppers. She said, "Everybody who eats them likes them." Some people have told her that she should enter the recipe in a contest or something, but she never has. When I asked her how she made them, Raymond said, "Well, first, she yells, 'Hey, Raymond, are there any peppers in the garden?'" And, then Raymond goes out to the garden so they can have,

POLLY'S STUFFED PEPPERS
6 green peppers, halved, cleaned and blanched
Pour the water off and cool the peppers
In a large mixing bowl combine:
1 can (6 oz.) white tuna in water, drained
4 - 6 boiled eggs, chopped
1 large onion, chopped
1 cup (or more to taste) grated cheese (colby or cheddar)
1 cup (or more) cooked rice
1 tomato, chopped
Salt and pepper to taste
Mayonnaise (enough to hold the mixture together)
Stuff the mixture into the pepper halves. Cut three slices of bread into tiny cubes. In a skillet, melt 1 tablespoon butter or margarine. Add the bread cubes and stir to toast them. Place the toasted bread on the stuffed peppers. Bake in a 350 degree oven for 30 to 45 minutes.

NOTE: I made these, and Raymond and Polly are right! They are wonderful!

When I was talking with Polly one day, she said that she had just put a meatloaf in for their supper. I told her that I was going to do a meatloaf, too. She said, "This is a good old recipe... I don't know how long I've had it, but it's good!" Here's her recipe:

POLLY'S MEAT LOAF
1½ pounds ground beef
3 slices of bread or the equivalent of saltine cracker crumbs

¼ of a chopped onion
2 eggs, slightly beaten
1 cup milk
1 teaspoon salt
pepper, to taste
1 teaspoon dry mustard, optional
½ cup catsup

Mix all ingredients together. Place in loaf pan or form into a loaf-shape in another pan or skillet. Place two uncooked bacon slices on top. Bake at 375 degrees for about an hour.

When the whole family has a meal together, Polly likes to make her Deviled Eggs. This is one of those "pinch of this," "tad of that" recipes.

DEVILED EGGS

Boil the number of eggs needed to feed your crowd. Peel off the shells. Cut the eggs in half (they will work better on a plate if you cut them vertically from end-to-end). Remove the yolks. Mash well. Add mayonnaise, pickle relish, a tad of prepared mustard, and salt and pepper to taste. Put the yolk mixture back into the hollowed-out eggs. Slice pimiento-stuffed olives and place a slice on each egg.

Raymond talked about the types of fun they used to have when they were young. He said, "We made our own fun! Kids around here were so bored not long ago, I got out a barrel hoop and showed them how to roll it using the stick." He said that they played for a while and then left it. A little while later, he heard a scraping noise and looked out the window. One of the dads was out rolling the hoop—perhaps reliving a part of those simpler, happy days.

Back in the late 1930s and early 40s, Raymond belonged to the American Federation of Musicians because he played with Elmo Morton's Orchestra. Raymond said, "George (the oldest brother) played the guitar, Elmo played the piano, Tater McNew played the trumpet, Shake Ganaway played drums, and I've forgotten the name of the guy who played the saxophone. Betsey Ross was the vocalist. And… I played the 'stand-up' bass." He said, "We played the 'Glenn Miller-type' music." I said, "Oh! The good stuff." Raymond said, "Yea…. We played for dinner-dance type things. We played a lot at Hotel Bristol, at the Country Club in Bristol and at the Country Club in Spruce Pine, North Carolina." He continued, "And, we played for the Jitterbug Contests they used to have at the Paramount Theater every Saturday…. They used to have those contests every week." I imagined they had a lot fun playing at those places. Raymond said, "Well, it was at first, but then it got old pretty quickly. Here we were up there playing and watching the people at these dinner-dance affairs. At first, they were fine and then when they started drinking, it wasn't fun to watch them. I just don't understand it…so, after awhile, it got old."

(Hotel Bristol used to be one of the landmarks in Bristol, Virginia, along with Hotel General Shelby. Hotel Bristol was where many high school proms and banquets were held. When "Urban Renewal" hit town with full force, both of these hotels were demolished to make way for what else—asphalt parking lots? The hotels went the same route as Bunting's Drug Store (in Bristol, Tennessee), but without the many voices speaking

Uncle Johnnie, Aunt Ida and Their Family

up trying to save them as Bunting's had. The Paramount, a movie theater at that time, was saved from the wrecking ball, probably because it was in one of the main blocks of State Street. It was still open for sometime when our children were small. Then, it closed. Now restored, it is open for special concerts, plays, and other activities. But, it is not the Paramount that most of us remember with so much fondness).

From our house, Raymond remembers the barn. He said that,

> One cold day, Hobart and I were out in the barn. Hobart started to do the milking and that cow started slapping her tail around. She hit Hobart once or twice in the face, and that tail was cold! Hobart couldn't get her to stop. She switched her tail into Hobart's face one more time, and he picked up a two-by-four and hit her on the side.

I asked, "What happened to the cow?" Raymond said,

> Oh, she fell over… but, she was O.K. The next thing I knew, Uncle Oscar had come out to the barn and picked up that two-by-four. And, the last thing I remember of that day was seeing Uncle Oscar chasing Hobart all over the yard with that board!

Raymond told us this story when Grandpa and Grandma Vance's descendants were having a picnic. We had never heard this but it was so like Hobart … and so like Daddy!

Hobart had a temper, and when he had enough aggravation from anybody or anything, that was enough!

The Daddy I knew, could not stand to see any body or any thing mistreated. It was sort of like Mother used to say to me if I had said or done something unkind to one of my little friends. When Mother heard it or found out about it, she would say to me, "How do you think that made them feel?" And, I heard myself repeating this to our daughters when they were young. I have heard that Daddy was pretty hard on Hobart sometimes. Maybe he mellowed a bit as he got older.

Raymond remembers Grandpa and Grandma Vance very well. He said that he didn't know what was wrong with Grandma—"She used to have these fainting or weak spells when she got upset and always had smelling salts or something that she used. But, sometimes, she would just take to her bed and stay there for days!" I told Raymond that I knew that Grandma had heart trouble, but I didn't know when that started. I further speculated that some of her "spells" possibly were not from her heart trouble, but just her way of dealing with or not dealing with the thing or person who upset her. I never remember my sisters, brother, or even Mother ever mentioning Grandma's "spells." Maybe my sisters didn't even know about them.

Just recently, Albert, Uncle Johnnie's third son, said that Grandma would just go to bed. "She would stiffen up and hold her breath and act like she was gone. Then, she would say in a weak trembling voice, 'You'd better call the children in because I'm not going to last much longer.'" Albert continued, "One day, she was going through one of these spells and Dr. Leavell came to check her out. He said, 'There's not a thing wrong with you except that somebody made you mad. Now you get out of that bed!' And, Grandma jumped up and told Dr. Leavell off!" Dr. Leavell's comment to Grandma partially confirms what I had told Raymond.

Raymond said that Grandpa and Grandma were almost religious fanatics. Family books we have or I have seen have a religious tone (among the books Grandpa had was a history of the Baptists from about 1400 A.D.). Raymond sent me a pamphlet written by B.F. Vance, a cousin of Grandpa's. The pamphlet, "The Gates of Hell," was priced at fifteen cents; and eleven thousand copies were printed. Raymond said that Grandpa got out on weekends and sold them or gave them away. Other smaller leaflets were stuffed inside its pages. Looking at some of the things written in these papers, I think it no wonder that some people in those days were scared to death of God! I never saw Him portrayed in these pamphlets as a God of love.

Both Raymond and Albert talked about Grandpa and the Holston Baptist Church and the church at Riverside. Some disagreement arose in the church, which is not unusual in Baptist churches, and some members left to start another church. They built directly across the road from the old church; and, the people "tried to outdo each other to see who could sing louder or make the most noise."

Raymond said that, "Grandpa hired a man in Bristol to drive a city bus which Grandpa rented every week. And, on Sunday morning, Grandpa would ride that bus and go pick up the relatives and others to go to the church at Riverside." Raymond continued, "Neither church had enough members to support the churches."

Most of the stories I heard about Grandpa were either about how strict he was or how religious he was or what a perfectionist he was. I wonder what his reaction was to the following episode. Hobart told me that,

Grandpa used to sell some kind of products door-to-door. He went up to this one house and knocked on the door and the lady came to the door. Grandpa told her what he was selling, and the woman didn't seem to want any of that powder. So, Grandpa said, 'It will be good for your drawers!' And, the woman slammed the door in his face!

When I told Reba this story, she said that Grandpa sold Blair Products one time. I told her that, "With all I've heard about Grandpa being so strict and so religious and everything, I can't believe he told that story on himself." She said, "Well, maybe he didn't. Maybe he told Grandma and Grandma told the story on him." Reba responded, "Grandma was funny sometimes. She would get tickled and laugh, but she sort of laughed through her nose and covered her nose and mouth while she laughed. It was just so funny!"

At one time, in the later 1920s and early 30s, Uncle Johnnie, Aunt Ida and their family lived in the same block of Carolina Avenue, on the same side of the street as my family later would live. Albert said that only one or two house were on the opposite side of the street, the Buckles house and one other. An open field lay down the hill between these houses and Virginia Avenue. Albert said that during 1930 or '31, the last big Klu Klux Klan meeting in Bristol was held in that field. Albert said that he and some of the other neighborhood boys watched the whole thing and that,

> The men drove into that field in their cars, got out, and immediately put on their white robes and hoods so they wouldn't be 'seen' although their cars could be identified. They had their meeting, then took off their hoods and robes and immediately got in their cars and drove away.

Uncle Johnnie's family moved to Kentucky Avenue after living on Carolina, also one block away from Virginia Avenue where Grandpa and Grandma lived. When Grandpa got sick, Grandma used to ask the grandchildren to come and stay with Grandpa when she had to go to town or somewhere else. Albert said, "I was always afraid to go stay because I was afraid something would happen while I was there with him." He continued, "Grandpa used to talk about the types of coal and the best type to burn in the furnace."

Raymond said that when Grandpa died, in 1940, the casket was so long they couldn't get it through the doors into the living room of Grandpa's and Grandma's house. At that time, few people had wakes or visitation at the funeral homes when people died. Grandma, determined to have Grandpa home, had the front window in the living room removed; the casket was

Grandma and Grandpa Vance At Their House
on Virginia Avenue

then put through the open space. Then, the window was replaced until time for the burial when the window was removed again to get the casket out. This must have been a very strenuous workout for the men involved because that front window is at least six feet above the yard.

When I was growing up, Mother seemed to be grieving, still, for Grandpa sometimes. She said that the doctor wouldn't let her go to Grandpa's funeral. She was expecting me in a few months, had become anemic, and perhaps had some other physical problems. For years, I felt guilty because I thought everything was all my fault.

Raymond said that when Grandpa died, his family moved in to live with Grandma because Uncle Cloyd and Aunt Blanche and Mother and Daddy

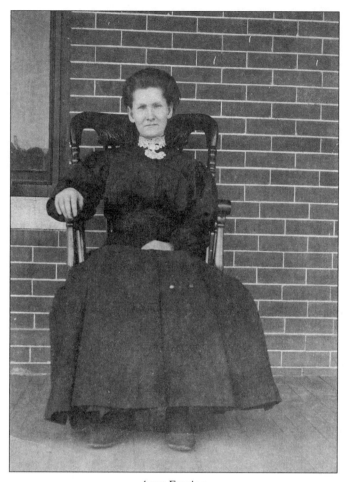

Aunt Ermine

already were settled in their homes. So, the house I remember as being Uncle Johnnie's family's is remembered by the older family members as first being Grandpa's and Grandma's.

Albert told me that one day some time after Grandpa died, Grandma and Aunt Ida were sitting in the dining room quilting. They heard the front door open and footsteps coming down the hall. The footsteps stopped at the stairs that went to the second floor. Grandma got up to see who was there. No one. The front door was closed, as it had been before, and no one was in the hall. She and Aunt Ida said it was Aunt Ermine's ghost. Aunt Ermine, Grandma's sister, had died in the front bedroom of the house. Albert said, "Or… maybe it was Grandpa coming back to see which type of coal was being burned in the furnace."

Years ago, Jim Buckles told Albert a story about Hobart, and Albert related it to me:

Hobart ordered a taxidermist's kit; and one day Jim and Hobart were sitting on the edge of the Buckles' porch talking. Hobart said, 'I sure would like to have something to stuff.' Then later, 'I really wish I had something to stuff.' About that time, Mrs. Buckles' old black cat came around the corner of the house. Jim picked up a board and whacked the cat in the head. Mrs. Buckles kept looking for her cat; but, she couldn't find it. Finally, after several days, she asked Jim if he had seen it. He said, 'Yes, Hobart's stuffing it.' Jim said that his mother gave him the awfulest 'wearing out' he ever had.

Thelma said that Hobart and Jim and Charlie Buckles used to like to hitchhike to the Holston Mountains when they were teenagers. Sometimes they went and returned several times a day. The just wanted to see how many times they could catch a ride.

I talked with Bernice, Jim's wife, recently and she said that sometimes when they hitchhiked to the mountains, they went fishing at Big Creek. Other times, they just hitched for fun. She asked me if Hobart ever told me about the time he was going to raise chickens. I told her that I had never heard about that. She said that Jim used to talk about it often and she said that she couldn't tell it like Jim did, but that,

One time Hobart decided he was going to raise chickens and ordered some through the mail. When the chicks came, it was cold and he was afraid to put them outside because he was afraid that they would freeze. So, he put them in one of the rooms of the house to keep them warm and started raising chickens in the house. Jim used to think that was the funniest thing!

Since I talked with Bernice, I was looking through some old pictures Hobart sent me in his later years, and found a photograph of him dressed in a white shirt and tie, and what looked to be new bib overalls. Hobart looked to be about 17 years old. On the back of the photograph, Hobart had written, "I won five dollars for raising chickens." Evidently, Daddy and Mother were so proud of him that they took his picture.

Bernice said, "Jim always loved you, didn't he?" I told her that I had been told by Mrs. Buckles that he did. Bernice said, "Yes, he used to drop in just to see you." Maybe he was checking on the kid that the duck delivered! When Jim died a few months ago, it was like Hobart dying again. Jim was kind of like a big brother to me even though after I grew up I never saw him often.

Albert's story about Hobart stuffing Haggi's cat reminded Raymond of another story:

> Hobart once sent off for a device he saw advertized in a magazine 'guaranteed to kill mosquitos.' When he got the device in the mail and opened it up, there were two blocks of wood. Oh! He got mad!

My sisters don't remember the stuffed cat or the mosquito killer, but they remember that Hobart used to catch and mount butterflies. I remember that some of his materials were still on the shelves in the old smokehouse when Daddy tore it down; then, they were moved to the barn. I don't know what happened to them. I just know that I was warned not to mess with Hobart's things, and I didn't. When we were older and talked often, he said that he ordered things from Carolina Biological Supply and had ordered some things from the same place for his grandchildren in more recent years.

Raymond or Albert also talked about Mr. Buckles' car that he kept in a garage in the empty lot next to the house. This was the car Daddy borrowed one Saturday so he could take me to where he worked and then on to town. I was four; this was the first trip I ever remember taking just with Daddy. I remember that I wore my little green wool coat with a darker green velvet collar. And, I wore a green crocheted tam with a white pom-pom on top and carried the little green purse to match the tam. The tam and purse had been gifts from Hobart. I felt so important! I don't remember anything about going on to town, but I still remember the smell of the wood in Daddy's little office at the lumber company. The Buckles' garage was torn down sometime when I was little. They always used their extra lot for their garden. And, now, the Buckles' house has been torn down. But, the memories linger.

Raymond said that J.C., his youngest brother, used to eat canned tomatoes with sugar sprinkled on them in beans. J.C. died of cancer in 1975. He not only sang with the quartet when he was younger, but was a member of the Charles Goodwin Orchestra for many years. He worked with the Boy Scouts and was the first in this area to have them learn and demonstrate the Native American dances. Some of the troops continue to do this.

J.C.'s wife, Daphne, who has remarried since J.C.'s death, remembered a dish that Aunt Ida made which she called Rhubarb Slump. From

Daphne's description of this dish, it sounds like another fruit dumpling, similar to a cobbler, that is cooked on top of the stove. Daphne said that she would experiment one day and try to fix this dish like she remembered it.

Albert has continued the work with the Boy Scouts, designing many of the special patches and conducting the training programs for the leaders. When I asked Albert about comfort food, his first response was, "Beans, cornbread, and fried potatoes." He said that Uncle Johnnie loved potatoes so much that he even took cold mashed potatoes with him to work for lunch.

Albert said that Sunday was meat day—and, "pies—berry, cherry, etc. After lunch, the food on the dining room table was covered with an extra tablecloth and you could go raise the cloth and eat those pies all afternoon!"

He remembers when the ice man delivered blocks of ice to people's ice boxes, before refrigerators. He and the other kids would see the ice truck coming and follow it and pick up the chips of ice left behind the truck. He continued,

> That was a treat! ... People had a three-corned sign they hung outside the front door. The sign corners had 25 lb., 50 lb., 75 lb. written on them. The iceman would look at the signs and whichever corner was up on the sign, he would bring that amount of ice in, carried by heavy iron tongs, and put it in the ice box.

Albert remembered Uncle Johnnie's quartet (before J.C. and Reba sang with them). He said that Aunt Ida would cook for Sunday on Saturday because the women didn't cook on Sunday. When they were going to have chicken to eat, the chicken's neck would be wrung to kill it. Sometimes they had beef instead. He said that, "Many times, the Saturday cooking would be to take to Sunday All-day Singings and Dinner-on-the-Grounds. The quartet and the family went quite often, and I enjoyed that."

I remember that Aunt Ida had a good voice. I believe she sang alto and sometimes sang in the choir, but I don't believe that she ever sang with the quartet. The one thing I remember most about Aunt Ida was that besides the fact that she altered my wedding dress for me, she made beautiful quilts. Once when I took our children to visit, she showed me a butterfly quilt she had designed. She said, "The butterfly pattern just didn't look like a real butterfly, so I made my own pattern!"

Even though we visited with Uncle Johnnie and Aunt Ida several times during the year, I don't remember talking directly with Uncle Johnnie very much. To me, he was a very tall, big-built, quiet man. He reminded me of the pictures I had seen of Grandpa Vance.

The first thing I was impressed by when I went to Uncle Johnnie's and Aunt Ida's house was the front door. It was ornately carved and had a large window in the upper part of the door. A doorbell was in the center of the door. It was a two-pronged finished iron or brass handle that you clasped your hand over and turned. Then, a "Bring-g-g-g" sound was heard. The sound was nowhere near the sound that the often-portrayed cosmetics lady heard as she rang more modern doorbells.

I remember sitting in Uncle Johnnie's and Aunt Ida's living room in front of the fireplace listening to the grown-ups talk. I just wish that I had remembered what they talked about and the stories they told. I do remember the fireplace. Theirs was oak with a large mirror in the middle framed on either side by large oak pillars. The face of the fireplace was framed with small rectangular shiny green tile. Two large Staffordshire dogs (I learned they were later) were always sitting on the hearth.

Albert said that a pork shoulder could be purchased for a couple of dollars when he was young. Aunt Ida made sausage and he loved that. He also mentioned liking peanut butter. In addition, he said that Aunt Ida made forty-eight biscuits every morning. When I asked, "Forty-eight?" He said, "Remember, she had Daddy and four growing boys to feed!"

When he went to school, Albert always wanted to buy his lunch because he thought if he took his lunch from home, the other kids would think he was poor. He said that he realized now that "because I was so proud, I missed out on a lot of good eating!"

He remembers that when they went to see Grandma Vance when Grandpa was still living. Albert said that, "in the cupboard next to the fireplace in the dining room, she had a lard can with one or sometimes two cakes in that can. Every time there was a visitor, she insisted that they have a piece of her cake."

One of the dishes that Albert and all of us like now is a vegetable casserole that Shirley, his wife, brought to our Vance family picnic two years ago, the first time I had ever known that this bunch ever got together just to have fun. And, if you don't have fun with this bunch of people, something is wrong! This is the casserole recipe:

SHIRLEY'S MIXED VEGETABLE CASSEROLE
¾ of a large bag of mixed frozen vegetables, cooked according to
 package directions
¾ cup chopped onion
1 cup chopped celery

1 cup grated Colby cheese
1 cup mayonnaise
2 cups snack crackers

Mix the vegetables, cheese and mayonnaise together. Place in a rectangular casserole dish. Top with 2 cups crushed snack crackers. Melt 1 stick of margarine and pour over crackers. Top with 1 additional cup of grated cheese. Bake at 300 degrees for 30 - 40 minutes until browned and bubbly.

Shirley also makes wonderful Starks Family Country Fried Steak and Gravy. She served this when the first cousins got together for a winter meal. It is a dish her mother taught her to make. Here's the recipe; I have called it by Shirley's family's name:

STARKS FAMILY COUNTRY FRIED STEAK AND GRAVY

Round steak, cut into serving-size pieces and pounded with a meat mallet until thin (1 pound of steak will serve three to four people, approximately)

Put all-purpose flour in a pan or plate. Add a sprinkling of salt and pepper.

Dredge the steak in the flour mixture until all pieces are well-coated.

In a 10- or 12-inch skillet, add vegetable oil and margarine (2-4 tablespoons).

Add the steak pieces to the skillet over medium-high heat a few pieces at a time. Brown the steak well on both sides. When fully browned, remove to a casserole dish with a lid.

Then, make the gravy:

To the drippings left in the skillet, add about 2 tablespoons flour. Stir to blend in thoroughly and to get any particles of meat or browned flour left in the skillet.

Mix together 2 cups milk and 1 cup water or a sufficient amount of the combined liquids to make almost a full skillet—in the proportions of twice as much milk as water

Add additional salt and pepper.

Let come to a boil, stirring continuously.

Immediately pour over the steak which has been placed in the casserole dish.

Cover and place in a 325 degree oven to bake for 1½ hours.

Shirley is about as funny or funnier than the other people in the family. She has such a way with words and she doesn't mince them, either! She told me a hilarious story about some of her following recipes. It seems that Albert was downstate somewhere at the place where he was involved in training Boy Scout leaders. It was a tradition that the person who conducted the training for this particular program provide a special meal for the other men. So, Albert planned "his" menu far in advance. But, here he was going to be "at camp" while Shirley was here, planning to do the cooking. The main dish he chose was one of their favorites—Rock Cornish Hens with Wild Rice Stuffing and Cherry Sauce.

Shirley said, "And, I had to stuff and cook twenty-six of those things—all in one morning! Now, you know that you cannot find twenty-six of those birds at one time in the same grocery store and so we went from grocery store to grocery store collecting the number we needed ahead of time."

On top of all that, during the week prior to this long-anticipated meal, the area Albert was in had experienced numerous severe thunderstorm and tornado warnings. And Shirley was about to stand on her head! She said, "Here I was sitting up at 3 o'clock in the morning watching the weather channel just about out of my mind!"

On the morning of the day she was supposed to deliver the stuffed and cooked birds downstate by one in the afternoon, we had a horrible storm. Shirley said that she was about to panic. And, she was ruing the day, to put it mildly, that Baden Powell had even started the Boy Scouts! (She, like a lot of us, will not do any cooking if we are having a major storm). She said, "I was thinking, 'What if the electricity goes off? What will I do?'" She continued, "I was racking my brain trying to think of someone I could get to cater something quickly."

Luckily, the power did not go off, but waiting for the storm to pass had wasted a lot of time. "I got my poor mother up here to help me stuff those birds and we finally got them done and loaded up in the car!" And, Shirley did make it downstate in time for the scheduled meal.

Shirley's extra special recipe for those stuffed birds and for her Chocolate Cherry Cake that was served as the dessert on this unforgettable day follow.

ROCK CORNISH HENS WITH WILD RICE STUFFING AND CHERRY SAUCE
4 Servings
4 frozen Rock Cornish Hens, thawed
Salt and pepper

Cherry Sauce: *(Can be made ahead and refrigerated or frozen)*

In saucepan, mix 4 teaspoon cornstarch, ¼ cup sugar, ¼ teaspoon each salt, dry mustard, and ginger.

Drain 1 (1 pound) can water-packed red sour pitted cherries, reserving the liquid.

Add the cherry liquid, ½ cup orange juice, and ¼ cup red currant or red cherry jelly, and a few drops of red food coloring to the mixture in the saucepan.

Cook over medium heat until mixture boils and thickens.

Add cherries.

Stuffing: *1 small onion, chopped*
  Butter or margarine
  ⅓ cup each finely diced ham and mushrooms
  ¾ cup cooked Wild Rice

Saute onions in 2 tablespoons butter until tender and golden brown.

Add ham, mushrooms and rice.

Bring hens to room temperature. Wash inside and out.

Pat dry with paper towels. Sprinkle inside and out with salt and pepper. Fill with Stuffing.

Put in shallow baking pan and roast in preheated 350 degree oven, brushing several times with melted butter. Bake for about 1 hour and 10 minutes.

To Serve: Reheat the Cherry Sauce, if made ahead, and pour over the top of the hens.

And, now for dessert:

CHOCOLATE CHERRY CAKE

1 box chocolate cake mix
1 can cherry pie filling
2 eggs
1 teaspoon almond flavoring

*Combine the above mixture **with a wooden spoon**. (This is very thick and hard to stir). Spread kind of thick in a greased pan (9 x 13-inch size). Bake at 350 degrees for 30 minutes. Let cool.*

Icing: **⅓ cup milk**
  1 cup white sugar
  5 tablespoons butter

Combine the above mixture and let come to a boil. Boil 1 minutes. Remove from the heat. Stir in 1 (6 oz.) package chocolate chips into the mixture. Stir until thick.

Spread on cooled cake. Refrigerate Shirley says that the icing gets thinned if allowed to stay at room temperature. About half-way through your meal, remove the cake from the refrigerator. Cut into squares to be served at the end of the meal. Return the cake to the refrigerator.

Shirley gave me the recipes for some of their other favorites dishes, but none of them have funny stories attached to them—yet. Here they are:

IRISH POTATO CASSEROLE

When Shirley gave me the name of this dish, I thought of how long it had been since I had heard potatoes called "Irish" potatoes. When I was little, I heard this a lot because people used "Irish" to distinguish plain old white potatoes from sweet potatoes. Shirley says that this is absolutely delicious!

8 to 10 medium potatoes
1 (8 oz.) package cream cheese, softened
1 (8 oz.) carton sour cream or a little less
½ cup margarine, melted
¼ cup chopped chives
**1 clove garlic, crushed and minced (or sprinkle in garlic powder
  to taste)**
1 teaspoon salt
Paprika

Cook potatoes until tender and mash. Beat potatoes and cheese with hand-held electric mixer until smooth. Add all other ingredients and beat until well mixed. Place in a 2-quart casserole that has been sprayed with non-stick cooking spray. Sprinkle paprika on top. Cover and refrigerate overnight. Take out of oven 15 minutes before baking.

Bake at 350 degrees for 30 minutes.

Shirley says that if she has refrigerated something like this that has to be baked later, when she takes the dish from the refrigerator, she sets it in warm water for a few minutes to take the chill off the dish.

SOUTHWESTERN TACO PIE

This is a quick, easy, and tasty meal-in-a-dish good for busy people!

½ pound ground beef
1 can (16 oz.) Mexican-style chili hot beans
1 (4 oz.) can chopped green chilies, drained

1 cup shredded cheddar cheese
1 (8 oz.) can crescent rolls
Shredded lettuce
Chopped tomatoes
Sour cream

Brown ground beef and drain. Add beans and chilies and simmer 15 minutes, stirring occasionally. Add ½ cup to ¾ cup cheese. Stir until melted.

Preheat oven to 375 degrees.

Separate crescent rolls into 8 triangles. Arrange the triangles in a 9-inch pie plate so that the wide edges form the rim and the points meet in the center of the plate. Press dough together to seal. Dock the dough with the tines of a fork by pricking the dough in several places to keep the dough from puffing up too much. Bake the dough for 10 to 12 minutes or until golden brown. Spoon meat mixture into prepared crust. Top with lettuce, tomatoes, and cheese. Garnish with sour cream.

I believe that everybody in this family loves chicken, just about any way it is prepared. This is one of Albert's and Shirley's favorite chicken dishes:

CHICKEN CASSEROLE
3 cups chopped cooked chicken
1 small can English peas or one (10 oz.) package frozen peas
1 cup chopped celery
3 boiled eggs
½ of a large jar pimientos or a little more
¼ cup chopped onion
1 can cream of mushroom soup
½ cup mayonnaise
1 teaspoon lemon juice
Salt and pepper, to taste

Mix ingredients together well. The frozen peas add more color. Place into a casserole dish that has been sprayed with non-stick cooking spray. Shirley adds about 1 cup grated cheese on top of the chicken mixture. Top with croutons. Bake at 350 degrees until bubbly.

STRAWBERRY NEOPOLITAN
This is a very good summer dessert... and it's pretty, too!

1 small box instant vanilla pudding
1¼ cups water
1 can condensed low fat milk (not evaporated milk)
1 quart fresh strawberries, sliced
Vanilla wafers
1 package any size miniature chocolate chips
1 (8 oz.) carton whipped topping

Beat vanilla pudding, water and milk together and set aside 5 minutes to thicken. Add whipped topping to preceding mixture and blend well. Layer pudding, wafers, strawberries, and chocolate chips. Repeat layers with pudding on top. Use remaining strawberries and chocolate chips on top for decoration.

BAKED PEARS

Shirley likes to make this close to Christmas. She uses red and green cherries, alternating the colors among the pear halves. It's very pretty.

Place canned pears with some of the pear juice in a rectangular baking dish. Fill the pear centers with cream cheese which has been mixed with honey, to taste. Put a maraschino cherry (red or green) in the center of the cheese-honey mixture. Sprinkle crushed vanilla wafers with cinnamon over the pears. Bake at low heat until pears get barely hot.

FOUR-HOUR BEEF STEW

This is the kind of recipe that is very good on a gloomy cold day when all you want to do is to put on a pot of tea, curl up in your favorite chair with a good book, and let supper cook itself! This recipe came from Shirley's mother.

3 pounds boneless stew beef
6 potatoes, peeled and cut into chunks, quarters, halves, or
 left whole, depending of their size
6 carrots, cut into chunks
6 stalks of celery, cut into 1-inch pieces
12 small onions or the equivalent of halved or quartered larger
 onions—but if you can find them, the small ones are better
2 teaspoons sugar
2 tablespoons tapioca
Pepper to taste

Mix all the above ingredients in a very large bowl. Then, transfer it to a large Dutch oven or pot with a tight-fitting lid. Pour 4 cups or more of vegetable cocktail juice over the meat mixture. Cover with lid. Place into a 275 degree oven. Let this bake for 4 hours. Do not open the oven door. Do not lift the pot lid. Don't even peek!

Sometimes, Albert and Shirley make a breakfast dish they say is wonderful. Here's the recipe:

COUNTRY MORNING BREAKFAST
Cook 6 slices of bacon until crisp. Drain. Crumble.
Cook 4 cups frozen hash brown potatoes in the bacon grease until the potatoes are lightly browned.
Add ½ cup chopped green pepper and 2 tablespoons chopped onion. Season with salt and pepper.
Place uncooked eggs over potatoes. Cover and cook until the eggs are done. This can be done on top of the stove or in a 325-to-350 degree oven.
Sprinkle with crisp bacon. Then, sprinkle with shredded Cheddar cheese.

One of Shirley's favorite menus, and what I believe is her "comfort meal," includes Mush Bread, another of her mother's recipes. She likes to serve this with Baked Pork Tenderloin, Greens (Mustard and Kale mixed) with Sliced Boiled Eggs on top, and Macaroni and Cheese.

MUSH BREAD
To 2 cups scalded milk, add ⅓ cup or a little more grits (quick grits, not the instant). Add ½ teaspoon salt. Cook until thick. Remove from heat. Add 2 beaten eggs and 3 tablespoons melted butter to the grits. Mix well. Place in a round glass baking bowl and bake at 425 degrees for 30 minutes.

I asked Albert about visiting with Aunt Cindy and he said that they didn't see her too often. He said that when he got out of school, he was working for Dunn & Bradstreet and had to go check on one of the country stores. He went down into the country and couldn't find the store. He stopped at a house to get directions and he said,

Aunt Cindy, Uncle Bob, and Grandma Vance in Their Later Years

When the woman came to the door, it scared me. I told her what I needed and she gave me the directions. I then apologized for reacting, or for looking at her the way I did and said to her, 'But, you look so much like my Grandmother!' The woman said, 'Who was your grandmother?' I said, 'Nettie Vance.' The woman said, 'Well, your grandmother was my sister. I'm Cindy.'

Being the last of the litter, "the least little Rather girl" as the Moody family on Carolina Hill called me, or as Lucretia has introduced me, "the youngest grandchild," I guess I always believed that all of the cousins were as close to Aunt Cindy as we were. Our second cousins probably were closer to Aunt Cindy since one of the parents was a brother or sister to Aunt Cindy and to Grandma.

Hazel, my great-uncle Clyde Greene's daughter, said that the main things she remembered about going to Aunt Cindy's for a meal were all the jams and jellies she served in pretty, different-colored dishes with lids.

When asked about her comfort foods, Hazel immediately responded, "Daddy made stack cakes!" I asked, "He made them?" She said, "Oh, yes! He got to be a good cook!" Hazel said that she was never able to make these cakes as good as Uncle Clyde. Stack cakes are a Southern Appalachian tradition which some people have said are probably of German origin. Cake, sometimes containing molasses, is made into thin layers and baked, cooled, and then sandwiched together with cinnamon-spiced apple sauce, cooked dried apples, or apple butter, and topped with the same filling. Following are two versions of Stack Cake, not Uncle Clyde's recipes, but some I have found to be good.

STACK CAKE (WITH MOLASSES)
1 cup firmly packed brown sugar
1 cup shortening
1 cup molasses
1 cup buttermilk
2 eggs, beaten
1 teaspoon baking soda
1 teaspoon ground ginger
Dash of salt
5½ cups all-purpose flour
6⅔ cups apple butter
   Additional apple butter (optional)
   Dried apples (optional)

Combine sugar, shortening, and molasses. Beat until smooth. Add buttermilk, eggs, soda, ginger, and salt. Mix well. Add flour, abut a cup at a time, beating just until blended after each addition (do not overbeat).

Divide dough into 10 portions and place on a greased cookie sheet. Pat into a 10-inch circle.

Bake at 350 degrees for 5-to-7 minutes. Remove to cooling rack.

Stack the layers, spreading about ⅔ cup apple butter between each. If desired, spoon a mound of apple butter on the top of the cake and garnish with dried apples. Yield: One 10-inch cake.

STACK CAKE (WITHOUT MOLASSES)

1 cup butter
2 cups sugar
2 eggs
½ cup milk
2 cups all-purpose flour
4 teaspoons baking powder
½ teaspoon freshly grated nutmeg
1 teaspoon vanilla extract

Cream shortening. Add sugar and cream again. Add eggs and mix well. Sift flour, baking powder, and nutmeg. Add to first mixture, alternating with milk. Add vanilla. Knead in more flour to make stiff dough. Separate dough into twelve equal portions and roll out each one ¼-inch thick. Pat into cake pans and bake in 450 degree oven until a tester inserted into the middle comes out clean. Set layers aside to cool.

Take 1 quart of sweetened applesauce or more if needed.

Add ½ teaspoon allspice and ½ teaspoon cinnamon. Mix well and put this mixture between the cookie layers

Note: Both versions of this cake are better made a day or two ahead of serving so the filling can seep into the cake a bit.

Hazel also mentioned that one of her favorite foods was Aunt Nettie's pumpkin pies. I found the following recipes among Mother's collection. I don't know whether either one is the pie that Grandma made.

PUMPKIN PIE

2 eggs
1½ cups pumpkin
1½ cups milk
⅔ cups brown sugar
Flavoring (amount and kind unspecified)
Butter (amount not given)

No other directions were given

PUMPKIN PIE
For 2 pies

4 eggs, slightly beaten
3½ cups pumpkin
1 ½ cups sugar
¾ teaspoon salt

2 teaspoons cinnamon
1 teaspoon ginger
½ teaspoon cloves
3⅓ cups evaporated milk

Mix ingredients except milk and add it last. Put into 2 uncooked pie shells. Bake at 425 degrees for 15 minutes, reduce to 350 degrees for 45 minutes or until the filling is set.

Hazel said that for Sunday dinner, what we now call lunch, Aunt Bessie, her mother, would wring the head off the chicken; then, Aunt Bessie would cook that chicken for their meal. And, she liked her mother's sweet potatoes and sweet potato pie. She also mentioned "Mama's Stingy Tom Cakes." I asked her what these were and she said, "When Mama made a cake with brown sugar icing, she never would tell us how she made it. All she would say was that she 'just threw it together;' so we started calling the cakes 'Stingy Tom Cakes.'"

The icing was poured over the cake while it was still warm and that's the way it was served and eaten.

Hazel continued, "We once had a goose or duck; anyway, it had blue meat, and I didn't like it!" Uncle Clyde used to set traps for rabbits. "He would fix the rabbits and fry or boil them and make gravy. He used to fish at night and he would fry the fish for breakfast the next morning."

Hazel told me that when they were young, Uncle Clyde and Aunt Bessie let them go to dances and everything. This was something that even my sisters and I couldn't do, a generation later. Mother was never allowed to go to dances; she and Daddy kept the same rule with us. I don't know whether Daddy ever went to a dance or not, but I never heard anything about it. Once when Thelma's or Marie's daughter was getting ready to go to a prom, Mother said, "Well, I used to think that dancing was wrong. I don't know why I thought that. I guess it was because Mama and Papa said it was and I never questioned them." I said, "Well, gee, thanks, Mother, you're about 30 years too late for me," and then we laughed. I don't think I was too warped for not having gone to dances. I wasn't alone; some of my friends couldn't go to them, either.

When the young people Hazel's age had parties, they played Spin the Bottle and Post Office. I was a little surprised by this because I had never heard anyone of her generation talk about games such as these. Of course, when we were younger, we never thought that the older people went through the same stages or phases, or that they even had feelings like we did! She said that she dated quite a bit when she was young and even dated one of Ralph's uncles, Herman, a few times. Ralph's mother's family lived

Left to Right: Conley, Lorena, Great-grandma Greene holding Lawrence, Anna (sister to Conley), Aunt Bessie holding Lester (Hazel's and Orville's brother), and, Hazel.

in the same general neighborhood as Hazel's family.

Hazel said, "Daddy was proud that he taught Ora Lee to be a good cook." Ora Lee was Hazel's sister who died several years ago. She and her husband owned Terry's, Inc., in Bristol, Virginia, a snack foods company. Uncle Clyde's teaching probably came in handy. I remember Ora Lee as always being such a gentle and quiet lady.

Hazel's daughter, Judy, said that some of the stories she had heard about some of the older people reminded her of when she stayed during the day with her Grandma and Grandpa Greene. Hazel's first husband, and Judy's father, Walter Minnick, died some years ago.

I did not know some of Uncle Clyde's children well. But, knowing Hazel, Ora Lee, and Orville, I saw, and still can see in Orville, much of Uncle Clyde and Aunt Bessie in them, especially in the soft voices and smiles.

Orville, the youngest of Uncle Clyde's and Aunt Bessie's children, said that his brother Haskell fell backward while he was sitting in the high chair and was killed. Orville was two or three years old when this happened.

When we talked about going to Aunt Cindy's, Orville said that he remembered when they spent some time at Aunt Cindy's and Uncle Bob's during the winter. "Uncle Bob would heat bricks and wrap them up in towels to keep our feet warm at night when we went to bed."

One person whose family rented Aunt Cindy's house and farm when she no longer lived there said, "That was home! But living in that house did have some drawbacks. For one thing, the house was not insulated, and it got awfully cold during the winter," She said that she used to play in the barn on the hill and that they caught many good fish in Uncle Bob's pond.

Orville said that when he was growing up, candy was his comfort food. When I asked him what kind of candy, he said, "Stick candy, or any kind, just so it was candy!" He continued

Once, when I was in school at Beidleman School, they gave us sample tubes of Pepsodent toothpaste. On the way home, I started eating that toothpaste! It was sweet and I thought it was so good, so I kept eating it as I walked through the fields going home. By the time I got home, I had it all eaten. I was kind of foaming at the mouth, but it tasted good!

Orville said that he remembered when he was little that they would use the milk cans as cars and roll on the bank. When he was six or seven years old, he and some of the other kids found a box of dynamite caps. One of the Morrell boys put one of the caps in a paper bag and lit it. When they lived across the road from Gammon's Mill, they used to play in the creek at the mill.

The first teacher Orville had when they lived in Hickory Tree was Blanche O'Dell (my Aunt Blanche who married Uncle Cloyd, Mother's brother). He said,

She was a good teacher. After school I would sometimes go down to her house and she would help me with my work. I was having trouble writing some of my letters, especially the 'q.' I never could seem to get it right until Blanche told me to remember that the 'q' always had a little curl on it. And, I always remembered after that.

One time when they lived in Hickory Tree, Raymond—Aunt Blanche's brother—pulled the buggy up in the field to a hill. "We got in it and rolled down the hill," Orville said. "When we built wagons," Orville continued, "we made the wagon wheels out of pretty good-size pine logs."

The Mill Pond at Hickory Tree Store was a popular place to play. Orville said, "One winter, I fell all the way through the ice and had to be pulled out. I was only about six or seven."

Some of the other foods Orville mentioned that he liked to eat when he was young, besides candy, were Uncle Clyde's vegetable soup, potatoes, tomatoes, rice, and cabbage. Either he or Hazel said that they could remember when Aunt Bessie made cornbread in a baker in the open fire place in their dining room. This was when they lived in Great-grandpa and Great-grandma Greene's house.

Lorena said, "Mama's creamed corn," was her comfort food. "I never could make corn like she did. And, the grandchildren always want corn," she said. I really doubt that the following recipe is anywhere near the way Great-aunt Julia cooked corn, but it is a creamed corn that is very good.

CREAMED CORN

Select the number of ears of corn you will need to feed your family. Estimate about two per person. Shuck the corn, removing all the silk. Rinse the corn off.

Over a bowl or container to hold the corn and corn milk, using a sharp knife and starting at the tassel end of the corn, begin cutting the kernels from the cob. When all the kernels have been cut from one ear of corn, scrape with a knife down the corn to remove the milk. When all the corn has been cut and milk scraped out, place the corn with some butter added into a saucepan over medium heat.

Sprinkle the corn with salt and pepper. Stir and cook the corn until it gets hot. Then, add some whole milk or milk mixed with half and half to cover the corn. Turn heat to medium-low, cover, and let the corn cook until most of the milk has been reduced to make a creamy-like sauce. Correct seasoning, and add more salt if needed. This is not even like our own Mother made; she cooked the corn in a little bit of salted water, added "thickening", etc. The method given here is much easier and still tastes good, even if this is not the traditional method.

Another favorite food Lorena mentioned was Peas and Dumplings. Since she was the second person in the family to mention these, I asked how they were made. She said,

Well, you cook your fresh peas until they are just about done. Put in butter and cream; and, then, drop in your dumplings, just like you do other dumplings. Of course, now, you can hardly get fresh peas, and the milk is 'blue John.'

"Blue John" is an expression I have heard Mother use; it means skim milk or milk which is not creamy—it is very low in butterfat.

If you would like to try these, I have devised a recipe which may approximate the dish Lorena mentioned. You may have to modify the cream sauce to get it as thick or as thin as you want.

PEAS AND DUMPLINGS

3 cups fresh peas
Water to cover
Salt to taste
Cook peas until almost done.
Add: 1½ to 2 cups or more milk mixed with 1 tablespoon flour
  2 tablespoons butter
   Bring to a boil.

DUMPLINGS

1 cup flour
2 teaspoons baking powder
1 teaspoon shortening
½ teaspoon salt
¼ cup water or milk
  Mix together the flour, salt, and baking powder. Rub in shortening with your fingers. Add water or milk to make a dough stiff enough to drop from a spoon. Drop onto the boiling peas and cover tightly. Cook for 10 to 12 minutes. Do not remove the cover until the end of the cooking period.

  Lorena says that these days, you can use canned biscuits, cutting them in half or quarters instead of making the dumplings from scratch. And, some people would not add flour to make the sauce thicker.

Lorena also mentioned that she liked brown beans, cornbread, and buttermilk, and, chicken and dumplings. One of her two daughters always liked vegetable soup and fried chicken. She said, "Of course, now, they like to have lasagna and those kinds of dishes, too."

At one reunion, Lorena's daughter, Carolyn, brought tabbouleh. She used an old crock as the serving bowl and said that she wanted to bring her mother's dipper as the serving spoon. Lorena told her that it was too big; so, Carolyn searched all the antique shops lining State Street trying to find another unusual piece she could use as a spoon. When some of my other relatives saw that crock and that salad, they thought that I had brought it because they said it looked like something I would do. Evidently, Carolyn and I both get tired of sameness in our food and we like to use unexpected serving pieces. This is a recipe for Tabbouleh that was given to me by my sister-in-law, Liz:

TABBOULEH
1 cup bulgur cracked wheat
¼ cup - ½ cup - 1 cup finely chopped fresh mint
1 cup finely chopped parsley
½ cup finely chopped onion
½ to ¾ cup chopped tomatoes
½ cup extra virgin olive oil
¼ to ½ cup lemon juice
Salt and pepper to taste

Soak the bulgur in water for one hour. Drain and squeeze out as much of the water as you can. Mix the bulgur with the onion, salt and pepper, crushing the onion into the wheat. Add parsley, mint, oil, lemon juice, and tomato. Start with the least amounts given and adjust to your taste. It is better to be able to add more mint and lemon juice than to put the full amount in and have it too minty or too sour. Sometimes, I leave out the mint, altogether, even though adding it makes the dish more authentic. Correct the seasonings. May be served immediately or refrigerated and served later. This can also be made using cooked white beans instead of the bulgur, but then I guess the name changes. But whatever the name, I love it! I think it is good, even, put into pita bread and eaten as a "sandwich."

Two stories Lorena told me about growing up follow:

When I was a little girl, we had a horse name Bird. We lived down on the river (Holston River) and were going to Hickory Tree to church; it was in the afternoon. Mama was on the side saddle; she put Lawrence, my brother, in front of her. I was behind her. When we got to the creek, there was ice on the creek. Bird got scared and dumped us off in the creek. We went back home and never made it to church that afternoon. Sometimes we traveled in a buggy.

Lorena with Her Dolls and Her Brother Lawrence.
Their Dog's Name Was "Old Lead"

Lorena talked about going to Aunt Cindy's and said,

We used to walk to Aunt Cindy's. The road was muddy. We would walk through the field and crawl through the fence to get to the house. It was about two or two-and-one-half miles from our house to Aunt Cindy's.

Lorena calls herself "the antique of the family" since she is the "oldest" of all the Greene cousins; and, I use the term "oldest" loosely here. Lorena is still very active and still likes to laugh. She is a family treasure and the best antique I know!

When asked about his comfort food, Conley, son of Grandma's sister Rosa (Rosie), said, "I'll always remember Mama's blackberry dumplings with whipped cream." Two recipes for fruit dumplings follow. The first one is done on top of the stove; the second one is baked. You might want to try one or both, but they may not taste like Aunt Rosie's did.

BLACKBERRY DUMPLINGS
In a large saucepan, combine:

3 pints blackberries, picked over and washed
¾ cup water
1 cup sugar, or more to taste
1 to 2 tablespoons butter

Mix together: 2 cups flour
3 tablespoons sugar
1 teaspoon salt
1 egg
3½ teaspoons baking powder
Milk—enough to make a stiff batter

Place the blackberries, water, sugar, and butter on the stove and bring to a boil. Drop the dumpling batter, a spoonful at a time into the boiling mixture. Cover with lid and cook over medium heat for about 15 to 20 minutes. Taste. Serve with cream, real whipped cream, or vanilla ice cream.

BERRY DUMPLINGS

⅓ cup sugar
⅔ cup water
½ teaspoon vanilla extract
1 cup all-purpose flour
2 tablespoons sugar
1½ teaspoons baking powder
½ teaspoon salt
4 tablespoons butter
½ cup milk
1 pint (about 2 cups), fresh berries—blackberries, raspberries, or
 strawberries
1 tablespoon sugar

In a saucepan, combine the ⅓ cup sugar and water. Bring to boil. Reduce heat and simmer, uncovered, 5 minutes. Stir in vanilla. Combine flour, 2 tablespoons sugar, baking powder and salt. Cut in butter till mixture is crumbly.

Add milk and stir, just till well combined. Place berries in a 1½ quart casserole. Pour hot sugar mixture over. Immediately drop dumpling dough in 8 to 10 spoonfuls over berries. Sprinkle dumplings with the remaining 1 tablespoon sugar. Bake in very hot oven at 450 degrees for 25 to 30 minutes, or till dumplings are done. Serve warm from casserole into individual dessert dishes. Makes 4 to 5 servings. Serve with cream, real whipped cream, or vanilla ice cream.

Conley also likes biscuits and gravy and hotcakes. He said, "You know, up until a few years ago, if you went to a restaurant and asked for biscuits and gravy, they thought you were crazy!" He also likes peas and dumplings and beans and dumplings. He said, "Why, you can make dumplings out of anything!"

Other favorite foods that he now misses are his wife's meat loaf and her sourdough rolls. He said, "You know, not everybody can make a good meat loaf. Beulah made hers with some vegetables in it. Dwight used to take a big dish of it to work with him when they had a meeting and those people had a feast!" About the sourdough rolls he said, "Oh... h...h. , they're good!" Beulah died several years ago, but was able to enjoy many of the family get-togethers; and, she enjoyed having company at their house.

Conley and Beulah lived with us when I was a tiny baby. Their daughter, Norma Jean, probably was just a few months younger than I. Like many in this family, Conley likes to sing and was choir director at River Bend Baptist Church for many years. Norma Jean played the piano really well and also sang. She died of cancer in the early 1980s.

Conley was one of the cousins who worked at Bristol Door & Lumber Company. Part of the time, he worked for Daddy. Daddy had to retire in 1962 after he had a stroke. Conley worked for years after that and became the superintendent of the company. Evidently, Conley has always liked to hunt, especially birds, and has been known to have his freezer well-supplied with quail and pheasant.

Talking with Gene, another of Aunt Rosie's sons, is always a treat. Just about anything I talk with him about somehow gets turned until we are talking about music; however, his first response about his comfort food was, "hot potato soup." He then mentioned cornbread, October beans, fat back or salt pork, and kraut on biscuits. "Kraut on biscuits" was a new one to me; or, as Mother used to say, "That's a new wrinkle on my horn!" However Gene said that it was good and that he used to take it to school for lunch.

Gene's wife, Jerlis, said that she knew what was meant by pretty white kraut. It is almost a pure white, not like the yellowish kraut most of us buy these days. Jerlis said that her mother used to use a cut cream can to chop her cabbage for kraut. Some people, years ago, also cut a can in half and used it as a biscuit cutter. The recipe for Jerlis' Kraut is as follows: Chop cabbage. Put into sterilized quart jars. Add 1 teaspoon salt, 1 teaspoon sugar, and 1 teaspoon vinegar. Cover with boiling water and seal.

I had been told that after Gene's mother died, when he was very young, he lived at Aunt Cindy's some. After he no longer lived there, he said that the special attraction for him in going to Aunt Cindy's for a visit was not the food particularly, but, that,

> ... it was Dilla's fiddle! They had ordered the fiddle for $3.45 from Sears and Roebuck. I used to try to play a song at night while I was sitting next to the stove in the kitchen. The fire showing through the grate in the stove gave the only light I had. They wouldn't let me turn on other lights—it was expensive. They were high class; they had carbide lights when other people used oil lamps. I would practice and go into where they were sitting in the living room and play what I thought was sounding like a tune. I would say, 'Does that sound like anything?' She would say, 'Lord, no, go back and practice some more!' ...And, do you know? She gave me that fiddle!

Then, he said, "I've been told Mama played the fiddle, but I never heard her play."

Gene is still playing the fiddle—not the same one—but a fiddle. When he, his brother, J. Lee, and some other people including Lawrence, Lorena's brother, were younger, they used to walk from their house in Hickory Tree to radio station WOPI in Bristol, Tennessee, to play. He said that they used to wade across Beidleman Creek holding their instruments above their heads so they wouldn't get wet. J. Lee played the fiddle and guitar. Lawrence also played the guitar and did up until he had a severe stroke.

WOPI was the only radio station in Bristol at that time. J. Lee says that this was back in 1938-39. They walked to the station to be on Saturday Afternoon Matinee which came on, live at 2 o'clock, for a half-hour show. The announcer for the program was Tennessee Ernie Ford. Also on the show was a comedian who was called "Chitlins," but whose real name was Guy Carroll, according to J. Lee. Mr. Carroll also played the banjo with the band. J. Lee said that the other members of the band were Ed Vance who played fiddle, Lonnie Carrier who played mandolin, and Frank Richards who played guitar.

When I related these stories to Reba, she said, "We used to sing on the Saturday Afternoon Matinee, too!" She and the older sisters sang songs like, "Blue Hawaii." Reba was a tiny little girl then and had just suddenly started singing the third part. Thelma was in the seventh or eighth grade. A girl who went to the high school and was a friend played the piano for them. Thelma said that when they first started singing together sitting in the swing on the front porch, they sang to the top of their voices. She said that Tom Warren, one of Aunt Blanche's relatives, said that he could hear them singing all the way over to his house on Cedar Street hill, several blocks from our house.

Gene has won numerous awards at various fiddling conventions over the years. Many of these awards, newspaper and magazine articles, autographed photographs of some of the now-famous people he has played music with, and other memorabilia line the walls of his barber shop, The Star Barber Shop & Stylist, in Bristol, Virginia.

One of the attractions at his barber shop is hearing the men who come in pick up their fiddles, mandolins, and guitars, and play bluegrass music. Because of the atmosphere in the barber shop and because of Gene's personality, he is now featured as a character in the "Gasoline Alley" comic strip. Some of the people who play with him in the shop and some who have played with him in various bands have been persuaded to come to our cousins' meetings to play for us; and, some flat footin' is done. I told Gene once that I couldn't play music by ear, he said, "I'll bet I could teach you!" And, I'll bet he could, too!

When I asked J. Lee about his comfort foods, he said, "An apple." Even when he was younger, fruit was his favorite. He said that Uncle Bob and Aunt Cindy used to raise huge watermelons. He also remembers the apples they used to have. He continued,

> When I was younger, I remember Uncle Bob going out behind the wood shed to get apples. He kept a barrel under the drip of the woodshed and put the apples in that barrel. The rain would drip into the barrel and onto the apples, but even if they froze, if left, they would not ruin. So, the apples were always good!

J. Lee said that the same process could be used to keep pumpkins fresh. He said that Aunt Cindy was a wonderful cook and he remembered her ham and gravy more than anything else.

Later, he also talked about the popcorn balls they used to eat when they were little. He said that the "formula for them was to mix together honey, molasses, and Karo syrup." He said, "I don't know whose formula it was, whether it was Aunt Cindy's, Aunt Nettie's (my Grandma's) or Aunt Ermine's." He also said that sometimes they had maple syrup over popcorn. I wonder if the "formula" was like the following recipe:

POPCORN BALLS
4 quarts popped corn, slightly salted
1½ cups sugar
¼ cup honey

¼ **cup corn syrup**
⅔ **cup water**
⅓ **cup sorghum molasses**
3 tablespoons butter
1 teaspoon vanilla
1 teaspoons vinegar

Pop the corn and remove the hard kernels. Combine the sugar, syrup, honey, molasses, and water. Bring to a boil, stirring only until sugar is dissolved. Cook to the hard ball stage when dropped in cold water, 270 degrees on a candy thermometer.

Add butter, vinegar, and vanilla and blend into the mixture. Pour hot syrup slowly over the corn, stirring to evenly coat each kernel. Shape into balls and let stand in a cool place. Wrap the balls, individually, in waxed paper.

Mary Lee, J. Lee's wife, is the person who told me what water gravy was. She said that her Mother made water gravy sometimes when the cow had gone dry or when they didn't have very much milk. "When she was running low on flour," Mary Lee said, "Mother made batter bread that used less flour and had the pouring consistency of cake batter."

When I first asked J. Lee if he remembered going to Aunt Cindy's, he said, "Oh! Yea! The big holly trees had leaves so thick you couldn't even see through them, and they had great big red berries!" I asked him if they ever did anything with those berries. He said, "Yea, we strung them using a needle and thread and hung them on the Christmas tree. Dilla (Sharp) taught us how to do that." That was a better way to use the berries than the experience Marie and I had, I thought; but, our experience was still fun. The last time I saw Aunt Cindy's front yard, the holly trees were still there. They didn't look quite as big as they did when we were little; but, we still remember. And, we hope the new owners of Aunt Cindy's house will take care of the house and those special trees.

Because of my experimenting in the kitchen, Ralph has learned to eat just about anything—including some of the gosh-awful messes I created. He has said that he is tired of being my guinea pig; but then, he still takes samples. The only things I cannot quite sneak by him, and I've tried many times, are eggplant dishes and anything that has artichokes or artichoke hearts in it. He also didn't like cauliflower until he ate some at a conference we attended in San Francisco one year and now he loves it. I keep hoping for the eggplant and artichokes because I love both of them.

From his childhood, he remembers banana pudding, rice pudding, and corn pudding. I can never make any of these dishes just the way he remembers them from home. He also liked biscuits with fried fat back and mustard. At least for awhile, I believe that one of his comfort foods was cubed steak. Then, I came along.

When I was going to cook the first real meal for him before we were married, I asked him what he wanted and he said, "Country style steak." I tried, but the steak stuck to the skillet; the green beans tasted raw; the mashed potatoes had lumps; and, the gravy tasted scorched! Poor man, he still married me.

Thelma says that Henry still laughs about the time I had made Tomato Aspic or something like that and took it to Mother's for one of our family meals. While everybody was eating, Ralph said about the aspic, "Well, it's like Brill Cream... A little dab 'ill do ya."

Ralph About Age 5
(The Closest He Ever Came to Riding on the Range)

One of Ralph's mother's favorite foods when she was growing was corn pudding. She also remembers that at Christmas they always had oysters which her daddy bought at the fish market in Bristol.

Our family likes oysters, too, but I have never fixed them at Christmas, particularly. Most of the time, everybody just likes them pan fried (unless we go out to eat and then they take them as they are fried at the restaurant). Pan-frying oysters is very easy. (I never, or rarely, dip meat into egg wash before dipping it into the dry mixture, as some people do. Sometimes the "crust" may not stay on too well, but it still tastes good).

PAN FRIED OYSTERS

1 pint (or more) oysters
All-purpose flour mixed with a little cornmeal
Salt (go easy on this)
Pepper
Shortening, butter, or oil for frying

Check the oysters to make sure that you do not fry any pieces of shell. Roll in the flour and cornmeal mixture. Melt the shortening or butter (or pour in a small amount of oil) in a heavy skillet. Add the oysters; sprinkle lightly with salt (if desired) and a few grinds of black pepper. Brown quickly (do not overcook).

Another oyster dish we like is Scalloped Oysters. I believe that I like these more than the rest of my family, though. Here's how I make this dish:

SCALLOPED OYSTERS

One pint of oysters, in this dish, will serve about 4 people

In a medium saucepan, melt about ½ stick butter or margarine.

Crush ¼ of a package (one stack) of saltine crackers into coarse crumbs.

Add the cracker crumbs to the melted butter. Toss to coat the crumbs.

In a small rectangular baking dish, put a layer of cracker crumbs, a layer of oysters (be sure to check and see that you don't add any shell pieces), another layer of crumbs. Pour the oyster liquor over the top layer of crumbs (check the liquid for bits of shell, too). Then, pour about ¼ cup of milk or half and half over the top.

Place in a 400 degree oven for about half an hour.

Ralph's mother, who we call Gran, said that her mother made all kinds of cakes for Christmas— especially Lady Baltimore Cake. She said that she hadn't had one of those in years. So, the next Christmas, I made her one. This is the recipe I used:

LADY BALTIMORE CAKE

3 cups sifted flour
3 teaspoons baking powder
¼ teaspoon salt
3 egg whites

½ cup shortening at room temperature
1¾ cup sugar
½ cup water
1 teaspoon vanilla extract
¼ teaspoon almond extract
¾ cup milk

Sift together the flour, baking powder and salt. Beat egg whites in a small bowl at high speed until stiff but not dry. In another bowl beat shortening and sugar together at high speed until fluffy. Add water, vanilla and almond extract; beat at high speed for 1 minute. Mixture will look curdled. Working quickly, add flour mixture and milk alternately while beating at low speed for 2 to 3 minutes. Fold in beaten egg whites and pour into two 9-inch round cake pans that have been greased, lined with waxed paper, and the paper greased. Bake at 375 degrees for 25 to 30 minutes or until cake tester inserted in center comes out clean. Leave cake in pans standing on cake racks for 5 minutes. Turn out on racks and remove paper. Cool completely before filling and frosting with Lady Baltimore Frosting.

LADY BALTIMORE FROSTING

1⅔ cups sugar
½ cup hot water
¼ teaspoon cream of tartar
¼ teaspoon salt
4 egg whites
1 teaspoon vanilla extract
¼ teaspoon almond extract
⅓ cup finely chopped figs
¼ cup chopped seedless raisins (golden)
¼ cup finely chopped pecans

In the top of a double boiler, mix together: the sugar, hot water, cream of tartar, salt, egg whites. Beat one minute with a hand-held beater or electric hand-held mixer. Place over boiling water and beat until the mixture will stand in peaks probably 4 to 5 minutes. Remove from heat. Stir in vanilla and almond extracts. Divide frosting in half. To half of it, add the figs, raisins, and pecans.

Set the cake on a plate to frost. Use the fig, raisin, pecan mixture to place between cake layers. Use the plain frosting to ice the top and sides of cake. Decorate with red and green candied cherries, the green cut in the shape leaves and the red ones, halved with cut sides down.

Ralph's daddy, Carl, was good at everything he tried, I think. He wrote poetry, songs, was an ordained minister, a master brick mason, had earned a degree from King College where he was Class Poet and had an advanced degree from East Tennessee State Teachers College, now East Tennessee State University. In addition to all these things, Mr. O'Dell was a teacher and a school principal. He also coached basketball. And, in his spare time one or two winters, he even made some snow shoes and some skis.

Ralph said that he thought that brains were probably his daddy's comfort food—"He loved them!" According to Ralph's mother, Mr. O'Dell cooked them, too! She said, with a laugh, "I didn't cook anything I didn't like, so if he wanted them, he cooked them!" Since he could do so many things so well, he probably cooked well, too. I'm sorry I never met him. He died before Ralph and I knew each other.

One of Mr. O'Dell's classmates at King College was Katherine Kesner who became a math teacher at Tennessee High. When Marie sang solos for the chapel programs there, Miss Kesner played the piano for her. When Ralph got to high school, Miss Kesner rode herd on him because she knew what he was capable of doing from having known his dad.

On my very first day at Tennessee High, I felt a peck-peck-peck on my shoulder and turned around. There was Miss Kesner (now Mrs. Bob Elliott). She said, "You're Marie's sister, aren't you?" I thought, "Oh, no! Not again!" All the way through school I seemed to live in the shadow of my brother and sisters and what they had done—from Hobart's aggravating the teachers with his pranks to my sisters' goodness—and here that shadow was again, or so I thought.

(One special teacher I believe we all had was Miss Mary Hedrick. She taught English when I was in the eighth grade. She had been Hobart's teacher years before and he had played jokes on her and Miss Wingfield, the social studies teacher. Miss Hedrick was a wonderful teacher, as was Miss Wingfield, but many thought they were too strict and expected too much from their students. They did expect much—they expected us to learn. Once, in Miss Hedrick's class, we had to memorize a poem and recite it in front of the class. At that time, I was very shy and hated to get up in front of people to do anything; and, in class, if I was called on for an answer, I turned every shade of red, even if I knew the correct answer to the question. Reba suggested that I do "Invictus" as my poem and she made me practice saying it in front of a mirror, using the pauses and tone of voice as she had coached me. On the day that we were to do our recitations, my hands got cold and clammy and I was a nervous wreck. I made it through the poem without any problem.

When I sat down, Miss Hedrick said, "You practiced in front of a mirror, didn't you?" All the kids in the class just stared at me while I turned purple. I responded, "Yes ma'am." And, I thought, "Oh, no! Reba taught me wrong!" Then, Miss Hedrick said, "That's what all of you should do!" Then, addressing me, she asked, "Who taught you to do that?" I said, "My sister." Miss Hedrick then smiled one of her quiet smiles. I know that smile now as a smile of satisfaction because she knew that she had been a good teacher].

I never had a class under Katherine, as she now wants us to call her, but I heard some of the students talking that she expected too much—she, too, like those in elementary and junior high, during those years, expected the students to learn and to earn their grades. And, we did.

During the summer before I returned to college after Lynette and Linda were in school, I asked Katherine if she could tutor me in algebra. She came to our house to get me on the right track again. (It had been eighteen years since I had the second year of algebra in high school and I didn't want to walk into a college algebra class practically cold turkey). One of the days she came to see how I was doing, I had made a Pound Cake. We had some of it and coffee during the afternoon and I forgot to give Katherine a spoon to stir her coffee. I'll bet she wondered then what kind of a wife Ralph had chosen and what kind of a daughter-in-law I would have made for Carl, had he lived. Here is the recipe for the Pound Cake I served Katherine. My sister-in-law, Liz, gave it to me and it is one of our favorites.

POUND CAKE

1 cup butter
2 cups sugar
4 eggs, unbeaten
1 teaspoon vanilla extract
1 teaspoon lemon flavoring
½ teaspoon almond flavoring
3 cups sifted flour
½ teaspoon baking soda
½ teaspoon baking powder
¾ teaspoon salt
1 cup buttermilk

Cream butter and sugar thoroughly. Add eggs one at a time, beating well after each. Add flavorings. Sift dry ingredients together and add to the creamed mixture alternately with buttermilk. Beat after each addition. Place in a greased and floured tube pan. Bake in a slow oven at 325 degrees for 1 hour and 10 minutes or until done. Let cool in the pan for a few minutes and then remove to a rack. When it has cooled, sprinkle with powdered sugar, if you want. This is better made a day ahead of serving; or, make in the morning and serve in the evening to give the lemon and other flavor a chance to develop more. Don't forget the spoons to stir your coffee.

We have seen Katherine and Bob many times since the days she came to help me out and cherish the small amount of time we get to share from attending concerts, to environmental meetings, to our high school classes' reunions. She will always be in our hearts just as she has carried all of her "children," as she calls the former students in her heart all these years.

Several years ago, Don, Ralph's oldest brother, said that he loved Tomato Gravy. At that time, I had never heard of Tomato Gravy. Sometime later, I thought of that and found a recipe that sounded like what he had mentioned. I made it and Ralph immediately asked, "What's that?" I said, "Tomato gravy." He responded, "That's not tomato gravy!" I had fried bacon and then dusted tomato slices with flour and browned them in the drippings. After removing the tomato slices from the skillet, I had made gravy with the remaining drippings and served all this over toast. Later, their mother told me that to make Tomato Gravy, "You fry the bacon, remove it, make gravy, and then add chopped, canned tomatoes to the gravy." I have never attempted to make tomato gravy again. I have heard since then, from people who are knowledgeable about Tomato Gravy, that you don't eat the gravy on toast. You pour it over opened biscuits.

Don was an executive with Raytheon in Massachusetts. Anticipating retirement, he bought a lobster boat and started a business. The boat was docked in Marblehead where they lived. One of our most memorable vacations just a few years before his early death, was spent on the boat setting and pulling the traps. Ralph and Liz had the job of banding the lobsters, which we took home for dinner. In addition, Lynette got to eat a small flounder she had caught while fishing off the boat.

One of our favorite New England foods is a Lobster Roll. We were introduced to them during our first trip there. Now, every once in awhile, when we wish we had one, we make them inland, but they are just not the same. Perhaps it's the atmosphere and the smell of the sea in the air that make the difference. Below is a recipe for a simple Lobster Salad to fill the roll. But, first, you have to cook the lobster.

To make two or three—and if you stretch it, four Lobster Rolls—you will need at least two lobsters weighing 1½ pounds each. Be sure that the lobsters are active when you buy them. In a large pot of rapidly boiling water, add some salt. Put the lobsters, head first, into the boiling water (turn your head away if you must) and immediately put a lid on the pot. Let the water come back to a second boil. Cook for about 10 minutes (if you have larger lobsters, add some additional time, but don't cook more than 20 to 25 minutes even if you have 3-pounders). At the end of the cooking time, remove the pot lid and retrieve the lobsters with kitchen tongs. Hold the lobster upside down to drain as much water out as possible. Let cool enough to handle with your hands.

Then, cut the underneath side of each lobster with kitchen shears. Take out the sand sac near the head and the intestinal vein and discard. Don't be alarmed by the greenish pate-like material you may find. This is toma-lley and is good eaten on saltines, some people believe. Twist off the claws and crack them. Twist the tail off. Twist off the little legs or feelers. Take the meat out of the claws and put into a bowl. Remove the tail meat and put into the bowl with the claw meat. Now, you have removed just about all the "real" meat you can—at least enough to make the salad. While you are making the salad, you can put the shell, the feelers, and any other parts except what you have discarded at the beginning, into a pot. Add water, half a stalk of celery, a bit of onion, and a carrot, and a pepper corn or two, if you want, and make a little lobster "stock" that you can use to make chowders or soups. After cooking for a few minutes, strain out the shell and vegetables. Let the liquid cool and then pour in a freezer container (or freezer bag) and place in the freezer. Now here's the recipe for salad:

LOBSTER SALAD FOR LOBSTER ROLLS

Cut the meat of two lobsters into about ½-inch chunks. The tail meat will probably be a bit tougher than the claw meat so you may want to cut it smaller.

Add a sprinkle of lemon juice to the lobster meat—just a tiny bit.

Then, add 1 stalk of diced celery.

Add mayonnaise, 1 tablespoon at a time, or less, until you have a mixture that is moist, but not overpowered with the mayonnaise.

Add salt and pepper, to taste. You will need very little salt.

Be sure you don't eat all the salad just tasting for seasoning.

Have on hand some Hard Rolls. Heat in the oven, wrapped in aluminum foil for a few minutes.

Slice the rolls in half, horizontally, and remove some of the soft part in the middle. That's just too much bread! Leave about a ½-inch shell. Then, put the lobster salad into the hollowed-out places in the rolls, dividing the salad among the number of people you are serving. All you need to offer with this is some potato chips and something to drink.

One of Ralph's favorite week-day meals for years now, especially during the winter, is an adaptation of a recipe I heard about from Marblehead. The recipe calls for haddock fillets that have been "salted down at the fish market." Since, in our area, we had no variety of salted fish and still rarely have even salt cod, I use fresh mild-flavored fish. Here's the recipe:

MARBLEHEAD FISH DINNER

Boil peeled and quartered potatoes in salted water to which some butter has been added. Keep the potatoes warm.

In a separate saucepan, boil quartered onions in salted water to which some butter has been added. Keep the onions warm.

If you have nice fresh small beets, cook them washed, but unpeeled, in slightly salted water. When done, cover with cold water and slip the skins off. Slice into ¼-inch thick slices, or open a can of tiny whole beets or sliced beets. Keep the beets warm. Prepare rashers: Fry out cubed salt pork until most of the grease is extracted and nice crunchy "cracklins" as result. Keep the rashers in the grease and keep warm—but do not leave sitting on the stove eye to scorch.

Cook the fish fillets in salted water until it flakes easily. Don't boil the fish furiously, just let it simmer.

Cook fresh fillets in salted water until done.

To assemble: On a large platter, place the fish in the center and surround with the cooked vegetables. Re-heat the rashers in grease if they have cooled too much. Pour the grease over the fish and vegetables and sprinkle the rashers over.

This may sound horrible, and the beets will begin to color the potatoes and the fish, but it is absolutely wonderful in flavor! It is a complete meal, with bread, of course. We have French bread with it.

When we were talking about comfort foods, Lynette, immediately said that her comfort food was, "Chicken and dumplings." Linda's comfort foods are, "Grandma Rather's fried chicken and gravy and green beans, but mostly her pies!" And, Linda remembers the special pie server that Mother always used to get the pie out of the pie plate.

Most Sunday afternoons, we went to visit Mother and Daddy. Just about every Sunday, Mother would have made at least one kind of pie to serve all of us, Thelma's and Marie's families included, and the pies were usually the meringue cream pies. After Daddy died in 1976, Mother continued the Sunday afternoon pies until later in life when she was not always able to do all the work involved. Still, most of the times, she had something sweet for everybody. The memories of those pies and the other sweets are still a comfort to many in the family especially on a cold, gloomy, Sunday afternoon. Among Mother's recipes was one for the filling for Banana Cream Pies. This, evidently, is the way she made it before the use of pudding and pie filling mixes became popular:

FILLING FOR TWO BANANA PIES
2½ cups milk (1¼ cups canned, or evaporated milk, diluted with water)
¾ cup sugar
a little salt ¼ teaspoon or less
4 tablespoons cornstarch
Yolks of 4 medium sized eggs. Reserve the whites for meringue
Cook until thick. Add 2 tablespoons butter and 1 teaspoon vanilla. Cool the filling.

Make 1 recipe Basic Pastry for Pies (see Index)
2 large bananas
When the crusts and filling have cooled, slice a banana into each crust. Cover with cooled filling. Make a basic meringue (See Index) to cover the filling and bake until golden brown. Cool before serving.

One of the sweets that Mother made, Apple Nut Pudding, became a favorite with the whole family. This is the kind of dessert that begs for cooler weather. Carol, one of my childhood friends, says that one of the first things she thinks about and makes in the Fall is this pudding. She makes it every year and is reminded of my family. I believe that Aunt Cindy gave the recipe to Mother, but to us, it was always Mother's. It is delicious!

MOTHER'S APPLE NUT PUDDING
Step 1: Mix together
         1 cup white sugar
         1 stick oleo margarine or butter
         1 egg
Step 2: Mix with the above ingredients
         1 cup flour
         ½ teaspoon cinnamon

¼ teaspoon salt
¼ teaspoon nutmeg
1 teaspoon soda
Step 3: 2 cups diced tart apples washed and peeled
2 teaspoons vanilla
Add this to the previous mixture.

Preheat oven to 375 degrees. Grease a 9 x 15-inch size baking pan. Pour the apple mixture into the prepared pan and sprinkle with about one cup of chopped pecans. Bake for about 30 minutes. Cut in squares to serve with ice cream or whipped cream. This is good warm or cooled. NOTE: If you prefer to use a glass pan, reduce the baking temperature to 350 degrees.

One of the quickest desserts Mother made was an Oatmeal Cake. This, too, was a favorite. Here is the recipe:

MOTHER'S OATMEAL CAKE

Pour 1 ½ cups boiling water over 1 cup oats
 (quick-cooking oats are fine; however, do not use
 today's instant oatmeal). Let cool.
Mix: 1 cup brown sugar
1 cup white sugar
½ cup vegetable oil or melted margarine
2 eggs
Mix with the above ingredients
1 teaspoon baking soda
1 teaspoon ground cinnamon
½ teaspoon salt

Fold in the oats. Bake in a greased pan at 350 degrees for 30 minutes.

Sauce for Oatmeal Cake:
Mix together ⅓ cup soft margarine
1⅓ cups brown sugar packed
¼ cup canned evaporated milk

Add coconut or pecans or both if desired. Mother always used both. Pour over the baked cake and put under the broiler until it bubbles.

One of the all-time favorites, especially of her grandchildren, that Mother made was her Chocolate Chip Cookies. These have filled many "care packages" and were always included in with the Christmas gifts sent to family members who lived away from home. Here's Mother's recipe:

MOTHER'S CHOCOLATE CHIP COOKIES

Cream together: **1 cup shortening**
½ cup white sugar
1 cup brown sugar, firmly packed
2 teaspoons vanilla
Fold in 2 eggs, well beaten.

Beat entire mixture.

Sift in: **2 cups plus 8 tablespoons all-purpose flour**
1 teaspoon baking soda
1 teaspoon salt

Add sifted dry ingredients to creamed mixture.
Stir in 1 cup pecan meats.
Drop by small spoonfuls onto greased baking sheets and bake in moderate oven at 350 to 375 degrees for 10 minutes.

While most of the following recipes are not our "comfort foods," they are dishes that the four of us like, as well as some of the other family members and friends including our daughters' high school and college friends. I suppose they could be called, "Recipes from Enie's Bar & Grille" or "Recipes from Hotel O'Dell," the nicknames given to our kitchen and to our house.

DINNER ROLLS

In a large mixing bowl: Pour 1 cup boiling water over 1 cup shortening; ½ cup sugar; 1 teaspoon salt. Blend and cool slightly. Add: 3 beaten eggs; 2 packages yeast dissolved in 1 cup warm water; 6 to 7 cups unbleached flour. Blend well. Cover the bowl tightly with plastic wrap and refrigerate for a few hours. Knead dough, roll out, cut like biscuits or form into the desired shape. I always dip the dough into melted butter and fold them over like "pocket book" rolls. Place in a baking pan (9 x 13-inches) or place on a baking sheet. Let rise until doubled. Bake at about 400 degrees for 15 to 20 minutes or until lightly browned. This makes 3 to 4 dozen rolls, depending on how thick you roll the dough. The dough will keep for about a week so you can take out what you need and keep the remainder in the refrigerator.

HOMEMADE LOAF BREAD

1 envelope dry yeast
½ cup very warm water
3 tablespoons sugar
2 cups milk
2 tablespoons butter
1 tablespoon salt
7 or 8 cups all-purpose flour (sifted)

Sprinkle yeast into water in a 1 cup measure; stir in ½ teaspoon sugar. Stir until yeast dissolves. Let stand, undisturbed, to proof until bubbly and double in volume—about 10 minutes.

Combine remaining sugar, milk, butter and salt in small saucepan; heat just until butter melts. Pour into large bowl; cool to lukewarm. Stir in yeast.

Stir in 3 cups flour; beat until smooth. Gradually stir in enough flour to make a soft dough 3 to 4 cups depending on the flour.

Turn out onto lightly floured surface. Knead until smooth and elastic, about 10 minutes, using additional flour as needed to keep dough from sticking.

Place in buttered bowl; turn to bring buttered side up. Cover with a clean baking towel. Let rise 1 hour or until double.

Punch dough down, turn out onto lightly floured surface. Knead a few times. Invert the bowl over dough. Let rest 10 minutes.

Divide dough in half and knead each half a few times. Shape into 2 loaves. Place into 2 buttered load pans.

Let rise again for 1 hour or until doubled.

Bake at 400 degrees for 40 minutes or until golden brown and loaves sound hollow when tapped. If loaves are browning too quickly, cover loosely with foil. Remove baked bread from pans to cool completely on a wire rack.

PINEAPPLE BAVARIAN CREAM

I rarely make desserts, but when I want something a little special to serve, I usually make this, especially in the summer time. The basic ingredients are pretty uniform from one Bavarian Cream to another. The fruit and the jello can be changed to suit your taste.

1 can crushed pineapple
½ cup sugar
1 package lemon jello
½ pint heavy whipping cream

½ teaspoon vanilla extract

Combine pineapple, with juice, and sugar in a saucepan. Bring to a boil. Remove from the heat and add jello. Stir to combine. Cool completely in the refrigerator.

Have the heavy cream thoroughly chilled. Beat with a mixer until thick and fluffy. Add ½ teaspoon vanilla. Mix in pineapple mixture. Do not beat, but fold it in. Pour into shallow 8-inch square dish or freezing tray. Let it freeze for 8 to 10 hours. Remove from freezer 10 to 15 minutes before serving. Cut into squares to serve.

Some of the traditional foods that are expected at certain times at our house originated simply because that is what I had cooked. One Christmas Eve, years ago, I made Shrimp Salad with Mother Leone's Shrimp Sauce for supper; I do a slight adaptation. This is Ralph's favorite, I think. Now, this is expected every year.

SHRIMP SALAD

6 slices of Italian salami ¼ inch thick
1 large green, red or yellow pepper
20 jumbo shrimps, boiled
2 celery stalks with leaves, diced
6 whole fresh green scallions, diced
3 hard-cooked eggs, quartered
3 medium-sized hard tomatoes, quartered
Pinch of salt
Pinch of freshly ground black pepper
6 heaping tablespoons Mother Leone's Shrimp Sauce (below)

Cut the salami into strips 1¼-inches long, and slice the peppers into long thin strips. Place in a large bowl with shrimps, diced celery and scallions; refrigerate. Refrigerate eggs and tomatoes separately. When ready to serve, add salt and pepper and toss. Arrange eggs and tomatoes over top. Spoon shrimp sauce over all. Serve on the antipasto or as a main course. Serves 4 or 5.

MOTHER LEONE'S SHRIMP SAUCE

2 whole green scallions or 1 tablespoon grated sweet onion
6 tablespoons finely chopped fresh green or red pepper
2 tablespoons Spanish capers, chopped fine
2 tablespoons prepared horseradish

1 cup mayonnaise, preferably homemade with virgin olive oil
½ cup chili sauce
½ teaspoon crushed red pepper
½ teaspoon freshly ground black pepper
½ teaspoon salt
1 garlic clove, mashed

Sliced scallions lengthwise and chop fine, or grate the sweet onion. Place scallions or onion, green or red pepper, capers and horseradish in a strainer and drain for 15 minutes. Combine mayonnaise and chili sauce in a bowl. Add red and black pepper, salt and garlic. Whip well together with a whisk. Add drained ingredients and beat or mix well. Taste for salt. Refrigerate. Use over shrimps, crabmeat, or cold chicken lobster. Makes abour 2 cups.

This is the way I serve the shrimp salad. Place the shrimp salad in a serving dish. In separate dishes, serve shredded lettuce, and if desired, hard-boiled egg halves and tomato wedges. Place the remaining half of the shrimp sauce in a small bowl or sauce boat. Each person then can make a bed of lettuce top it with some shrimp salad, add the eggs and/or tomatoes to the side and top it all off with more shrimp sauce. This is a complete meal when served with Italian or French Bread and maybe a simple dessert… Sometimes, we just eat more salad.

One expected dessert at our house during Thanksgiving is Pumpkin Pie. This is one of the traditional foods that I have not copied from Mother's recipes. I like the following recipe much better than the really spicy and stiff pumpkin pies. This one, to me, is mild, creamy, and soothing.

BASIC PASTRY FOR PIES

For one double crust 9-inch pie or two single crust pies

2 cups flour
½ teaspoon salt
⅔ cup shortening
8 tablespoons ice water, or more depending on the flour

Mix together salt and flour. Cut in shortening until it is the size of small peas. Sprinkle water over. Stir with fork. This should not be so dry that all flour is not absorbed; but it should not be "wet," either. Form into a ball. Wrap in plastic wrap and refrigerate up to one day. To use, divide in half and roll out on lightly floured board. Bake as directed by individual recipes.

TAWNY PUMPKIN PIE

1¼ cups cooked fresh pumpkin
¾ cup sugar
½ teaspoon salt
¼ teaspoon ground ginger
1 teaspoon cinnamon
1 teaspoon flour
2 eggs, slightly beaten
1 cup evaporated milk
2 tablespoons water
½ teaspoon vanilla
1 unbaked 9-inch pie shell

Combine pumpkin, sugar, salt, spices, and flour in mixing bowl. Add eggs; mix well. Add evaporated milk and vanilla. Mix. Pour into unbaked pie shell. Bake at 425 degrees for about 50 minutes.

A dessert that is expected at Thanksgiving or at Christmas, or anytime for that matter is Pecan Pie. The recipe follows:

SOUTHERN PECAN PIE

This is the best recipe for Pecan Pie I have ever found.

1 cup pecan halves
1 9-inch unbaked pie shell
3 eggs
1 cup light corn syrup
1 tablespoon melted butter
½ teaspoon vanilla
1 cup sugar
1 tablespoon flour

Into the unbaked pie shell, arrange the pecans, rounded side up. Beat the eggs. Add and blend in the syrup, butter, and vanilla. Combine the sugar and flour; blend into the egg mixture and pour over the pecans in the pie shell. Let this sit until the nuts rise to the top. Bake at 350 degrees for 45 minutes.

While the tree is being trimmed before Christmas, there has to be egg nog and cookies, either Moravian Christmas Cookies or one of the other kinds which have become traditions at our house. We started making the Moravian cookies when Lynette was about two years old. She began learning to roll them out and cut them; but, she especially liked the decorating stage. When Lynette and Linda got a little bit older, at least in kindergarten, some of their younger cousins and some friends came over and spent afternoons cutting, decorating, and baking cookies.

I used to keep homemade cookies in a large plastic container in an upper cabinet. When Linda was little, even if it wasn't Christmas, she knew where I stored cookies. Sometimes, she would stand and point up to the cupboard and say, "Kookie, Kookie." Following are some of the recipes that are expected at our house during the Christmas season:

MORAVIAN CHRISTMAS COOKIES

1 cup butter or margarine, softened
1½ cups granulated sugar
2 eggs
1½ teaspoons brandy flavoring mixed with 1½ teaspoons water,
 or, 1 tablespoon brandy
3½ cups all-purpose flour
½ teaspoon cinnamon
¼ teaspoon nutmeg
¼ teaspoon salt

Cream butter and sugar together. Add eggs and brandy flavoring/water mixture. Beat. Sift together dry ingredients. Gradually add to creamed mixture. Chill overnight; or, make up in the morning, chill, and bake at night. Preheat oven to 400 degrees. Roll out dough on very lightly floured surface to ¼-inch thick. Cut with cookie cutters. Sprinkle with decorative sugar, if desired. Bake 6 to 8 minutes or until the edges of the cookies are just slightly golden brown. (If you use a lot of extra flour in rolling these out or if you bake these too long, they will be very hard).

NUT GEMS

2 cups flour
1 cup butter
4 tablespoons sugar
1 cup chopped pecans
2 teaspoons water
2 teaspoons rum flavoring or vanilla extract
Confectioners sugar

Sift flour; measure; sift again. Cream butter; add sugar. Cream together. Blend in flour. Stir in nuts, water and flavoring. Mix well.

Chill for several hours or overnight. Shape into 1-inch balls. Bake on ungreased baking sheet at 350 degrees for 20 minutes or until golden. While warm, roll in confectioners sugar. Makes about 60 cookies.

SWEDISH FILBERT-BRANDY CRESCENTS

1 cup butter
Confectioners sugar
1 tablespoon brandy OR 2 teaspoons brandy flavoring
 mixed with 1 teaspoon water
2 teaspoons water
1 cup chopped filberts or hazelnuts
2 cups flour

Cream butter; gradually add ½ cup sugar. Add the liquid. Add the nuts and flour. Form into a ball and wrap in plastic wrap. Chill several hours or overnight. Shape small pieces of the dough into crescent shapes and put on ungreased cookie sheet. Bake at 350 degrees for 12 to 15 minutes or until the edges are slightly tan. While still warm, roll in confectioners sugar. Makes about 4 dozen.

QUICK RUSSIAN TEA

Mix together in a blender or food processor:
3 cups instant tea with lemon and sugar
1 (1 lb. 10 oz.) jar orange-flavored instant drink mix
1 cup sugar
2 teaspoons ground cinnamon
1 teaspoon ground cloves

For a 1 cup serving, add 1 tablespoon or a little more of the tea mixture to 1 cup of boiling water.

BARBECUED CHICKEN WINGS

3 pounds chicken wings, cut into three pieces or; even better,
 3 pounds chicken drumettes
¼ cup soy sauce (optional)
3 tablespoons brown sugar
3 to 5 tablespoons vinegar
½ teaspoon ground ginger
2 garlic cloves, minced, or more to taste
½ cup chicken broth or water

Freshly ground black pepper to taste
Salt to taste
Cayenne pepper, to taste
Hot sauce, to taste

Make the marinade using all ingredients except the chicken. Wash the chicken and pat dry. Place the chicken in the marinade and refrigerate for at least 2 hours. Place on large baking sheets with a rim and bake, uncovered, for 1 hour or more in a 350 degree oven. Serves 25 as an appetizer. Serve with celery sticks, carrot sticks, and Roquefort cheese dressing.

ROQUEFORT CHEESE DRESSING

1 pint of your favorite mayonnaise
4 ounces of Roquefort cheese (or any bleu cheese), mashed or
 crumbled
½ cup or more sour cream
Garlic salt to taste

If this needs more salt after sitting awhile, add regular salt because you don't want the taste of the garlic to overpower the cheese flavor

Combine all ingredients in a quart jar and thoroughly mix with a fork (or with a skinny whisk). If you have about half a quart jar of mayonnaise remaining in your refrigerator, just make this dressing in the mayonnaise jar—it's easier.

MINIATURE TURNOVERS

This is a very versatile recipe. You can use the type of meat you like and vary the seasonings and other ingredients to come up with all kinds of "international" turnovers.

Make 2 recipes of Basic Pastry (see Index).

Filling: (The one I use most of the time)
¾ pound ground round
½ cup finely chopped onion
1 teaspoon butter
3 cups finely chopped fresh mushrooms
1 tablespoon all-purpose flour
¾ cup sour cream, or more
2 to 3 tablespoons dill weed

2 to 3 teaspoons Worcestershire sauce

In a large skillet, saute beef and onion in butter until meat is no longer pink. Add mushrooms. Cook until tender, stirring often. Pour mixture into a colander to drain off the fat. Return the meat-mushroom mixture to the skillet.

Add remaining filling ingredients and simmer, stirring constantly, until the mixture thickens. Let cool before making the turnovers. This can be refrigerated and the turnovers made the next day.

To assemble turnovers: Roll the pastry very thin—approximately ⅛-inch thick. Cut into 3- or 4-inch circles—if you have one of the fluted or scalloped cutters, use it.

With water, brush the edges of each circle.

Then, put about 1 tablespoon of the filling in the center of the circles. Fold the pastry over and seal the edges by pressing with the tines of a fork.

To bake: Preheat the oven to 400 or 425 degrees. Bake for about 15 minutes or until the crust is done and lightly browned. Makes about 4 dozen turnovers.

Additional Fillings: (1) Cheddar or other cheese (2) Ground turkey or beef, and any or all of the following: Green chilies, garlic, oregano, sliced green olives. (3) Ground beef mixed with taco seasoning mix and water. Cook until thick. Add shredded Monterey Jack cheese. (4) Peach Butter or Pear Butter mixed with pinon nuts. (5) Dried apple filling (see Index for Fried Apple Pies).

The possibilities are endless. Use your imagination!

STUFFED MUSHROOMS
1 large package (1 pound) fresh whole mushrooms
8 oz. cream cheese, softened
1 cup shredded sharp Cheddar cheese
8 to 10 slices bacon, crisply fried, drained and crumbled

Clean mushrooms and remove stems. The stems can be used in the Miniature (Meat) Turnovers, above. Mix together the cream cheese, Cheddar, and bacon pieces. Stuff mushroom caps. Place on a rimmed baking sheet or place in a baking pan or rectangular baking dish large enough to hold all mushrooms without crowding them. Put a little water in the bottom of the pan or baking dish. Sprinkle the tops of the filled mushrooms with a bit of seasoned salt. Bake at 350 to 400 degrees, depending on your oven, for about 20 minutes or until the mushrooms have cooked a bit and the cheese filling is nice and hot. Serve as an appetizer. Again, this is one of those things that you can vary according-ing to the kind of stuffing you would like. Have fun — experiment!

ALL-PURPOSE MARINARA SAUCE

Any time you need an Italian sauce, this is good to use. It is easy and tastes much better than the sauces that come out of a jar from your grocery store. It can be frozen into the portions you use most and put into freezer containers or freezer bags and brought out when you need it.

¼ cup olive oil or a little more
¼ cup butter
4 garlic cloves, crushed
A handful of fresh Italian parsley leaves, chopped
4 1-pound cans chopped tomatoes, or 4 pints home-canned ones
1 tablespoon dried oregano
1 to 2 teaspoons chopped basil, or more to your taste
½ teaspoon leaf thyme, or more to your taste
¼ teaspoon or more crumbled rosemary
1 bay leaf
Salt and freshly ground pepper, to taste
Half a small can of tomato paste
A sprinkling of granulated sugar, if needed, to take out any
  "bitter taste"

In a large saucepan, combine the olive oil and butter. Heat until the butter melts, over medium heat. Add the garlic and cook until just tender. Do not brown. Add the tomatoes, juice and all, and the rest of the ingredients. Bring to a boil, cover the pan, and reduce heat to medium-low. Simmer for 45 minutes to an hour, stirring occasionally. Add the tomato sauce, if you are using it. Taste and correct seasonings. Add the sugar, a tiny bit at a time, if needed. You can use this right away or cool and place in freezer containers for later use. Makes 6 to 7 cups.

EXTRA SPECIAL BARBECUE SAUCE

This sauce is all-purpose. I have used it on ribs, pork chops, chicken, and combined it with leftover boiled pork roast and leftover boiled beef for barbecue sandwiches served on hamburger buns. It is a combination of parts of several recipes and some new surprises. I usually double or triple the recipe here when I make it to have some on hand for later use.

2 cups catsup
3 cups water
2 tablespoons flour
6 tablespoons cider vinegar, or more to taste
3 tablespoons Worcestershire sauce
2 garlic cloves, crushed
¾ teaspoon Greek oregano
½ teaspoon marjoram
½ teaspoon thyme
¼ teaspoon tarragon
½ cup brown sugar, or to taste
1¼ cups molasses, or to taste
1 to 2 tablespoons liquid smoke, or to taste (Hickory flavor or
  a combination of Hickory and Mesquite)
Salt and freshly ground black pepper, to taste

Combine the flour with a little bit of the water and mix with some of the catsup. Then put this and all other ingredients into a large saucepan. Bring to a boil and immediate reduce heat to low or medium-low. Simmer for about half an hour. Adjust seasonings and simmer for an additional 5 minutes. This will keep for a long time kept in a screw-top jar (I use one of my canning jars) in the refrigerator.

One year, on Christmas morning, I was trying to cook some food for the family dinner at Mother's. For breakfast, I sliced some Cranberry Nut Bread I had made, boiled some eggs, and reheated some sausage balls leftover from the previous night's snacks. This is now a tradition. I do vary this sometimes by making Scotch Eggs instead of having boiled eggs and sausage balls. I almost started another tradition, by accident, when for several years, I served cream cheese, smoked salmon, and bagels for New Year's Day breakfast.

WELSH CHRISTMAS BREAD
Makes 2 loaves

1½ cups milk
¾ cup granulated sugar
½ teaspoon salt
2 packages active dry yeast
6 tablespoons lukewarm water
1 egg, beaten
1 cup raisins

1 cup currants
¼ cup chopped candied orange peel, or a bit more
¼ teaspoon ground cinnamon
⅛ teaspoon freshly grated nutmeg
About 5½ cups all-purpose flour
3 tablespoons melted butter, cooled to lukewarm

Scald milk; add sugar and salt. Stir to dissolve. Cool to lukewarm. Dissolve yeast in water. Add to milk mixture. Stir in egg, fruits, spices, and 2½ cups flour. Beat until smooth. Add 3 cups flour and melted butter. Mix thoroughly. Form dough into a ball. Turn out onto a lightly floured board and knead well. Place dough into a large buttered mixing bowl. Turn the dough over to make sure the top is also buttered. Cover with a baking towel (I use the white towels made from flour sack material) or plastic wrap. Let the dough rise until it is doubled in bulk. Divide dough in half. Form each half into a loaf. Place into two greased loaf pans. Cover and let the dough rise in a warm place away from drafts until doubled in bulk. Bake in a 375 degree oven for 40 minutes or until done. Turn out onto racks to cool. When thoroughly cooled, wrap tightly in plastic wrap. If you want to make this ahead, wrap in the plastic wrap and then in aluminum foil. Place each loaf into a large plastic bag and freeze until it is to be used.

NOTE: You may vary the fruits used in the recipe to suit your taste— figs, mixed candied fruit, candied cherries and/or candied pineapple, etc. Also, if you use the newer dark-colored loaf pans, the bread may tend to brown quicker than if you use the regular aluminum pans. You may need to adjust your oven temperature accordingly.

SCOTCH EGGS

Hard-boil 6 to 8 eggs. Let them cool and then shell them under cold running water. Let drain on paper towels. Refrigerate.

Portion out 1 pound bulk pork sausage to cover the number of eggs you have boiled. Remove the eggs from refrigerator. Make sure that the eggs are dry. You may need to blot them with paper towels.

Mold a portion of sausage around each egg, enclosing the entire egg.

You can mix a slightly beaten egg with the pound of sausage and this will keep the sausage from cracking, or you can dip the sausage-covered egg into 1 egg that has been beaten with a little water. I usually don't do either. The sausage may not stay on the egg perfectly, but they still taste good and who needs another egg when these can be habit-

forming. Roll the egg in dry bread crumbs. I cheat and use the prepared crumbs now; sometimes I even use the prepared "Italian-Style" crumbs. Place the eggs in a shallow pan and bake at 350 to 375 degrees for about 30 minutes or until the sausage is done. Cool. To serve, cut into halves or slices. These are better if they are just warm or even cold. Some of the recipes you may find for these have other added ingredients such as thyme and other herbs and are deep-fried. I keep it simple and we like the version given here.

The first Christmas we no longer had Mother with us, and we were just the four of us, we decided that we shouldn't try to imitate things as they always had been. So, we had some semblance of an English meal— with Standing Rib Roast, Yorkshire Pudding, the traditional vegetables, and I even tried to do a Plum Pudding which turned out to be horrible. The best part of the day, probably, was the "Tea." Some of the "Tea" recipes I used follow. Incidentally, we still like to go to Tea.

TEA SANDWICH FILLINGS

For all sandwiches, I use the very thin-sliced home-style breads with the crusts removed. Sometimes, I have made my own Herb Bread. You can vary the breads by using pumpernickel, etc., but you will need a firmer type of bread than regular "sandwich bread."

Smoked Salmon, Cream Cheese, Dill: In a small bowl, thoroughly combine 1 small package of smoked salmon (chopped) with 3 ounces of cream cheese that has been softened. Add about 1 teaspoon dried dill weed (unless you have some fresh; use about 1 tablespoon of the fresh, chopped).

A variation of this filling: Make the sandwiches open-face. Spread the bread with cream cheese that has been mixed with dill. Top with two thin strips of smoked salmon criss-crossed over the top. Garnish with a tiny sprig of fresh dill, top with a thin slice of unpeeled cucumber If the only cucumbers you can find are the waxed ones, I would just go with the first filling given here.

Ham: Use very thinly sliced ham. If you can get smoked ham, use it instead of the regular sandwich ham, or use both. Make Chive Mayonnaise: To about ½ cup of your favorite mayonnaise, add about 1 teaspoon chopped chives. Let this sit in your refrigerator to blend the flavors. Taste to see if you need a bit more chives added or if you need to add more mayonnaise. Spread a thin layer of the chive mayonnaise on one side of two slices of bread. Top one piece of bread with a slice or two of the ham and top with the other slice of bread.

Cucumber with Dill Butter: To ¼ cup softened butter, add ½ teaspoon dill weed or 2 teaspoons fresh dill; add a drop or two of lemon juice.

Buy small un-waxed cucumbers. Slice as thinly as possible. Sprinkle the cucumber slices lightly with salt. Let stand for 5 minutes. Drain the cucumbers on paper towels. Spread the bread with the dill butter and top with the cucumber.

HERB BREAD
Makes 1 loaf

1 package dry yeast
1¼ cups warm water
3 tablespoons butter or margarine, softened
2 tablespoons or a little less sugar
2 teaspoons salt
4 teaspoons mixed herbs (parsley, sage, rosemary, and thyme)
3 cups unbleached flour

Dissolve yeast in warm water in non-metallic mixing bowl. Add 2 tablespoons butter, 1½ cups flour. Beat for about two minutes, or if you are doing this the old-fashioned way, which I do, beat until your arm gets tired. Add remaining 1½ cups flour. Stir until smooth. Scrape batter from sides of bowl. Cover with a damp baking towel. Let rise in a warm place until doubles in bulk.

Stir batter 20 to 25 times. Place in a greased 9 x 5 x 3-inch loaf pan. Let rise until batter is almost to the top of the pan.

Bake at 350 degrees for 45 to 50 minutes or until golden brown and the loaf sounds hollow when tapped on top.

Remove from pan immediate to cool.

Melt remaining 1 tablespoon butter. Add some additional herbs, if you want. Brush on top.

Slices better the next day. This can be frozen, thawed, and sliced anytime you decide you need or want to have a Tea—or just some good bread with a meal.

SCONES
Plain Scones—The Easy Way

Measure out two cups of biscuit mix. Add 1 tablespoon granulated sugar. Add milk to make a stiff dough. Knead on lightly floured board. Roll out or pat out to about ½-inch thickness. Cut with a tiny cutter about 2 inches in diameter or use a small juice glass, or lid about the same size. Place on lightly greased baking sheet and bake at 425 degrees until golden brown. Serve with Almost Devonshire Cream, below, and raspberry jam.

ORANGE AND CURRANT SCONES

Plump about ¼ cup or more if you like currants in boiling water for 5 minutes. Drain. Cool a bit. Measure out the biscuit mix and sugar, as above. Add the grated rind of one orange and a little bit of orange juice; you may want to add a sprinkle of ginger. Then, add the plumped currants. Add milk, as above.

Roll the dough into a circle and cut into wedges. Bake as above. Serve with Almost Devonshire Cream, below, and orange marmalade.

ALMOST DEVONSHIRE CREAM

Combine 1 (8 oz.) package of cream cheese, softened, with a small amount of heavy cream or half and half. Blend in about 2 teaspoons sugar.

SCOTTISH SHORTBREAD

1 pound real butter (don't substitute margarine here)
1 cup granulated sugar
¼ confectioners sugar
4 cups (or a little more) all-purpose flour

Soften butter. Cream thoroughly with the sugars. Add flour a little at a time until you have a dough that will hold together, but is still a bit dry. Form into a ball. Divide in half. Place each half on an ungreased baking sheet. To make "Petticoat Tails," form into a circle and cut small scallops around the edge or just leave the circle plain. Dock the dough with the tines of a fork and then, beginning at the edges use a sharp knife and make tiny marks through the dough to the center of the bread, as if you are cutting a pie or cake, forming wedges, so the bread can be broken apart after baking. To make "squares" or other shapes, dock the dough with the tines of a fork, and make the lines for breaking according to the shapes you want.

Refrigerate until cold. Bake at 300 to 325 degrees for 30 to 40 minutes, or until the shortbread is sand-colored. Let cool. Break apart into serving pieces if you have not cut the dough prior to baking.

The following recipe is one of our favorite breakfast casseroles. The dish can be made with different ingredients to suit a menu for breakfast, lunch, or supper. That's why I call it Versatile Cheese Strata. Here's the basic breakfast recipe along with suggested ingredients for other meal options:

VERSATILE CHEESE STRATA

12 to 16 slices white bread, buttered, and crusts removed
2 cups shredded sharp Cheddar cheese
1 pound bulk sausage
6 eggs, slightly beaten
½ to 4 cups milk
1 teaspoon salt
½ heaping teaspoon dry mustard

Brown sausage in skillet, breaking it apart into crumbles. Drain on paper towels or in a colander or large sieve to remove the grease.

In the bottom of a 13 x 9 x 2-inch greased baking dish, put one layer of the buttered bread, buttered side up. Then, layer half the sausage. Distribute 1 cup of the cheese evenly on top of the sausage. Cover with another layer of buttered bread. Then, layer the other half of the sausage.

Combine eggs, milk, salt, and dry mustard. Beat together with a whisk. Pour this mixture over the entire casserole. You should have enough liquid to barely cover all the layers; if you don't, add a bit more milk. Cover the casserole tightly with plastic wrap and refrigerate overnight (or for six hours if you are going to serve this for a lunch or supper).

In the morning, replace the plastic wrap with aluminum foil. Put the casserole into a cold oven. Preheat the oven to 325 degrees. When the oven has preheated, remove the aluminum foil. Allow the casserole to bake for 55 minutes. Sprinkle with the remaining cup of shredded cheese. Bake for an additional 5 minutes. Let stand 10 minutes before cutting. This serves up to 12 people or as few as 6, depending on how big you cut the serving sizes.

Variations for lunch or supper: Instead of sausage, substitute:
(1) 2 cups diced ham and 1 cup of broccoli or asparagus
(2) 1 or 2 cans chopped green chilies
(3) Browned ground round and green chilies
(4) Cooked, chopped chicken, mushrooms, and sweet red peppers

Although I make few desserts except for special occasions or holidays, I do make the following cake quite often. This is a very good way to use up really ripe bananas; it freezes well; and, best of all, it is very to good to eat anytime—morning, noon, or night. Here's the recipe:

BANANA CAKE

5 medium bananas, mashed
¾ cup vegetable oil
½ cup sugar
1 box of yellow cake mix
5 eggs
½ teaspoon vanilla extract
½ teaspoon rum flavoring
½ to 1 cup chopped pecans
1 teaspoon ground cinnamon
3 to 4 tablespoons brown sugar

In a large bowl, mash the bananas. Whisk in the oil. Stir in the sugar and cake mix. Beat vigorously with a spoon or with an electric mixer. Add eggs, one at a time, beating after each addition. Then, add flavorings.

In a small bowl, combine the pecans, cinnamon, and brown sugar.

Grease and flour a large tube pan. Pour in half of the cake batter. Distribute the pecan mixture evenly over the batter. Then, pour in the rest of the batter. Bake at 350 degrees for 50 to 60 minutes.

One of the recipes my students request the most is one of my variations of Greek Spinach Pie. So, here, especially for them, is the recipe:

SPINACH PIE

2 pounds frozen spinach, thawed thoroughly, water squeezed out
  You can cook this for about 5 minutes in a little water, if you like
About 4 green onions or about ½ cup "regular" onion, finely chopped
1 large clove of garlic crushed in garlic press
½ cup fresh (flat leaf) parsley leaves, chopped
6 eggs, beaten
½ pound cottage cheese
1 pound Feta cheese
1 tablespoon (or less) dill weed

Salt to taste (you won't need a lot because of the Feta)
1½ cups good olive oil (I use extra virgin olive oil)
2 sticks butter or margarine
1 pound filo pastry sheets

In a large bowl, combine the thawed (and slightly cooked) spinach, onions, garlic, parsley, eggs, the cheese, dill, and ½ cup olive oil. Melt the butter with the 1 cup of olive oil in a small saucepan.

Brush a large rectangular baking dish with the melted butter-oil mixture.

Unfold the filo and place under a damp cloth. One at a time, on a waxed paper-lined work surface, butter a sheet of the dough and put it into the baking dish. Do this with 8 to 10 sheets. If you have trouble with this, just pick up a sheet, put it into the dish, brush it and then add another layer. If you pick up two or more sheets at a time, nobody is watching, and nobody will really know the difference when the dish is finished unless experts on this type of cooking. If the dough starts cracking and tearing, don't worry about it. Just remember to keep the dough you are not working on at the time covered by the damp cloth.

Finally, after you get the first 8 to 10 layers of dough into the baking dish, spoon in the spinach filling.

On top of the filling, start 8 to 10 layers of filo again, brushing each sheet and layering. Tuck in any edges of the dough and after brushing with the butter and olive oil one more time, sprinkle the top with water.

Bake at 350 degrees for 15 minutes. Reduce the heat to 300 or 325 degrees and continue baking for about an hour until the pastry turns golden brown.

Working with filo dough, at first, seems a little bit tricky. But, don't let it scare you. After all, it's just dough. If it does come apart in places, it will not really show in this pie because of all the layers. And, the olive oil and bread make the dough smooth out. Just remember to keep the dough you are not using covered with a damp—not wet—clean dish or tea towel.

When fall comes and blends into winter, I believe I could eat home-made soup and homemade bread every day and never tire of either! The only soups I remember Mother making were potato, potato-tomato, and vegetable-beef; but, oh, how good!

The first time I ever made vegetable-beef soup for Ralph, he asked, "Where's the macaroni?!" I said, "You don't put macaroni in this soup." He said, "Well, it's not vegetable soup without macaroni." So, now, I have learned to add that ingredient just for him because that's the way his mother made it. The way I make this soup these days shares few similarities with the version I first made in Clara Barton's House.

VEGETABLE-BEEF SOUP

You can adjust the amount of ingredients here according to the number of people you plan to serve. The proportions given here will serve at least 4 people with leftovers.

Boil at least a 1 pound chunk of beef pot roast in slightly salted water until it is really tender, adding more water as needed. Remove the beef from the broth. Wash, peel, and cube 2 or 3 medium potatoes. Add to the broth. Chop 1 large onion. Add to the broth. Bring the broth back to a boil. Boil slowly until the potatoes are fork-tender. Chop the beef, removing any fat. Add to the pot. Then, add 2 cans chopped tomatoes, 1 can mixed vegetables, ½ of a large green pepper (chopped), and 1 rib of celery (finely chopped).

Simmer for awhile to give the flavors a chance to blend. Then add 1 to 2 cups precooked drained, and rinsed elbow macaroni (optional). Taste for seasoning; adjust if needed.

Simmer for about 15 minutes. Taste for seasoning again; adjust. Serve with buttered cornbread wedges. (This is good reheated the next day. It can be frozen, but if you do this, remove any macaroni first because those noodles just don't hold up too well to being cooked, simmered, frozen, and reheated. Also, if you like the taste of the beef broth, but don't want to add meat, use a can or more of beef broth and follow the rest of the recipe. The soup is still very good and this version is very quick!

Another soup that my family likes is Broccoli Cheese Soup. After several attempts to get it just the way I wanted it, this is my standard recipe give or take an additional "pinch of this" or a "smigdin' of that":

BROCCOLI CHEESE SOUP

1 large potato, diced
1 large onion, diced
¼ to ½ cup celery, diced
1¼ to ½ cup carrots, diced
1 cup water
1 can chicken broth

2 cups grated sharp cheddar cheese
½ to 1 cup half and half
Salt and pepper to taste
¼ teaspoon leaf thyme optional
A dash or two of garlic powder, optional
1½ to 2 cups pre-cooked fresh broccoli, chopped into tiny pieces

In a medium saucepan, simmer vegetables except the broccoli in water and chicken broth until very tender. Puree in the blender or leave as is, if you like. Put the mixture back into the saucepan. Add the thyme and garlic. Stir in the cheese and half and half. If you like really thick soup, add 1 tablespoon cornstarch to the cold half and half before adding to the vegetable mixture. Heat slowly until the cheese has melted. Stir in pre-cooked, chopped broccoli. If the soup is too thick, add a little bit of water. Taste for seasoning again, adding more salt, pepper, thyme or garlic, if needed. Let this rest on very low heat for about 10 minutes. This amount should serve 4 to 6 people.

Sometimes when I was ill, which was often when I was a little girl, I would ask Mother for potato soup with noodles. Many times she thought I shouldn't have the soup, and especially the noodles. Mother made the noodles for soup by mixing flour with some milk until the tiny noodles formed similar to the Amish rivels. These were then dropped into the simmering pot of cream and potatoes to cook. How good!

Sometimes I got a scraped apple instead. Mother took a paring knife and scraped the apple so that it was practically of applesauce consistency. We had canned applesauce in the cellar; but, this apple was fresh which meant "better for me."

In addition to soup being a comfort food, the boiled beef with broth over biscuits and potatoes, pork with sauerkraut and potatoes, chicken and dumplings, and even scrapple are comfort foods to me. And, sometimes, I still yearn for a real Bunting's hot dog. I guess you could say that I just like good old-fashioned food. My family and I also like some of the newer ways to serve some of the traditional meats and vegetables. Some of these recipes follow.

MARINATED VEGETABLES
2 carrots, cut into 1 to 1½-inch long sticks
1 cup broccoli flowerets
1 cup cauliflower flowerets
1 small zucchini, cut into sticks

1 small red (or other) onion, sliced horizontally and separated
  into rings
1 sweet green or red pepper, seeded, ribs, removed, cut into thin
  strips
½ cup vegetable oil
3 tablespoons tarragon vinegar
1 tablespoon cider vinegar or wine vinegar
1 teaspoon dried dill weed or about twice as much fresh,
  chopped, or more to taste
1 teaspoon salt
¼ teaspoon freshly ground pepper

In saucepan, blanch the carrots until crisp tender; drain; refresh in cold water; drain. Repeat this process with the broccoli, then the cauliflower. If the zucchini is really young and tender, it really does not need to be blanched. Combine the vegetables with the sweet pepper strips and the onion in a large bowl. Whisk together the oil, vinegars, dill, salt, and pepper. Pour over the vegetables. Toss gently. Cover and refrigerate at least 8 hours, stirring occasionally. You can adjust the amount and variety of vegetables given here to suit you. The amounts given here will make about 6 servings. This is good to serve if you are doing a buffet meal and it is very good to take on picnics.

POTATO SALAD (MY WAY)

Peel and cube 6 to 8 medium-large potatoes. Put into cold water to cover. Add a bit of salt. Bring to a boil. Reduce the heat to medium. Cover and cook until the edges of the potato cubes begin to round off. This may sound funny, but that's the way I judge the cooking.

Drain the water off. You can leave the potatoes in the saucepan to do the mixing—fewer pots/dishes to wash. To the hot potatoes, immediately add one chopped onion, one large chopped dill pickle (kosher dills), about ¼ teaspoon celery seed, about ½ cup mayonnaise added a little at a time, and about 1 tablespoon prepared mustard. Stir this together. Taste for seasonings. If you need to, add more mayonnaise, mustard or salt. Spoon the mixture into a serving dish, cover tightly and refrigerate until ready to serve. If you just can't wait for hours, this is even good a bit warm. This amount will serve about 6 people, usually with some leftovers for the next day.

HASH BROWN CASSEROLE

1 large package (about 2 pounds) frozen hash brown potatoes, thawed (I like to use the ones cut in small cubes)
¼ cup melted butter
1 can cream of chicken soup
2 cups grated sharp Cheddar cheese
2 cups sour cream
2 tablespoons dried onion flakes
1 teaspoon salt, or a sprinkling more
½ teaspoon pepper
2 cups corn flakes, crushed to crumbs
½ cup melted butter

Combine all the ingredients except the corn flake crumbs and the ½ cup melted butter. Place the potato mixture in a large rectangular baking dish which has been sprayed with non-stick cooking spray. Distribute the corn flake crumbs evenly over the top. Drizzle the ½ cup melted butter over the corn flake crumbs. Bake at 350 degrees for one hour. This may be made up and refrigerated the day before serving, or it may be frozen before baking. Be sure to start a glass baking dish that has been refrigerated in a cold oven. Allow more time for baking if you have refrigerated this and even more time if you have frozen it. Place aluminum foil over the top so it doesn't get too brown while the oven is preheating.

NEW POTATOES WITH HERB-BUTTER SAUCE

1½ pounds new red-skinned potatoes, as small as you can get them
¼ cup melted butter
3 tablespoons chopped Italian flat leaf parsley
2 tablespoons snipped fresh chives
2 or 3 teaspoons fresh lemon juice
1 to 3 teaspoons chopped fresh dill or half this amount of dried dill weed
Salt and pepper to taste

Wash the potatoes well. Peel a narrow strip around the center of each potato, but leave the rest of the skin on the potato. Place potatoes into a medium saucepan, cover with cold water; add a bit of salt. Cover the saucepan. Cook potatoes at a slow boil for 15 to 20 minutes, or until the potatoes are fork tender. Test with a toothpick stuck into a potato— don't use a fork or the potato will crack. Drain potatoes and keep in the saucepan, covered. Combine the butter, herbs, and lemon juice in a small saucepan. Heat slowly, stirring well, until the butter melts. Pour the butter sauce over the potatoes. Toss to coat. Add salt and pepper to taste. These proportions can be changed to fit the number of people you are serving. You want to have plenty of the butter sauce to coat the potatoes well.

SAVORY COTTAGE CHEESE PIE

1 9-inch deep-dish pie crust, unbaked (see Index for Basic Pastry)
2 or 3 fresh tomatoes, washed, cored, sliced, dredged in flour
½ teaspoon or more dried oregano or ½ teaspoon or more dried
  basil (If you have fresh, use twice the amount of herb)
1 or 2 tablespoons fresh Italian flat leaf parsley, chopped
1 tablespoon or less of minced onion
½ teaspoon or more of salt
2 teaspoons Worcestershire sauce
1 cup cottage cheese
1 cup sour cream
1 tablespoon flour
3 eggs
2 cups or more shredded sharp Cheddar cheese

In a large skillet saute tomatoes in butter until lightly browned. Place on paper towel to drain. Into a medium bowl, place the cottage cheese, sour cream, herbs, onion, salt, flour, and Worcestershire sauce. Blend with a whisk. Add the eggs, blending well. Into the bottom of the unbaked pie shell, place half the Cheddar cheese. Add half the cottage cheese mixture. Place half the tomato slices on top.

Cover with the remaining cottage cheese mixture. Top with the remaining tomato slices. Sprinkle more sharp Cheddar on top. Bake at 350 degrees for 25 to 30 minutes.

OLD FASHIONED SLAW

This slaw is similar to the German-style slaw without the added flour and eggs.

1 very small head of green cabbage or half a large head
1 medium onion
2 tablespoons sugar
½ cup vegetable oil
½ cup cider vinegar
1 tablespoon sugar
1½ teaspoon dry mustard

¾ teaspoon salt
Black pepper to taste

Coarsely shred the cabbage. I just use my knife and cut the cabbage into thin strips. Peel and slice the onion into thin horizontal slices; separate the rings. Sprinkle the 2 tablespoons of sugar over the cabbage and onion. Into a small saucepan, put the oil, vinegar, the other sugar, dry mustard, salt, and pepper. Bring to a boil, whisking with a small whisk or fork. Pour over the cabbage/onion mixture and let it sit for about 5 minutes. Toss and refrigerate. This will make enough slaw for 4-6 normal servings, with some left, when serving a meat and at least one other vegetable.

SPECIAL CHICKEN SALAD

4 freshly boiled chicken breasts cooked in salted water
1 or 2 stalks celery, finely chopped
2 to 4 tablespoons very finely chopped onion
1½ or more teaspoons curry powder mixed with 1 to 2
    tablespoons milk or half and half
Additional salt and pepper, to taste
Mayonnaise

Cook chicken until very tender. Cool until you can hold it in your hands. Cut into small pieces. Add the curry powder to the milk and mix. Add to the chicken.

Add the chopped celery and onion. Add mayonnaise; begin with about ½ cup. Mix into the chicken mixture. Then, add a little more at a time until you have the consistency you like. Taste for seasoning. You may want to add more curry powder, salt or pepper. Cover tightly and refrigerate until ready to serve.

NOTE: This can be made a day ahead of serving. Because of the curry powder, the salad will turn yellow, but don't be alarmed. It is WONDERFUL!

We like this with fresh tomato wedges, wedges of boiled eggs, and toasted French bread with butter. It is good to take on picnics, too. You can also use it as a filling in pastry puffs for a party.

PASTRY PUFFS

1 cup all-purpose flour
½ teaspoon salt
½ cup shortening (butter or margarine works, too)
1 cup hot water
4 eggs

Bring shortening and hot water to boil in saucepan. Add flour and salt all at once, stirring constantly. Continue cooking until mixture leaves sides of pan and follows spoon around sides of pan. This will take about 15 minutes.

Remove from heat and let cool about a minute.

Add eggs, one at a time, beating vigorously after each, before adding another egg. Beat again until smooth.

Preheat oven to 450 degrees.

Drop the pastry dough from a teaspoon about 2 inches apart on a lightly greased baking sheet. Bake at 450 for 10 minutes. Then, reduce the heat to 350 degrees and bake for an additional 15 minutes. Cool on a wire rack. Cut open and fill with the salad of your choice. This makes 3 to 4 dozen puffs. These can also be filled with pastry cream or a pudding-type filling to make Cream Puffs.

BOUNTIFUL BAKED BEANS

You may cook dried beans for this dish by washing, sorting, and soaking them overnight, draining the water off in the morning, and then cooking them in fresh water, OR you can take the easy way out and use canned beans, without meat seasoning, if you can find them. The recipe given here is the easy way out.

1 can light red kidney beans, rinsed and drained
1 can pork 'n beans, pork removed
1 can butter beans
1 can pinto beans
1 large onion, chopped
1 sweet green pepper, chopped
½ cup brown sugar, packed firmly
½ cup catsup, or more to taste
1 teaspoon Worcestershire sauce, or to taste
1 clove of garlic, crushed or ½ teaspoon garlic powder, or to taste
¼ cup or more apple cider vinegar, to taste
1 to 2 teaspoons dry mustard
1 to 2 teaspoons liquid smoke, or to taste
Salt and pepper to taste
6 strips bacon, fried and crumbled

Fry bacon, drain, and crumble. Set aside. In a large saucepan, in bacon grease, or margarine, saute onion and green pepper until tender.

Dump in the beans.

Add the other ingredients except the crumbled bacon.

Heat and taste to make sure you have enough of this and that to your liking. Correct seasoning.

Place the bean mixture into a large casserole dish.

The beans can be prepared up to this point, covered, and refrigerated ready to bake the next day.

Preheat oven to 350 degrees.

Bake the beans until bubbly and the mixture just begins to thicken. Then, sprinkle the crumbled bacon on top. Bake an additional 10 minutes or so. (Total baking time: 30 to 45 minutes).

EASY ROAST BEEF

This method will NOT work in a gas oven! I tried it in Reba's kitchen in Albuquerque purposely to make sandwiches the next day for a picnic and had to finish cooking it the next morning. Since I had not used gas for cooking for over 30 years, I had forgotten that when you turn the gas off, the oven cools quickly. If you do not like medium-rare beef, you will not like to use this recipe.

Buy at least a 3-pound solid cut roast with very little fat such as eye of round.

Wash the meat and pat it dry with paper towels. Have the roast almost at room temperature. Don't try this with a roast that is still frozen. Preheat the oven to 500 degrees. Place the roast, unsalted and unseasoned, into an ungreased baking pan or skillet.

Place the roast in the oven. IMPORTANT NOTE: After you put the roast into the oven, do not open the oven door at all! Turn to bake and bake at 500 degrees for 5 minutes per pound. At the end of the cooking time, turn the oven off. Do not open the oven door. Leave the roast in the oven for two hours. During this two hour-period, don't open the door. If you need to, you can leave this in even longer than the two-hour resting period. It will not overcook. After two hours, you can open the oven door and remove the roast. If you serve this for supper one night, then you can make sandwiches from the leftovers the next day.

To make gravy: To any drippings in the pan or skillet, add a can of beef broth, about 2 tablespoons of cornstarch mixed with ¼ cup of water. Blend thoroughly and let cook until it get to the desired consistency. Add salt, pepper, and Worcestershire sauce to taste.

To Make Sandwiches: Refrigerate the roast. Slice very thinly.

Use on Hoagie buns, French bread, or your choice although regular sandwich bread will not hold up to the following fillings. Cut the bread.

Fillings: 1. Spread the inside with sour cream, cream cheese, and horseradish and salt to taste mixed together. Layer on the thinly sliced beef. Add leaf lettuce and any other toppings you like. 2. Spread the inside with butter and/or mayonnaise. Layer on the thinly sliced beef. Then, layer on thin slices of onion, roasted sweet red pepper strips and a mild easy-to-melt cheese, Monterey Jack, Muenster, or American. Wrap each sandwich tightly in aluminum foil and place in a 375 degree oven for about 10 minutes. Make sure the cheese melts. You can still take these on picnics... just put them, still wrapped, in one of the keep warm insulated containers.

FRIED CHICKEN

In a large cast iron skillet, begin to melt one stick of margarine or butter over medium heat. Wash the number of chicken pieces you need to serve your crowd and place them, one or two at a time, in plain all-purpose unseasoned flour in a brown paper bag or a large plastic food storage bag. Close the bag and shake to coat the chicken. Place the chicken pieces in the melted butter or margarine. Sprinkle the tops of the chicken pieces with seasoned salt. Brown the chicken over medium heat, or medium-low heat, depending on your stove, until the bottom is golden brown. Add more butter if the skillet begins to look dry.

Turn the chicken over. Sprinkle on a bit more seasoned salt. Continue to brown the chicken until all sides are golden brown and the chicken is good and done, turning the heat down if it begins to brown too fast. Frying the legs will take quite a bit longer than some of the other pieces, so start them first if you are doing different pieces. It will take about 45 minutes to an hour to cook the chicken properly. Drain on paper towels. To serve, place on a platter for the table or load it up in your basket and take off for a picnic. This is good cold the next day.

QUICK, EASY, AND DELICIOUS BAKED CHICKEN

Buy enough skinless, boneless chicken breasts to feed your crowd. Wash the chicken and blot dry with a paper towel. On a plate or platter, place about ½ cup of your favorite mayonnaise. Roll each chicken breast into the mayonnaise, coating well. Replenish the mayonnaise on the plate as needed.

Then, roll the coated chicken breasts in crushed corn flakes. Place the chicken into a large rectangular glass baking dish sprayed with non-stick cooking spray.

Melt half a stick of butter (or more if you're really feeding a crowd) over low heat. Pour over the chicken. Bake at 325 degrees for about 45 minutes or until dark golden brown and the thickest part of the breasts are very tender. Delicious served hot, warm, or cold.

BAKED PORK IN WINE SAUCE

Purchase about 3 pounds whole pork tenderloin or a 3-pound pork loin roast. Wash the roast. Pat dry with paper towels. Sprinkle with salt and pepper. Place the roast in a large rectangular baking dish that has been sprayed with non-stick cooking spray. Preheat oven to 325 degrees. The meat will need to roast for at least an hour and a half. About halfway through the roasting, place into a small sauce pan:

1½ cups dry white wine
1 or 2 cloves crushed garlic
2 or 3 teaspoons snipped fresh chives
½ to 1 teaspoon chopped fresh basil
1 tablespoon chopped Italian (flat leaf) parsley
A sprinkle of salt

Bring the mixture to a boil. Reduce heat to low. Begin basting the meat every 15 minutes, using all the wine mixture by the time the roast is done. Remove from the oven. Remove the meat from the sauce and place on a cutting board or platter. Let the roast sit for 10 to 15 minutes before slicing into thin slices. Strain the pan juices and serve as a sauce to pour over the meat if using as the meat for a meal.

To serve as an appetizer: First, for this, it is better to use the pork tenderloin. Prepare the tenderloin the day before serving. Let cool. Slice into very thin slices. Into a casserole dish that fits over a warmer, place the strained sauce.

Place the meat slices into the sauce. Cover and refrigerate. On the day of serving, remove the casserole dish from the refrigerator and re-heat the meat with sauce in the oven or in the microwave. Place the casserole in the chafing dish or warmer container and keep warm. To accompany the meat: Slice a French Bread Baguette into thin diagonal slices, spread with softened butter. Toast in the oven. Place in a tea towel-or cloth napkin-lined basket. Have on the table a small dish of Dijon mustard to which you have added a sprinkling of curry powder to your taste. Your guests can spread some of the mustard onto the bread slices and then add one or two slices of pork.

Some of our treasured memories are of Ralph's mother's relatives in Grayson County, Virginia. Hiley and Johnson were elderly cousins. Their small house, hidden from the road, was filled to the rafters with their spirits. Both were of small stature, but they had boundless energy and love.

On one of our visits, we took a hike up the steep hill behind the house and pasture, to the family cemetery. There, at least three generations of the Cole family ancestors are buried. Charlie and his wife, Nancy, were the first of the family to come to America "from across the waters."

Hiley still had remnants in her speech of old pronunciations or meanings for certain words, and she used some specific words I had not heard in years. Hiley used terms such as "hain't", for "ain't" or "haven't," "hit" for it," "yander" for "yonder," or "down there/over ther," and "nary" for "none" or "not any." The words she used are just considered "old-fashioned" today. When she talked about going to Independence, just a little piece down the road, we understood what she meant. Independence is a small town not far from where Hiley and Johnson lived. A fur piece or a fer piece—far piece—is another matter; that means a pretty good distance away, or in general understanding, a long distance.

Many of us living in the Southern Appalachians use, in our speech, even today, some of the older words or expressions we heard our families use. Michael Montgomery* has found that while "yonder" and "hit," as Hiley used, are among the words brought with people from various parts of the British Isles, some of our words or expressions, including "piece," as used above, are of Scotch-Irish origin rather than of English origin, as some people have claimed.

Examples are found even in my writing which is not intentional—that's just part of me—or in people's quotations given here, such as when my friend Barbara said that she thought that she and her sister grew up with their heads in a poke. A poke, as spoken of here, is what most people refer to as "bag" or a "sack." And, then, we could get into people's different usages for the word "sack." In the Southern Appalachians, a "sack" may be referred to as a "gunnysack," while in other parts of the country, it may be referred to as a "crocus sack," the meanings are the same—a bag made of a coarse material such as burlap. Sometimes, the word "sack" is used interchangeably with "bag," meaning a "paper bag."

*Michael Montgomery is Professor of English and Linguistics at the University of South Carolina, Columbia. He has been the editor of several books and is the author of numerous articles on Southern Appalachian speech and its connection to the speech of our ancestors. A widely acclaimed speaker, he is in demand both at home and abroad. His current project (which he began with Joseph Hall) is editing *The Dictionary of Smoky Mountain English*, which Michael has expressed may be his "life's work." After this book went to edit, Michael retired and is now Distinguished Professor, Emeritus. He continues his writing.

Another example of the Scotch-Irish influence is when Raymond, my cousin, stated, "…you just don't have those anymore.…" Natives to our area or those who have been here a long time would know that "anymore" as used here means "these days" or "nowadays."

People back in the earlier days rarely distinguished between afternoon (after the noon hour) and what we now refer to as evening (between 6:00 and 9:00 p.m.). Any time after the noon hour was referred to as evening, usually pronounced "evenin'". If they are going to visit people, they might let the people know by saying, "We'll be over sometime this evenin'." This would be unacceptable to most people these days because we would want to know a more precise time the visitors would be arriving. And, while literally, "muley" meant a hornless cow, when we were growing up, we understood that if Mother or someone else described us as being muley, they meant we were being stubborn. We also knew that if people said, "It's gettin' a little airish in here," it meant that the room was getting too cool and more wood needed to be put into the fireplace or more coal put into the furnace.

Other common terms in our speech include "backset," meaning that before someone is sufficiently over (has recovered from) an illness, the person goes back to the usual routine and quickly becomes ill again—except we never said "ill," we always said "sick." Ill, in earlier years, was interpreted as meaning that someone was in a bad mood, was hateful, or that the person had spoken in a hateful manner. Sometimes, even today, someone may be described as being ill-tempered. This means that the person always seems to be hateful or to be in a bad mood. I try to avoid these people, they must be awfully unhappy inside. This may get confusing because we have learned that when a person is what used to be referred to as "sick," we now say that the person is "ill." "Sick" has a different connotation these days, even here.

We didn't "turn" our ankles or "sprain" them; to some people, we "creeled" them, and with all my gracefulness, I had several creeled ankles over the years. We also knew that to build a fire, first we had to put down a layer of kindling, usually pronounced "kindlin.'" Kindling is small strips of quick-burning wood—known as "fat wood" in some part of the country—and is one of those collective nouns. If more kindling was needed for the fire, I have heard some people say, "Hand me another piece of kindling." So, distinctions were made.

I remember one of my sisters, especially, saying "Well, I'll swan!" "Swan" replaced the word "swear." We never said the word "swear," and any "swear" words, so commonly used today, were avoided. The first time the word "darn"—which was considered too close to another four-letter word—slipped out of my mouth in front of Mother when I was a teenager, I thought, "Oh, no, I've had it now."

If we had our feelings hurt by someone, or knew something that shouldn't be broadcasted to other people, Mother sometimes said, "Don't you let on that you are hurt." In other words, just overlook it and go on like nothing happened. Sometimes she said, "Don't you let on that you have heard anything about it." In other words, we were not to take part in a conversation about that particular topic. I interpreted this to mean that in some cases, at least, we were not to let people really know how we felt and that we were not to spread gossip. These words and others are still in our understanding and part of our speech.

Sometimes people say that they can't understand us because of our accents. When you add some of the terminology we use, just imagine that confusion in trying to translate what we say. And, evidently, we owe many of these words and expressions to our ancestors who came from the Northern Ireland Counties of Antrim, Armagh, Londonderry, and Tyrone, as did Hiley.

Prior to a visit one summer, Hiley and Johnson asked us to come eat dinner with them. Ralph's mother, Pauline, his Aunt Nan and I cooked some food so Hiley wouldn't have to do it all, but I don't remember now what we took with us.

We ate at the trestle table in the dining room. The table and the benches that pulled up to the table for seating were probably made by one of the Cole ancestors. When the food was ready, among other foods placed on the table were large dishes filled with mounds of fresh green beans and cornbread made from stone-ground cornmeal, baked in an iron skillet. I tasted the other foods, but, I ate so much of the beans and cornbread, I was embarrassed—well, almost.

While we were eating, I learned that although Hiley had an electric stove, she had purposely cooked this meal on her old wood cookstove even though this was the middle of the summer. "Because," she said, "the food just tastes better." And it did! I had forgotten how good food prepared on these old stoves really was! I had not tasted any prepared this way since my younger childhood on Carolina Hill. So, in a sense, I had gone home, again.

This, then, is the flavour of home experienced, in part, by my family. We never thought that we as individuals or as an extended family were atypical of others in the Southern Appalachians. And, in reality, were we?

Now, when we have our family gatherings, as someone begins to ask the blessing, just for an instant, some of us wonder what it must have been like to hear Preacher George Barker say his special blessing at other family dinners:

> Oh, Lord, smile upon us in tender mercy,
> Pardon and forgive us of our sins and
> enable us to be thankful for these and
> all other blessings. We ask in Your name.
> Amen.

EPILOGUE

Some of the family members included in this book are no longer with us. Anna Mae, the daughter of Daddy's sister, Virgie, died before I began working on this book.

Lawrence, Lorena's brother, who had dealt with the aftereffects of a stroke for several years, died not long after I began this writing.

The home of Nelma Greene Moore and her husband was the site for some of the first Greene cousins' get-togethers. Nelma, my Great-uncle Clyde's daughter, died before I began to gather the information included here, as did Dilla Sharp Godsey, Aunt Cindy's daughter.

Another of Uncle Clyde's daughters who was a dear person to all of us, Hazel, and her husband, Fred, have now gone away for awhile. Fred went ahead of her. Hazel was so excited about what I was doing and they enjoyed reading a shortened version of this work that I had completed by December 1995. She said that she loved it so much that she shared it with her daughter and stepdaughter.

In October 1998, Zillah Webb Rhea, at 99 years, Mother's best friend and the closest person to a sister Mother ever had, has left us for a happy reunion with her husband, Karl, and other family members who preceded her on this journey. I believe that she and Mother will have a wonderful time visiting with each other again.

My hope is that all of those who have gone before us would have been pleased with this effort.

ERO
October 23, 1998

AFTERWORDS

After the Epilogue was written and while this book was going through the initial edit, other life changes occurred.

In November 1998, another of the cousins, Conley, left us to join Beulah and other family members and friends. Conley's son said that he could not have picked a better daddy if he had been given the choice. Nor could we have chosen a better cousin. Conley made many lives happier by his being here.

The week before Thanksgiving 1999, my last aunt, Aunt Beulah Kirkland Rather, died at 88. Her only daughter, who we called Susie, died the month before. Aunt Beulah, like Mother, loved beautiful flowers. We will miss her sense of humor and her wonderful stories. Her two sons, Gilbert and Ken, and their families still live near the old Rather home site.

Two days following Thanksgiving 1999, Ralph's mother, Edythe Pauline Cole O'Dell, went away to join all of her brothers and sisters, her husband, and the other family members who have passed. Sometimes in her later years, Gran, as we called her, wondered why, out of all her family, she had been left here. Sometimes I told her that she was left just to aggravate us. Then she would laugh. Other times she would say that it was her time to go. At those times, I told her that her going was not up to her— that this was not her decision; then, she would settle down and say, "I guess you're right." Two years ago, during the recovery period from major surgery, she told me that she would like to live to be 90. And she did!

To everything there is a season...

REFERENCES

Alexander, Rhea.
1993 Personal conversation. Lenoir City, Loudon County, Tennessee.

Arthur, John Preston.
1915 *A History of Watauga County, North Carolina*. Richmond: Everett Waddey Co. Reprinted 1976 Easley, SC: Southern Historical Press.

Ball Blue Book®: Easy guide to tasty, thrifty home canning and freezing. 1936, 1969 Muncie, Indiana: Ball Brothers Company, Inc.

Barker, Herbert.
1998 Personal conversation. Bristol, Tennessee.

Biographical Directory, Tennessee General Assembly 1796-1969. Preliminary, No. 38-A, Greene County, Hawkins County, Sullivan County, Washington County to 1861. Nashville, Tennessee: Tennessee State Library and Archives.

Buckles, Bernice.
1998 Personal conversation. Bristol, Virginia.

Dowd, Clement.
1897 *Life of Zebulon B. Vance*. Charlotte, North Carolina: Observer Printing & Publishing House.

Family Records. Personal possession.

Frigidaire Division General Motors Corporation, Frigidaire Products of Canada, Ltd. 1943 *Wartime suggestions to help you get the most out of your refrigerator*. Dayton, Ohio; Toronto, Ont.

Leone, Gene.
1967 *Leone's Italian cookbook*. New York: Harper & Row, Publishers.

Lerma, Barbara Hartley.
1944 Personal conversations.

Montgomery, Michael
1995 "How Scotch-Irish is your English?" in *The Journal of East Tennessee History* 67:1-33.

Nichols, Nell B., ed.
1959 Farm *Journal's country cookbook*. Garden City, New York: Double-
day & Company, Inc.

Personal conversations with family members.
Summer 1995- Conley Boyd, Jerlis and Gene Boyd, Mary Lee and J. Lee
Boyd, Hazel Greene Minnick Carrier, Lucretia Vance Gilmer, Orville
Greene, Carolyn O'Dell Hooker, James William Maiden, Jr., Marie
Rather Maiden, Linda O'Dell, Lorena Boyd O'Dell, Lynette O'Dell,
Pauline Cole O'Dell, Ralph E. O'Dell, Reba Rather Ragan, Tunis R.
Ragan, Sr., Beulah Rather, Mena and f Rather, Judy Minnick Stump,
Henry C. Taylor, Thelma Rather Taylor, Albert Vance, Claude S. Vance,
Jr., Pauline ("Polly") (Vance) Vance, Raymond Vance, Shirley Starks
Vance

Taber, Gladys
1972   *My own cook book: From Stillmeadow and Cape Cod.*
Philadelphia: J.B. Lippincott Company.

Three Forks Baptist Association of North Carolina.
1882 *Minutes of the Forty-second Session of the Three Forks Baptist Association of North Carolina Held with The Church at Flat Top, August
31st and Sept. 1st and 2nd, 1882.* Compiled by D.C. Harman, Clerk,
Sugar Grove, N.C. Raleigh: Edwards, Broughton & Co., Steam Printers and Binders.

Three Forks Baptist Association of North Carolina
1883 *Minutes of the Forty-third Session of the Three Forks Baptist Association of North Carolina Held with The Church at Mulberry, August
30th and 31st, and September 1st, 1883.* Compiled by D.C. Harman,
Clerk, Sugar Grove, N.C. Raleigh: Edwards, Broughton & Co., Steam
Printers and Binders.

U.S. Bureau of the Census.
1790-1880 Various years and various states and counties. *Census of the
population: Summary of the population of the Unites States.* Washington, D.C.

Wilson, Rex.
1993-94 Personal conversations and correspondence. Richmond, Virginia.

Appendix
Additional Family Recipes

FROM MOTHER'S KITCHEN:

BAKING POWDER BISCUITS
I never knew Mother to make these, but the recipe was in her little box.
2 cups sifted flour
3 teaspoons baking powder
1 teaspoon salt
2 to 3 tablespoons shortening
⅔ cups (sweet) milk

Sift flour, baking powder and salt together. Cut or rub in shortening. Add milk to make a soft dough, stirring just enough to make ingredients hold together. Turn out on lightly floured board, knead gently for a half minute. Roll or pat out ¼ inch thick. Cut. Bake on ungreased baking sheet in hot oven 425 to 450 degrees, depending on your oven for 10 to 12 minutes. Makes about 18 two-inch biscuits.

ORANGE DONUTS

4 cups flour
1 cup orange juice
2 eggs
¼ teaspoon soda (baking soda)
¾ teaspoon baking powder
1 teaspoon nutmeg
1 cup shortening
2 cups sugar

Fry in deep fat.

Mother had no other directions for making these donuts. But, you follow the usual procedure: Cream the shortening and sugar together, add eggs. Mix dry ingredients together and add alternately with the orange juice. Roll out on lightly floured board and cut with a donut cutter. After frying, drain on a paper towel. Sprinkle with confectioners sugar or granulated sugar, if you want).

YEAST BREAD (2 LOAVES)

2 pkgs. dry yeast
¼ cup lukewarm water
1 cup sweet milk
1 cup hot water
2 tablespoons shortening
2½ tablespoons sugar
1 tablespoon salt
7 to 8 cups all-purpose flour

Dissolve the yeast in the ¼ cup warm water. Scald the mixing bowl and pour 1 cup hot water into it. Dissolve salt, sugar, and shortening in the hot water. Add the cup of sweet milk.

When the mixture is lukewarm, add the yeast. Stir in enough flour to make a batter. I add an egg, too. I think it makes it better. (NOTE: If you are going to add the egg, it should be at room temperature, not straight from the refrigerator).

Beat well and add rest of flour to make a dough. Knead until smooth and elastic and until it does not stick to the board.

Brush the top with water to keep it soft. Cover and let set in a moderately warm place until the dough is double in bulk, about 1½ hours.

Work down, let rise and divide in half. Shape into two loaves and place in well-greased pans.

To get a good and crusty top, brush the top with melted butter. Cover and let rise until doubled in bulk.

Bake in a hot oven at 425 degrees for first 15 minutes. Reduce heat to 325 degrees or less if bread browns too quickly. Bake about 45 minutes in all. I put a cookie sheet over it after it browns while it finishing baking.

SWEET APPLE PRESERVES

5 pounds prepared apples *(peeled, cored, cut into pieces or sliced)*
(To prevent the sliced apples from turning brown, place into about 1 quart of water to which you have added the juice of half a lemon)
5 pounds sugar
4 cups boiling water
½ level teaspoon alum
½ level teaspoon Salicylic Acid
7 drops cinnamon oil if desired

As soon as syrup boils drop in apples and boil for 1 hour. Makes about 8 pints.

BOSTON CREAM PIE

This is an easy recipe I gave to Mother. It doesn't require the usual making of pastry cream, etc.

1 box yellow cake mix (2 layers)
¼ teaspoon salt
1 small box vanilla instant pudding
¼ cup whipping cream (measure out and reserve 1 tablespoon of cream before whipping)
¾ cup chocolate icing

Prepare cake per box instructions, adding salt. Bake as directed on the cake mix box. While cake is baking, make instant pudding according to directions. When the pudding has chilled, whip the cream and add to the pudding. Spread pudding between and on top of cooled cake layers. Ice with:

2 cups powdered sugar
1 tablespoon margarine, softened
1 tablespoon cocoa
Pinch of salt
1 tablespoon cream (reserved above)
1 teaspoon brandy flavoring or vanilla extract (or ½ teaspoon of each)

Combine ingredients and spread over top of pie.

BROWNIES (ANOTHER RECIPE)

Brownies were popular at our house, as you can see.

2 cups sugar
2 sticks margarine
1½ cups flour
4 tablespoons cocoa
4 eggs, unbeaten
2 teaspoons vanilla
1 cup nut meats

Cream sugar with margarine. Add salt, flour, cocoa, eggs, and vanilla. Stir in nut meats and pour into greased large pan. Bake at 350 degrees about 25 minutes. Cool and cut into squares.

BROWNIE PIE

I gave this recipe to Mother years ago and she still had it in her little box where she kept her recipes. I haven't made this in years; but, it is good.

3 large eggs, well beaten

½ cup sugar
¾ cup light or dark corn syrup
¾ cup chopped pecans
2 squared unsweetened chocolate melted with two tablespoons
butter

Pour into unbaked crust and bake 40 minutes at 375 degrees.

BUTTERSCOTCH COOKIES

Mother had written this recipe on the back of one of Thelma's eighth grade English papers from October 17, 1938, on which she had written the parliamentary procedures. Thelma believes that she was in Mrs. Marney's English class then. I was in Mrs. Marney's English class in the seventh grade. Her accent was different from ours; she was from the eastern shore somewhere and said "hoose" for house, "oot" for out, etc. We thought it was quite amusing at the time. Mrs. Marney's husband, Sam, worked with the YMCA where I took swimming lessons during the '50s.

2 cups butter or lard, melted
1 egg
1 cup brown sugar
½ teaspoon vanilla
2 cups flour
2 teaspoons baking powder

Melt butter, add sugar then egg and beat well. Add flour, baking powder and vanilla and (nuts if desired). Make a stiff dough. Form a roll about 2 inches in diameter. Let chill 2 hours or overnight. Slice ⅛-inch thick. Bake until light brown at 350-375 degrees.

BUTTERSCOTCH PIE

2 cups brown sugar
4 tablespoons flour
4 egg yolks, beaten (reserve the whites for meringue, below)
¼ teaspoon salt
2 tablespoons butter
2 teaspoons vanilla
2 cups sour cream

Mix ingredients together and pour into an unbaked pie shell. Bake for ten minutes in a hot oven until when tested with a knife it will come out cleam. When nearly done, top with meringue made with 4 beaten egg whites, 8 tablespoons sugar and return to the oven to brown.

NOTE: I suggest beginning the pie at 425 degrees and then reducing the heat to 375 to finish baking, especially if you are using a glass pie plate. This make take more time baking, but the crust will not be too dark.

CHOCOLATE COOKIES

1¼ cups flour
½ teaspoon soda
¼ teaspoon salt
¾ cup sugar
½ cup shortening
1 egg
2 squares chocolate
½ cup canned cream (evaporated milk)
pecans

Melt chocolate in double boiler over boiling water. Combine flour, soda, salt, and sugar. Cream together sugar and shortening. Stir in beaten egg. Add dry ingredients alternately with cream. Remove chocolate from heat. Stir into batter. Stir in chopped pecans, if desired.

Icing: Combine:
1½ cups confectioners sugar
2 tablespoons butter, softened
¼ cup canned cream (evaporated milk)
½ teaspoon vanilla
  Top with crushed peppermint candy, if desired.

CHOCOLATE FROSTING

¼ cup butter
1½ cups confectioners sugar
1 square (1 oz.) melted chocolate
2 tablespoons (about) milk
  Cream butter and sugar together. Add melted chocolate. Add enough milk to make frosting consistency to spread. Makes enough frosting to cover tops and sides of two 8-inch layers.

CHOCOLATE ICING - UNCOOKED

1 box powdered sugar (confectioners sugar, xxxx)
½ cup cocoa

4 tablespoons butter, softened
⅛ teaspoon salt
1 teaspoon vanilla
6 tablespoons hot coffee, or any hot liquid

Mix together until smooth and of spreading consistency. Use to ice layer or sheet cakes.

COCOA SYRUP

We used to spoon this over vanilla ice cream and also put it in our milk to make chocolate milk or hot chocolate.

1 cup cocoa
1½ cups water
1 cup hot water
Dash of salt
2 teaspoons vanilla

Mix sugar, salt and cocoa dry. Add sufficient water to make a paste, then add the remainder of the water. Bring to boil, stirring constantly. Boil 3 minutes and add vanilla. Pour in jar. Store in the refrigerator.

COFFEE SPICE CAKE

This recipe and the recipe for Ginger Creams, below, were in Mother's recipe box, on a light green 3 x 5-inch card — "Compliments of the Rawleigh Dealer." When I was very little, an old man, thin and tall, dressed in a loosely fitting brown suit and floppy hat used to come by our house selling Raleigh Products. Later, in school, when I read about "Ichabod Crane," I imagined that "Ichabod" looked like the "Rawleigh man," only younger. I don't remember Mother using Rawleigh's products in her cooking, so if you happen not to have this specific brand of flavorings and spices, just substitute your usual brand. Ralph's Mother used to use Rawleigh's Salve to grease throats and chests when the people in her family had bad chest colds. She swore that this was what "opened them up."

½ cup shortening
1 cup sugar
2 egg yolks (separated from whites)
2 egg whites, well beaten
⅔ cup strong, cold coffee
2 cups (all-purpose) flour
3 teaspoons baking powder
⅛ teaspoon salt

1 teaspoon cinnamon
¼ teaspoon cloves
¼ teaspoon allspice

Cream shortening, add sugar and beat until light. Beat in egg yolks; add coffee slowly and add flour sifted with baking powder, salt, cinnamon, cloves and allspice. Mix well; fold in well beaten whites of eggs. Pour into two oiled and floured square layer tins and bake in a moderate oven at 350 degrees 25 to 35 minutes.

CUSTARD PIE

3 cups milk
¼ teaspoon salt
6 tablespoons sugar
3 eggs, beaten
1 teaspoon vanilla (extract)
Pastry for bottom crust

Heat milk over boiling water. Add salt and sugar to beaten eggs gradually. Add the milk to the egg mixture. Add vanilla. Pour into uncooked pie crust and sprinkle lightly with nutmeg.

Bake in a moderate oven (350 degrees) for 30 to 40 minutes , or, until custard is set.

DEVIL'S FOOD CAKE

This is the recipe Mother used for her Devil's Food Cake, one of the family's favorites when I was little.

½ cup shortening
2 cups light brown sugar
2 eggs
2¼ cups flour
¼ teaspoon salt
½ cup sour milk
½ cup boiling water
1 teaspoon soda
1½ squares chocolate
1 teaspoon vanilla
1 teaspoon baking powder

Cream shortening. Add 1 cupful sugar gradually creaming mixture thoroughly. Beat eggs until light. Add the other cup of sugar to the eggs, mixing well. Add this egg mixture to the creamed shortening and sugar, beating hard. Sift flour once; measure. Add baking powder, salt and sift three times. Then add to the first mixture, alternating with the sour milk, beating batter hard. Into the boiling water, stir the soda and melted chocolate or cocoa and mix into the cake. Add the vanilla. Bake in two layers in a moderate (350 degree) oven.

Devil's Food Icing: Cook 2 cups brown sugar and ¾ cup of water until it spins a thread. Pour in stiffly beaten egg whites of two eggs and beat until creamy. Add one teaspoon salt and two teaspoons vanilla.

FILLED COOKIES

⅓ cup shortening
1 cup sugar
½ cup sweet milk
3½ cups flour
1 egg
½ teaspoon salt
3 teaspoons baking powder
1 teaspoon vanilla

Combine shortening and sugar. Cream. Add egg and beat well. Sift dry ingredients together. Add alternately with milk. Refrigerate until chilled. Roll out on lightly floured board; cut with cookie cutter.

No assembly instructions were included with this recipe. I have found two different methods: (1) Bake cookies first and then sandwich the cooled filling (recipe follows) between two cookies OR (2) Place 1 to 2 teaspoons cooled filling (recipe below) on half the cut cookies. Cover with the remaining cookies. Press edges together with a fork and cut one or two small vents in the top of each cookie and then bake.

Bake cookies in a 375 degree oven until golden.

FILLING FOR COOKIES (ABOVE):

Cook together until thick
2 tablespoons flour
1/2 cup sugar
1/2 cup water
1/2 cup raisins
1/2 cup dates, chopped finely
1/2 cup nut meats

GINGER CREAMS

See note under Coffee Spice Cake, above

1 cup sugar
½ cup molasses
½ cup dark corn syrup
1 cup butter
1 cup sour milk
2 eggs
1 teaspoon baking soda
½ teaspoon cinnamon
½ teaspoon ginger
½ teaspoon nutmeg
½ teaspoon baking powder
½ teaspoon salt
3½ cups all-purpose flour

Use cake method of mixing. Spread thin on an oiled baking sheet. Bake at 375 degrees until very lightly browned. Cut in squares or oblongs. Ice with a powdered sugar icing. Simple Powdered Sugar Icing or Glaze: To 1 cup or more sifted confectioners sugar, add hot milk, a tablespoon at a time until the mixture is to the spreading or glazing consistency. (I tend to like a simple glaze more than a lot of icing.)

HAND ME DOWN CHOCOLATE CAKE

¾ cup margarine
1¾ cups sugar
2 eggs
1 teaspoon vanilla
2 cups flour
¾ cup cocoa
1¼ teaspoon soda (baking soda)
½ teaspoon salt
1⅓ cups water

Cream margarine and sugar until light. Add eggs and vanilla. Beat 1 minute at medium speed. Combine flour, soda, salt, cocoa. Add alternately with water to creamed mixture. Pour batter into 2 greased and floured 8-inch cake pans. Bake at 350 for 30 to 40 minutes. Cool. Frost with Chocolate Frosting.

ICE CREAM

The foundation:

½ teaspoon salt
6 tablespoons flour or cornstarch
½ cup cold water
5 cups boiling water
2½ cups sugar
2 eggs, beaten
2 tablespoons vanilla

Mix flour, ½ the sugar, the salt, and cold water. Add to boiling water. Boil 3 minutes. Mix with remaining sugar and beaten eggs. Let cool and store for future use, all except 2 cups.

2 cups foundation
1 large can chilled, whipped cream
Add vanilla
Freeze until chilled around edges
Whip again, freeze.

JAM CAKE

1 cup strawberry or blackberry jam
1 cup sugar
½ cup shortening
2 eggs
3 cups flour
½ cup milk
1 teaspoon baking soda
2 teaspoons baking powder
½ teaspoon salt
2 teaspoons vanilla

Cream sugar and shortening. Add beaten eggs. Sift flour, soda, baking powder, and salt together. Add (to creamed mixture) alternately with milk. Add jam and vanilla. Bake in greased and floured tube pan at 325 degrees until tester inserted into the center comes out clean.

KIFLINS

Mother and Aunt Blanche both had this recipe.

1 pound butter
⅔ cup sugar
½ pound ground almonds

1 quart flour
1 teaspoon vanilla

Mix in the order named. Make into small crescent shapes with the hand and bake at 375 degrees (until light tan around the edges). (NOTE: I have a similar recipe, using different nuts and flavorings which calls for rolling the cookies, while still warm, in confectioners sugar. You may want to do the same with these cookies. Some people make essentially the same recipe given here these days, mold them into balls, roll them in the powdered sugar, and call them Mexican Wedding Cookies).

LACE COOKIES

2 cups brown sugar
1 cup butter
2 cups oatmeal
1 egg
1 teaspoon vanilla

Mix in order named. Drop in small amounts on a greased pan. Bake in 400 to 425 degree oven.

MAPLE NUT CAKE

Sift together:
1 cup sifted flour
1½ teaspoon baking powder
2 tablespoons white sugar
½ teaspoon salt
Mix in 6 tablespoons brown sugar, firmly packed
Form a well (in the above ingredients). Add:
¼ cup vegetable oil
3 unbeaten egg yolks
6 tablespoons cold water
1 teaspoon maple flavoring

Beat until smooth: 1 cup egg whites (about 4) and ¼ teaspoon cream of tartar. Beat until it stands in peaks. Pour first mixture into egg white mixture. Fold in ½ cup chopped nuts. Pour into 2 ungreased loaf pans. Bake 50 - 55 minutes at 325 to 350 degrees. Let cool in pan. Ice with:

BROWN BUTTER ICING

Melt ¼ cup butter
Blend in: 2 cups confectioners sugar
1 teaspoon vegetable oil
1½ teaspoon maple flavoring or vanilla extract
Stir in 1 tablespoon hot water.
Stir the mixture until it is of spreading consistency.

PEAR HONEY

This recipe was written in a letter to Mother from Thelma Cole West, Mother's first cousin. Thelma and her family lived in North Carolina. When I was very young, she and her daughter came and stayed with us a few days during two or three summers. After Thelma died, we lost track of the family.

22 cups ground pears
12 cups sugar
One pound coconut
1 can crushed pineapple
Cook until thick and watch closely as it burns easily. (Put into hot sterilized jars and seal).

PENUCHI

Mother and Aunt Blanche both had this recipe.

3 cups brown sugar
1 cup milk
2 tablespoons butter
1½ teaspoon vanilla
1½ cups nut, (chopped), if desired
Cook milk and sugar to the soft ball stage (234 to 238 degrees) or to test it without a candy thermometer, put about ½ teaspoon of the candy mixture in cold water; supposedly, if it flattens out a bit, it is ready. (I trust a candy thermometer rather than testing the old-fashioned way.) Remove from fire and add butter, vanilla, and nuts. Beat until creamy. Pour in pan and cut in squares.

PEANUT BUTTER FROSTING

Cream together ¼ cup peanut butter and ½ cup butter or margarine. Add slowly 2 cups powdered sugar, creaming until mixture is light and fluffy. This is delicious on white, spice, or chocolate cake. Makes frosting for 24 cup cakes.

QUICK CHOCOLATE FUDGE

When marshmallow cream came on the market, Mother never used her old recipe for making fudge again. The old recipe called for beating the candy for awhile and Mother said that she never could get it right—it was usually too sugary to her. This is the fudge that became a Christmas tradition at Mother's and Daddy's house.

2 sticks margarine
5 cups white sugar
1 large can evaporated milk

Mix above ingredients in pan. Boil 8 minutes, stirring constantly. Set off heat and add 3 packages (small) or 1½ large or 1 large and 1 small chocolate chips, 1 pint marshmallow cream and stir until melted. Add 1 cup of nuts if desired Mother usually used pecans. Pour into greased pan. Let set until hard.

SUN GOLD COCONUT CAKE

4 eggs (separate yolks from whites)
3 cups flour
2 cups sugar
1 cup butter
1 cup sweet milk
3 teaspoons baking powder
4 teaspoon salt
2 teaspoons vanilla

Cream butter. Add sugar and mix well. Add egg yolks which have been beaten. Add milk alternately with flour which has been sifted three times with baking powder and salt. Add 2 teaspoons vanilla. Lastly, add egg whites which have been stiffly beaten. Bake at 375 degrees until cake tester comes out clean. This makes 3 large (round) layers. Ice with white icing and sprinkle with coconut.

THELMA'S CAKE

This recipe was not named for my sister or for Thelma Cole West, Mother's first cousin. This was just the name given to the recipe which was popular during earlier years.

2 cups sugar
½ cup butter
2 egg whites and yolks beaten separately
1 cup buttermilk
½ cup cocoa dissolved in ¾ cup boiling water
2 scant teaspoons soda dissolved in cocoa and water
2½ cups flour
2 teaspoons vanilla

Cream margarine and sugar. Add beaten egg yolks and buttermilk. Add cocoa mixture and beat. Add flour. Lastly, add beaten egg whites. Bake at 350 degrees until tester inserted in the center tests done in layer cake pans and ice with white icing. Sprinkle with coconut if desired.

MOTHER'S WHITE ICING

When I first remember Mother making white icing, boiled custard, or anything she had to beat well, it seemed that she stood for hours in front of the stove using one of the old rotary beaters. Of course, the electric mixers didn't become popular until later.

2 cups sugar
6 tablespoons cold water
4 egg whites
½ teaspoon cream of tartar
2 pinches of salt

Mix all together. Beat over boiling water in double boiler with electric mixer until stiff enough to spread between layers and outside of cake.

CABBAGE RELISH

This recipe came from Mother's cousin, Thelma Cole West.

4 cups shredded cabbage
1 cup chopped red peppers (sweet peppers)
1 cup chopped onions
2 cups vinegar
4 tablespoons white mustard seed
3 tablespoons salt
4 cups chopped green peppers
1 cup sugar
1 tablespoon celery seed

2 cups water

Combine vegetables. Cover with boiling water. Let stand 5 minutes. Drain. Add remaining ingredients. Simmer 5 minutes. Pack in sterilized jars. Seal.

HORSERADISH MUSTARD RELISH

This recipe came from Mother's friend, Grace Simerly Boyd. It is written here as Grace wrote it down for Mother.

6 large cucumbers
6 large onions
6 green tomatoes
6 pimientos (2 red—2 yellow—2 green to give nice color). Note, or if I don't have pimiento I use red, green and yellow peppers to give color.
1 bunch celery

Grind this and add handful salt and let stand two hours. Let boil 10 minutes and drain.

Then make a dressing of:

1 cup horseradish mustard
4 cups sugar
1 cup flour
1 teaspoon turmeric
1½ pints vinegar diluted with water to suit taste

Cook 10 minutes. (Boil). Seal while hot.

PEPPER RELISH

I believe that this recipe also came from Thelma Cole West, judging from the handwriting.

12 green peppers (sweet bell peppers)
12 red peppers (sweet bell peppers)
6 large onions
1 bunch celery
3 teaspoons salt
1 pint vinegar
2 cups sugar

Grind peppers, onions, and celery through food chopper. Cover with boiling water. Let stand 10 minutes. Drain. Cover (with water) again. Let boil a few minutes and drain again. Add salt, vinegar, and sugar. Boil 15 minutes. Put into sterilized jars and seal at once. Makes 6 pints.

SANDWICH SPREAD

This recipe was written on the back of a sheet of paper that Hobart had started using to do his Writing homework when he was in the fifth grade. I never remember Mother making this, but I think the ingredients and the wording are interesting.

Grind six red and six green sweet peppers, (Peppers can be all green if no red ones are to be had), six medium-sized onions. Then grind enough green tomatoes to make four quarts. Mix tomatoes, onions, and peppers together with one cup salt and let stand overnight.

In the morning, squeeze out of brine. Then make a salad dressing of three cups of granulated sugar, two cups flour, one tablespoon turmeric powder and one ten-cent box of French's ground mustard. Mix all ingredients to a thin paste with water, then stir it slowly into two quarts of boiling vinegar.

Cook until thick and add to tomato mixture. Stir thoroughly and heat thoroughly (not boil). Put in cans and seal while hot. This recipe makes seven and one half pints.

SANDWICH SPREAD (ANOTHER RECIPE)

This recipe was given to Mother by Grace Simerly Boyd, one of her class-mates at Cedar Grove. Grace married Lorena's half-brother, Lee Boyd. Lorena's dad, Robert Boyd, married Aunt Julia (Greene) after his first wife, Mattie Carrier, died. (Mattie was Lee's mother). I think it's interest-ing that green peppers are called mangoes here.

1 dozen green tomatoes
2 dozen mangoes (sweet peppers)
3 cups sugar
1 cup flour
1 cup prepared mustard
1 pint vinegar
1 quart salad dressing
2 tablespoons salt

Grind tomatoes and mangoes. Combine salt, sugar, flour, mustard, and vinegar and add to ground vegetables. Cook (slowly to prevent burning) 20 minutes from the time it begins to bubble up. Remove from fire and add dressing. Can in hot sterilized jars. A note written and circled at the bottom of the page on which this was written states, "Watch this closely to prevent burning."

SWEET PICKLES
Make in a non-reactive pot, such as an enamel one

1 gallon cucumbers soaked in 1 gallon water and 1 cup salt.
   Let stand 24 hours.

Simmer together: 3 pints vinegar
                             3 cups sugar
                             1 cup water
                             1 tablespoon mixed spices

   For 30 minutes.
   Pour (the vinegar mixture) over the cucumbers and simmer 15 minutes.
   Let stand 2 days.
   Pour off (drain off and reserve) vinegar and add 3 more cups sugar.
   Boil this mixture and pour over cucumbers. Put in sterilized jars and seal.

FROM AUNT BLANCHE'S KITCHEN:

AUNT BLANCHE'S BREAD PUDDING

   Butter 6 pieces of day-old bread. Place buttered side down in baking a dish. Sprinkle ½ cup raisins over bread. Then, butter 6 more slices of bread and place on top of raisins.

   Mix together: 2 eggs, 1 pint milk, ⅓ cup sugar, and 1 teaspoon vanilla extract. Pour over the bread. Bake in a 350 degree oven for 30 minutes. Cover with sauce (recipe follows).

   Sauce: *Mix together in a saucepan: ½ cup sugar, 1 tablespoon cornstarch, a pinch of salt, and 1 cup boiling water. Stir and bring to a boil. Cook until thick and clear. Add 1 tablespoon butter and ¼ teaspoon (ground) nutmeg. Pour sauce over baked bread pudding.*

FROM MY KITCHEN:

PEARS GRENADINE

Use as a relish with meat or poultry. Daddy really like this dish. I sometimes took it to family dinners.

Drain 1 can (1 pound) pear halves, reserving syrup. Put syrup in saucepan with 2 tablespoons grenadine syrup. Heat. Add 2 tablespoons sherry (optional), a few drops of red food coloring and pour the syrup over pears. Put into jars, cover and refrigerate.

WEDDING PUNCH

This is really not my recipe. Reba gave it to me. I have served it, as she did, at bridal showers. Makes 25 punch cups

½ **cup sugar**
1½ **cups water**
1 **2-inch stich cinnamon**
1 **tablespoon whole cloves**
¾ **cup grenadine syrup**
3 **cups grapefruit juice**
2¼ **cups pineapple juice**
1 **cup orange juice**
1 **bottle (12 oz.) sparkling water**
Ice cubes or fruited ice block

Combine sugar, water, cinnamon, and cloves in saucepan. Bring to boil, stirring occasionally, and boil 5 minutes. Strain and cool slightly. Add to grenadine syrup and fruit juices. Chill. Just before serving, pour into punch bowl; add sparkling water and ice.

FRUITED ICE BLOCK

Arrange a layer of strawberries, orange slices and mint sprig in a mold or coffee can. Add just enough water to cover and freeze. Repeat layers until mold is filled. To unmold, dip in hot water.

ZUCCHINI SQUARES

These are popular with Marie's and Jim's grandchildren—Katie, Andrew, Crissy, and Derrick.

1 **cup biscuit mix**

½ cup finely chopped onion

½ cup freshly grated parmesan cheese

2 tablespoons chopped Italian (flat-leaf) parsley

½ teaspoon salt

½ teaspoon Greek oregano (or ordinary oregano if you don't raise your own)

⅛ teaspoon pepper

1 medium-large clove of garlic, pressed with a garlic press or mashed and chopped finely

¼ cup vegetable oil

4 eggs, beaten

3-to-4 cups coarsely shredded zucchini

Combine all ingredients except zucchini, mixing well. Stir in shredded zucchini. Spread in a 13 x 9 x 2-inch baking pan that has been sprayed with non-stick cooking spray. Bake in a preheated 350-degree oven for about half an hour. Cut into small square. Serve warm or at room temperature. Refrigerate leftovers. These can be served as an appetizer or as part of a meal.

BUTTER PECAN COFFEE CAKE

I used to make this frequently when our daughters were little, but I doubt if they remember it now. It is very good fresh from the oven—at breakfast or for a coffee or tea break later.

2 tablespoons sugar

2 cups biscuit mix

1 egg

¾ cup milk

½ teaspoon vanilla

⅔ cup brown sugar

2 tablespoons flour

1 teaspoon cinnamon

½ cup chopped pecans

¼ cup cold butter

Combine first 5 ingredients and beat about 1 minute. Spread batter in greased 8-inch square pan. Combine remaining 5 ingredients and blend with a fork until crumbly. Swirl half of this mixture through the batter in the pan; sprinkle the remainder on top. Bake at 400 degrees for 20 to 25 minutes. If you use a glass pan, reduce the oven temperature to 350 or 375 degrees.

CARAMEL PECAN ROLLS

(This is Mother's recipe that she gave me years ago).

Caramel Coat: Into each ring of a muffin pan, put ½ teaspoon melted butter, 1 teaspoon brown sugar and a drop or 2 of water. Place several pecan halves in rings.

Rolls:

2 cups flour
3 teaspoons baking powder
1 teaspoon salt
4 tablespoons shortening
1 egg
½ cup milk
2 tablespoons butter
½ cup brown sugar

Sift flour, baking powder and salt together. Cut in shortening. Beat egg and add milk. Add to first mixture. Turn out on a lightly floured board and knead gently for ½ minute. Roll out ¼-inch thick. Brush with melted butter. Sprinkle with brown sugar. Roll jelly roll-fashion and cut into 1-inch slices. Place slices, cut side down, in prepared pans. Bake at 425 degrees for 20 to 25 minutes. Let stand in pan for 1 minute before turning out. Makes 16 to 18 rolls.

CARDAMOM CAKE

I used to make this cake when Lynette was little. The recipe has been misplaced for years. Just so history doesn't repeat itself, I'm putting the recipe in here. This cake is very good! Perhaps some of our Scandinavian ancestors enjoyed something similar. It's not likely, but cardamom is a popular ingredient in their more modern recipes.

2⅔ cup all-purpose flour
1 tablespoon ground cardamom (if you find the whole seed pods, you can grate them using a nutmeg grater)
2 teaspoons each ground cinnamon, cloves, ginger
1 teaspoon baking soda
½ teaspoon salt
1 cup butter, softened
2 cups sugar
6 eggs
2 cups sour cream
Confectioners sugar

Sift flour with spices, baking soda and salt. Set aside. In a large bowl, cream butter.

Gradually add sugar. Add eggs, one at a time, beating after each.

Stir in flour alternately with sour cream.

Spoon into greased 3-quart bundt pan or tube pan and bake at 325 degrees for 1 hour.

Remove from the oven. Cool 10 minutes. Turn cake out.

Store in an airtight container in a cool place.

Before serving, sprinkle with confectioners sugar.

CINNAMON ROLLS

This is the recipe Mother gave me for her Cinnamon Rolls.

2 cups flour
3 teaspoons baking powder
2 tablespoons sugar
1 teaspoon salt
1 teaspoon cinnamon
4 tablespoons shortening
⅔ cup milk
¼ cup milk
¼ cup sugar
1 cup seedless raisins

Prepare square cake pan. In the pan, melt 2 tablespoons shortening (butter) and add ½ cup brown sugar, sprinkling evenly. Sift dry ingredients together. Cut in the 4 tablespoons shortening. Add milk. Turn out and knead for about 30 seconds. Roll out to ¼-inch thick. Sprinkle with ¼ cup sugar and raisins. Roll jelly roll fashion and cut in 1-inch slices. Arrange rolls in pan with cut sides down. Bake at 400 degrees for 20 to 25 minutes. Let stand in pan for a minute. Turn out. Makes 16 to 18 rolls.

SPINACH CREPES

This another of those versatile recipes. Instead of making the filling "savory," as in the spinach filling, you can make the filling sweet or with fruits. This is one of those recipes that you can make when you are sick and tired of the ordinary things. It is also one that can be made from things you probably have in your pantry, refrigerator, or freezer. (You can, if you have to, even use well-drained canned spinach). And, it can be stretched into a meal with a salad, but I usually serve another vegetable, also. They can be made ahead, put into the baking dish and frozen and then baked.

Leftovers can also be frozen. These crepes are very good, are filling and satisfying, and they give you a "comforting feeling."

Crepes: **1⅓ cup all-purpose flour**
        ¾ teaspoon salt
        4 eggs, beaten
        2 tablespoons vegetable oil
        1⅓ cup milk (I use the ½ percent)

Combine flour, salt and eggs, mix well. Blend in oil and milk, beating until smooth. Refrigerate at least 2 hours.

Brush the bottom of an 8-inch crepe pan or heavy skillet with vegetable oil (or use a non-stick skillet). Place pan over medium heat until just hot, not smoking.

Place 3 tablespoons batter into pan. Quickly tilt pan in all directions (like you are making an omelet) so batter covers the bottom of the pan in a thin film. Cook crepe about 1 minute.

Lift the crepe to see if it has turned a golden brown (if it is too brown, you will need to lower the heat). Turn the crepe over and let cook for about half a minute on the other side.

Remove and stack between layers of waxed paper.

Repeat with all batter. After finishing the crepes, you can keep the waxed paper between each, place in large freezer bags and freeze until you want to use them. So, this is something you can do far ahead of time and just pop them out when you are thinking—what's for supper.

Filling: **2 pounds spinach, drained** (fresh if you have it in your garden or prefer to cook it fresh, or chopped frozen spinach, or in a bind—about 3 cans of chopped spinach, thoroughly drained)
        1 onion, chopped
        1 clove of garlic, crushed and minced
        1 tablespoon olive oil (I use extra virgin olive oil)
        16 oz. cottage cheese
        1 cup shredded Mozzarella cheese
        ½ cup (or more) freshly grated Parmesan
        3 eggs, beaten
        1 tablespoon fresh lemon juice
        ½ teaspoon salt
        ¼ teaspoon freshly grated nutmeg
        Freshly ground black pepper to taste

Cook spinach in a little bit of water for about 5 minutes. Drain in a sieve, pressing out as much of the water as you can.

In a large skillet, saute onion and garlic in olive oil until translucent (do not let the garlic get brown). Dump in the spinach and all the other filling ingredients. Mix well.

To Assemble the Crepes: Place 2 or 3 tablespoons on one side of each crepe. Roll the crepe up over the filling. If you can, fold the ends under a little bit. Place, seam side down, into a 13.9.2-inch baking dish which has been lightly oiled with additional olive oil or sprayed with a non-stick cooking spray.

To Bake: Cover with aluminum foil. Bake at 350 degrees for about 30 minutes. Remove the foil. Spoon 1½-to-2 cups All Purpose Marinara Sauce (See Index) over the crepes. Return to the oven for about 5 more minutes. Remove from the oven again and sprinkle with additional Parmesan and Mozzarella cheeses. Return to the oven for 5 minutes.

NOTE: In addition to freezing the crepes ahead, if you will need only half the amount
of finished crepes for one meal, before baking, put half of the full recipe into two smaller rectangular baking dishes and freeze one (tightly wrapped).

ADDITIONAL NOTE: These crepes, without the spinach filling, of course, also can be used as Dessert Crepes and filled with cottage cheese, an egg, a bit of sugar, and your spice of choice. Then, bake, covered, at 350 degrees for about 10 minutes. until the filling is cooked together and is hot. Serve topped with a fruit filling (one that will go with the spice you have used) and a dollop of whipped cream.
Alternately, you can put a fruit filling or raspberry jam in the center and after heating for about 5 minutes, top with Almost Devonshire Cream or your topping of choice.

INDEX OF RECIPES